"Branson and Martínez discuss the issues of culture and ethnicity in the life of the church, and of leadership within the context of these issues, in a more thorough and yet more accessible and practical way than any other book I know. This is a must-read book for any who are really concerned for the mission of the church in the future that now opens before us."

Justo L. González, author of *The Story of Christianity*

"*Churches, Cultures and Leadership* is one of the most significant books on the work of racial and cultural reconciliation yet published. Branson and Martínez have written a comprehensive work that integrates biblical research and social science analysis with highly practical suggestions for application in congregations and communities facing intercultural realities. They make the complexities of diversity understandable, accessible and even exciting. This thoughtful, engaging and substantive book by two practitioner scholars is a must-read for anyone interested in creating intercultural community."

Curtiss Paul DeYoung, Bethel University

"Part biblical study, part handbook on ministry, for use in the classroom or in small groups, *Churches, Cultures and Leadership* is a foundational text that meets the need for a broad, interdisciplinary and substantive perspective on intercultural ministry. From years of experience, Mark Lau Branson and Juan Martínez offer unique insights and a range of practical resources. May it help us toward a church in the power of the Spirit!"

Mark R. Gornik and Maria Liu Wong, City Seminary of New York

"This book provoked my mind theologically, historically, practically and spiritually. Branson and Martínez do a masterful job in communicating the complexities that conjoin church, cultures and leadership."

David A. Anderson, author of *Gracism*

"Given the phenomenal demographic changes in our nation (e.g., cultural diversity of our communities and congregations), *Churches, Cultures and Leadership* is a very important and rich resource for engaging the multicultural challenges facing the church. Via an interdisciplinary approach (i.e., Scripture, practical theology, social anthropology, cultural studies, philosophical hermeneutics, leadership theory and communication) Branson and Martínez have gifted the church with an unique—the only one of its kind—work for practical and faithful intercultural life and for helping the church reflect the diversity of America."

Eldin Villafañe, Gordon-Conwell Theological Seminary

"A book on the intercultural formation of congregations that integrates theology and cultural anthropology. This book is not a 'how to' but a humble and profoundly informative presentation that facilitates coming to the transparency needed for moving toward intercultural relations and ministry. Culture, language, worldview, theology and the unconscious assumptions that shape these are defined and examined so that we can understand our habits of ethnicity, class and social status. Awareness exercises are provided for facilitating conversations and the doing of theology. Leadership issues are then discussed in light of all of these aspects. The vignettes provided keep it real, and resources are provided with every chapter for further reading and viewing (movies). Finally, a book that's 'real' about these complex matters. Read it, share it, and you will be ushered into lasting change."

Elizabeth Conde-Frazier, pastor, Esperanza College of Eastern University

"If I were teaching today, this would be my basic and required text. If I were a pastor, this would be my chief source for leading my congregation into the future. Since I am a congregant, I will read this to better understand how to function in a changing urban society. This is a timely offering, crafted out of field experience, classroom disciplines and deep personal commitments. Great stuff!"

William Pannell, Fuller Theological Seminary

CHURCHES, CULTURES & LEADERSHIP

A PRACTICAL THEOLOGY OF CONGREGATIONS AND ETHNICITIES

Mark Lau Branson
& Juan F. Martínez

IVP Academic
An imprint of InterVarsity Press
Downers Grove, Illinois

InterVarsity Press
P.O. Box 1400, Downers Grove, IL 60515-1426
World Wide Web: www.ivpress.com
E-mail: email@ivpress.com

InterVarsity Press® is the book-publishing division of InterVarsity Christian Fellowship/USA®, a movement of students and faculty active on campus at hundreds of universities, colleges and schools of nursing in the United States of America, and a member movement of the International Fellowship of Evangelical Students. For information about local and regional activities, write Public Relations Dept., InterVarsity Christian Fellowship/USA, 6400 Schroeder Rd., P.O. Box 7895, Madison, WI 53707-7895, or visit the IVCF website at <www.intervarsity.org>.

Scripture quotations, unless otherwise noted, are from the New Revised Standard Version of the Bible, *copyright 1989 by the Division of Christian Education of the National Council of the Churches of Christ in the USA. Used by permission. All rights reserved.*

While all stories in this book are true, some names and identifying information in this book have been changed to protect the privacy of the individuals involved.

Table 9.2 on p. 193 is taken from Jürgen Habermas, The Theory of Communicative Action, *trans. Thomas McCarthy, 2 vols. (Boston: Beacon, 1984, 1987). Used by permission of Beacon Press.*

Design: Cindy Kiple
Images: Song Speckels/iStockphoto

ISBN 978-0-8308-3926-1

Printed in the United States of America ∞

Library of Congress Cataloging-in-Publication Data

Branson, Mark Lau.
  Churches, cultures, and leadership: a practical theology of
congregations and ethnicities / Mark Lau Branson, Juan Francisco
Martinez.
      p. cm.
  Includes bibliographical references (p.   ) and index.
  ISBN 978-0-8308-3926-1 (pbk.: alk. paper)
  1. Multiculturalism—Religious aspects—Christianity. 2. Church and
minorities—United States. 3. Pastoral theology—United States. I.
Martinez, Juan Francisco, 1957- II. Title.
  BV639.M56B73 2011
  259.089'00973—dc22

                                                                                                2010052959

P   23   22   21   20   19   18   17   16   15   14

Y   30   29   28   27   26   25   24   23   22   21

We dedicate this book to

the churches (usually anonymous) noted throughout these chapters,

and to other congregations
that are leading the way toward intercultural life.

We are also grateful for the students in our classes
who not only demonstrate a commitment to intercultural life
but also teach us about their own cultures.

CONTENTS

LIST OF BIBLE STUDIES

LIST OF PERSONAL REFLECTION/ GROUP EXERCISES

List of Figures and Tables

INTRODUCTION

Mark Lau Branson
and Juan Francisco Martínez

Oakland—About sixteen seniors waited to welcome the new pastor. Half of them were in the kitchen, the others in the sanctuary. Six months earlier they had voted to close their sixty-year-old church, but the bishop wanted one more attempt. In the 1930s the members had decided on a second relocation, following the pattern of congregations moving when ethnic demographics affected their neighborhoods. Changes had also occurred in this new neighborhood, so most members had moved to the suburbs and commuted back to the city for Sundays. They obviously had relational connections with each other, but they seldom saw each other between Sunday gatherings. The neighborhood, with its people and networks, knew little about the church other than it was the site for a couple of 12-step recovery groups hosted in the church basement. Over the next ten years the church became culturally diverse and deeply committed to its urban environment.[1]

Houston—After several decades of growth as a suburban, Caucasian, Baptist church near Houston, a congregation experienced a significant decline in the mid-1980s. Later, when the economy recovered and the community regained residents, those residents were ethnically diverse (80 percent non-White by 1990). The pastor shaped activities that he hoped would add members. Since he believed in the homogeneous unit principle, which taught that growth was most likely when churches remained racially-specific, he asked members to knock on doors in the next suburb. Then, consistent with his vision, he proposed that the church move to a location that matched his ethnic strategy. Some of the church's leaders were troubled by this strategy. They eventually de-cided they would stay in the diverse community and reach out to new

---

[1]Mark Lau Branson, "Forming Church, Forming Mission," *International Review of Mission* 92, no. 365 (April 2003): 153-68.

neighbors; and they called a pastor who would work with them in this challenge.[2]

INTRODUCING OUR THEME

Moses left Egypt with a "mixed crowd," and the earliest followers of Jesus learned that the Holy Spirit was leading them to cross cultural borders. The scriptural narratives are loaded with references to the strangeness of strangers and the discomforts of participating in God's love for the world. This book is about that strangeness, those discomforts. It is about God's call on the church to love our neighbors, and we acknowledge that such love is a matter of grace and of work.

Our focus is on churches in the United States and how we can be faithful to God's call on our churches in this context. We live in a culturally diverse nation—and many of our cities and neighborhoods exhibit that cultural pluralism. Ethnic diversity is evident in the media, at shopping malls and in many schools. Such diversity is less evident in our churches, but it is growing. We wish to promote more attentiveness, wisdom and faithfulness concerning intercultural life in and among churches, and between churches and their neighbors.

We have all been shaped in a historical context of prejudice and racism. We carry the influences of our environment in our minds and hearts; too often our actions, choices and words perpetuate ethnic biases. There are many prejudices, rooted in racism, built into our institutions. We believe that God's love for the world is definitive in Jesus' inauguration of God's reign, and therefore we believe that the church's identity and agency should be characterized by reconciliation. Such reconciliation, if it is defined and empowered by the gospel, must be personal, interpersonal, cultural and structural. When persons of different cultures share life, once we get beyond music and food, the complexities increase.

We claim that "paying attention" is important and difficult. Just as a competent painter, carpenter or teacher learns, over many years, how to attend—how to train their senses and responses to their environment and their work—church leaders need to pay attention to cultural characteris-

---

[2]Michael Emerson, *People of the Dream: Multiracial Congregations in the United States* (Princeton, N.J.: Princeton University Press, 2006), pp. 1-4, 28-29.

tics and the work of shaping intercultural life. And that is the purpose of our writing: to help men and women in our churches to see differently and to gain the skills and competencies needed for multicultural contexts. We want to encourage church leaders to create environments that make God's reconciling initiatives apparent in church life and in our missional engagement with neighborhoods and cities.

HISTORY MATTERS

History reminds us that many of the colonists who crossed the Atlantic and eventually formed the first states of the new United States were people seeking religious freedoms that they were denied in Europe. These colonies were established by people who wanted the space to develop their own specific vision of church and society, without the interference of a European government committed to its own state religion. The degree of establishment (the official connections between governing structures and churches) varied throughout the colonies, and some who fled persecution in Europe initiated their own oppressive practices in the New World. Those with primarily religious reasons for migrating were mixed with others who sought economic opportunities or political freedom, and these motivations were often overlapping because religion, politics and economics were overlapping factors in Europe.

These various colonial projects developed their distinct vision free from the interference or persecution they had experienced in Europe. They brought their theologies and practices from Europe and adapted them to life in the New World. Their experiences included opportunities and threats, and these new churches offered familiar experiences, dialects and practices. All of these immigrants valued their own familiar and distinctive theology, social relationships and worship practices. So churches and ethnicities were linked from colonial days, be they English Puritans in New England, Dutch Reformed in New York, English Anglicans in the mid-Atlantic or Swiss-German Mennonites in Pennsylvania. Most colonists arrived in the New World with church life thoroughly embedded in ethnic culture.

Most nineteenth-century immigrants to the United States continued with some version of this pattern. When they migrated to the States they tended to bring their ethnic-specific religious expressions with them.

Once in the United States they usually formed ethnic enclaves, and the churches were usually one of the central underpinnings of these new communities. They might have similar theological backgrounds, but one could clearly identify the differences between Irish, Ukrainian and Italian Catholics, or between German, Swedish and English Baptists. Some of these ethno-religious communities formed their own denominations, while others created joint structures, even as they maintained their clearly defined ethnic-specific churches.

As the nation grew, there were succeeding waves of immigrants in the new cities and towns, and neighborhoods went through ethnic transitions. It became increasingly common for a church facility to be turned over to a more recently arrived national/ethnic group as a previous tenant moved to a newer neighborhood. There were occasions, in the interim, in which some new arrivals investigated an unfamiliar church, especially in Puritan, Methodist and Baptist congregations, but this overlap was usually temporary and did not tend to change the culture of the church unless there was a complete handoff of the organization.

Thus ethnic homogeneity in American churches has been the norm from colonial days. Throughout the nineteenth century and into the twentieth, these ethno-religious churches adapted in numerous ways of life, responding to factors like language shift, new immigration patterns and continuing connections with homelands. The churches also dealt with realities that were unfamiliar: the frontier, close contact with those who are different and shifts away from the European norms of state churches. Yet even as Euro-Americans began relationships and eventually church affiliations that crossed the boundaries of national origins and culture, such changes were slow. The European pattern of national churches within denominational traditions continued in the United States well into the twentieth century. Even as the United States became a place of numerous cultures, this diversity was not significant within specific churches or denominations. There were practical reasons (language, existing associations, theological and liturgical biases) and affective preferences (accents, familiarity, a place and time in which one could be at ease among those who were "similar" to oneself).

In the midst of the European migrations there were also other peoples on the North American continent, such as Native Americans, African slaves, descendants of earlier Spanish and French migrations, and immigrants from Asia and Latin America. These peoples were treated differently than the European immigrants who landed on the Eastern seaboard. Many U.S. Christians questioned the humanity of African slaves and Native Americans, who were subject to annihilation and abuse by many who called themselves Christians. But African slaves and Native Americans were also the objects of Christian mission. During the colonial years some of these converts were invited to join the existing churches. But that practice quickly ended and the Christian converts were "encouraged" to form their own ethnic-specific churches. (This same pattern prevailed in the evangelistic efforts among the "Mexicans" of the Southwest and the Asian immigrants on the West Coast.) The issue of slavery also created divisions in many denominations and ended up defining Christian faith and practice in the United States well into the twentieth century and beyond.[3]

Those who became Christians among these groups were often organized into ethnic-specific churches that were placed under the direction of existing denominations. Most of these churches tended to be dependent on the denominations and churches that formed them. This dependency was usually only broken when these "ethnic" Christians formed their own denominations and church structures far from the control and direction of Euro-American churches and structures.

These patterns of ethnic specific religious interaction continued in the United States, even as people learned to speak English and as they adopted the dominant-culture (English American) norms and attitudes. When Milton Gordon published his *Assimilation in American Life* (1964) the subtitle of the book *The Role of Race, Religion, and National Origins* made abundantly clear that religion played a strong role in the complex intercultural interaction in the United States.

Gordon does a thorough analysis of the various theories of U.S. cultural interaction: Anglo-conformity, melting pot and cultural pluralism. He concludes that all three have existed as ideals in U.S. history but that none has ever been fully imposed as the norm. He describes U.S. reality as structural pluralism, where there is a fair amount of acculturation along

---

[3]See C. C. Goen, *Broken Churches, Broken Nation: Denominational Schisms and the Coming of the Civil War* (Macon, Ga.: Mercer University Press, 1985), for an analysis of the impact of the slavery issue on Christianity in the United States.

with continuing separation among peoples, particularly in the religious sphere. He also recognizes that the "excluded" peoples, African Americans, Native Americans and Latinos (he specifically mentions Mexican Americans), probably push beyond structural pluralism into cultural pluralism.[4] He calls on people in the United States to quit insisting that these "ideal" categories have ever existed as a historical reality. He calls for a willingness to develop a conversation about which of these models would work best in the United States. But he recognizes that none of them has ever been the "official" policy of the country.[5]

Throughout the history of the United States there have also been efforts to think differently about this issue. Voices in both North and South America questioned the racist European (Christian?) attitudes toward native peoples and those of African descent. As early as 1514 Fray Bartolomé de las Casas challenged the Spanish (Roman Catholic) mistreatment of native peoples and later worked for equal rights for native peoples in the Spanish colonies. In colonial North America (1688) the Mennonites in Germantown, Pennsylvania, were the first to begin protests against slavery that would later spread through many churches and denominations. There have also been occasional efforts in intercultural and interracial worship. For example, Richard Allen and Absalom Jones, both African American converts, worshiped and taught classes in St. George's Methodist Episcopal Church (Philadelphia), but they eventually left because of segregated seating and other humiliating experiences. Later they formed the African Methodist Episcopal denomination (1816). There are a few notes about biracial worship among frontier Methodists and Native Americans in the early 1800s, but overall the record is that mission efforts were continually undermined by prejudice, greed and violence. Much later (1906), the Azusa Street Revival was marked by multiracial worship. Several churches that developed in that movement attempted to form multi-

---

[4]We recognize that various terms are used regarding ethnicity and gender in reference to people in the United States who have a heritage in the Spanish-speaking world. Generally we will use the word *Latino;* others prefer *Hispanic.*

[5]Milton Gordon, *Assimilation in American Life: The Role of Race, Religion, and National Origins* (New York: Oxford University Press, 1964). In 2004 Samuel Huntington quoted Gordon in his book *Who Are We? The Challenges to America's National Identity* (New York: Simon & Schuster, 2004), but he ended up illustrating Gordon's concern by attempting to impose his Anglo-conformity interpretation on Gordon's thought and on the history of the United States (see Huntington, *Who Are We?* pp. 182-84).

cultural life, but most found themselves in a situation similar to that of Church of God in Christ. They started as a multicultural denomination, but in 1914, as they faced laws that forbade interracial worship, their leaders decided to avoid confrontation with the society's racist standards. Other denominations formed around specific ethnic groups or around majority-culture leadership with ethnic-specific churches and substructures.

This tendency toward ethnic-specific churches has often been seen by some as an asset for evangelization in the United States and beyond. The Homogeneous Unit Principle (HUP) states that people respond most effectively to the gospel in ethnic or culturally specific churches. On the one hand this means that the gospel can be embodied in any human culture. But often it has been used as a way to reduce the gospel's claims on us and on the ethnocentricity of cultures.[6] To this day the vast majority of churches in the United States tend to be ethnically or culturally specific with the related values and practices. Even churches that have intentionally gathered a multiracial congregation still exhibit the dominance of one culture.

The history of our country raises many theological and social questions for us as we attempt to be faithful churches in the midst of a rapidly changing ethnic and cultural environment. It shows us that without God's initiatives that transform us personally and as groups, our behaviors tend to be limited by cultural and human habits. Encounters with those who were different often led people to withdraw and to protect what was familiar. We will be addressing theological questions raised by this history throughout the book, believing that God's grace counters our habits and that Scripture and the Holy Spirit give witness and power to the shaping of a people who live transformed lives.

But we also have to ask ourselves the questions Milton Gordon raised almost fifty years ago: Which model (or models) best reflects both the diversity (all peoples, languages, ethnicities) and the unity that is appropriate for the United States? (Our church discussions and efforts are embedded in the national experiences.) Even more central to this book, what is the call of the gospel on churches? How can churches model gospel reconciliation and be agents of reconciliation and justice in our cities and in our nation? We believe that God's grace calls us beyond racism and

---

[6]See Donald McGavran, *Understanding Church Growth* (Grand Rapids: Eerdmans, 1980) for a thorough description of the Homogeneous Unit Principle.

Bible Study: Acts 2—Pentecost, Languages and Cultures

[1]When the day of Pentecost had come, they were all together in one place. [2]And suddenly from heaven there came a sound like the rush of a violent wind, and it filled the entire house where they were sitting. [3]Divided tongues, as of fire, appeared among them, and a tongue rested on each of them. [4]All of them were filled with the Holy Spirit and began to speak in other languages, as the Spirit gave them ability.

[5]Now there were devout Jews from every nation under heaven living in Jerusalem. [6]And at this sound the crowd gathered and was bewildered, because each one heard them speaking in the native language of each. [7]Amazed and astonished, they asked, "Are not all these who are speaking Galileans? [8]And how is it that we hear, each of us, in our own native language?

1. Use maps in your Bible to find the geographical locations listed in verses 9-11. What do you know about how and when Jews migrated to those locations? (This is one phase of what was called the "Diaspora.")

2. What was the Pentecost festival—or the Feast of Weeks—about?

3. In this Holy Spirit initiative, what can we discern about God's priorities concerning the gospel and cultures?

   Since this holiday lasted for only one or two days, and the season was one of intense agricultural work, most pilgrims would be from nearby regions. So the "devout Jews from every nation" were not primarily pilgrims but people who had relocated and were now "living in Jerusalem," and it is likely that a significant number of them were retirees (who wanted to be in Jerusalem for their last years and for burial). There is another interesting cultural factor: throughout the Roman Empire, Greek was the established language, and the assumption would be that everyone could speak Greek. So, discuss the following:

4. Does it make any difference in the meanings of the passage if the Holy Spirit's work was significantly aimed at retirees? What opportunities does this create?

5. Since Greek was available to everyone, why would the Holy Spirit initiate proclamation in the local languages of the Diaspora? What might this demonstrate about how God wishes to encounter cultures?

ethnocentrism. The question is how to express the new reality of the gospel in ways that both celebrates our differences and draws us toward unity in Jesus Christ.

CULTURAL AUTOBIOGRAPHIES: BRANSON AND MARTÍNEZ

In writing a textbook about ethnic identity we are aware that our own stories have shaped the ways we think about church and ethnicity, the ways we perceive our worlds, and the priorities we place on various approaches to ministry. We believe that the leaders and participants in any church can benefit from the process of researching, writing and reflecting on their own cultural and ethnic narratives. Without self-awareness we are more prone to misunderstanding others and to underestimating the impact that our own heritage has on how we perceive and think and act. The writing of a personal cultural autobiography is always selective, and the benefits can be extended when we revisit memories or engage research after the original narrative is written. For the purposes of this book, both of us will provide only an initial narrative. Throughout the chapters we add details that are appropriate to particular topics.

Mark. How does a white boy from Kansas receive an ordination from an African American Pentecostal church in San Francisco? What is the relevance of marrying someone who is Chinese American? Or teaching in Peru? Or coaching pastors in the Philippines? Or being a member of a Japanese American church? Or teaching and writing with a Mexican American colleague?

I was born in Wichita, Kansas (both names have roots in Native American tribes), with a mixed European ancestry that is predominantly Scotch-Irish.[7] In the postwar ethos my playground activities included chants about Japanese and African Americans that I later learned were racist. Our family was self-consciously American, with relatives connecting with the earliest Virginia settlements, then to Benjamin Franklin, Mary Todd Lincoln and the Hoovers. In our neighborhood school I gratefully remember an African American teacher, Mrs. Woodard, who as the librarian helped me find a way into books. (In 1970, her husband, A. Price Woodard, became

---

[7]James Leyburn, *The Scotch-Irish: A Social History* (Chapel Hill: University of North Carolina Press, 1962). I have also traced roots to British, German, Prussian, Dutch and Native American origins.

the first African American mayor of Wichita.) As the neighborhoods continued to change, the first African American kids arrived at my primary school in the fall of 1957.

My father was a carpenter and contractor, and Mr. Gibson, an African American carpenter, was one of his most skilled and dependable employees. When Wichita faced an economic downturn, and our family moved to a farming community near the Colorado border, Dad asked Mr. Gibson to join him on some projects. As a ten-year-old I was unaware of the oppressive social norms that required Mr. Gibson to leave the town boundary every night at sundown. Dad, a creative manager, would buy lots at the boundary so he could provide a trailer house for Mr. Gibson adjacent to the construction project. And because Mr. Gibson could not eat in the local restaurants, he would on occasion join us for holiday meals. I was witness to their working friendship, and only later did Dad explain to me the racism of the town.

My teenage years were influenced by the civil rights movement. On television I watched demonstrations, heard Martin Luther King Jr., and saw African American teenagers and children get knocked over by water canons as they prayed. When I saw the poverty of Mexican farm workers in my town, who often lived in railroad boxcars, I became curious about what I now understand are the social and economic arrangements of our society. I also became aware of how racial prejudice had been a force in my own extended family, bringing alienation and sorrow.

During graduate studies I was involved in campus ministry at the Claremont Colleges (California), first with the chaplain's office and then with InterVarsity Christian Fellowship (IVCF). I am still grateful for the cross-ethnic friendships that brought so much cultural diversity into my life: an African American student with whom I regularly shared the pulpit in campus worship, a Chicano student who introduced me to the farm workers movement and to folk masses (Roman Catholic worship), and several Asian American students who deepened my appreciation for the diversity of Asian cultures. I began to read the Bible differently—attending to cultural diversity and how the gospel of reconciliation addressed human barriers.

When I was thirty, I married Nina Lau, who had been born one year after her mother left China to join her husband in Texas. (When Nina was in middle school the family moved to Hawaii, where their extended family lived.) As Nina became the national coordinator for InterVarsity's Asian American staff (a total of six persons throughout the United States), we were finding deep friendship and ministry partnership among the other non-Euro-American staff of the organization. For several years I worked on a committee that restructured management and financial procedures in order to more equitably serve a multicultural ministry. As the director of IVCF's Theological Students Fellowship, I initiated connections with African American and Latino professors, and cochaired an international conference on biblical hermeneutics in Tlyacapan, Mexico, and edited the collected essays with René Padilla.[8]

In 1984, at the invitation of Samuel Escobar, a Peruvian theologian, we spent four months in Lima, Peru. I taught a seminary course, and we were enriched by the friendships and conversations. Brief weeks in Ecuador and Nicaragua also expanded our perspectives on those cultures and on the United States.

When Nina's work drew us to Oakland, California, I became the dean of an African American Bible institute. Located in San Francisco since the early 1950s, it was part of an organization that included a preschool, grade school and middle school. Later that year I was ordained at San Francisco Christian Center, an African American Pentecostal church. It was a profound privilege to work in this ministry and to be welcomed into homes and friendships. In Oakland our family became involved in the church described at the beginning of this chapter—a church that would become significantly multicultural as it reinvented itself to mirror the neighborhoods around it. During this time Nina and I were gifted with a son by birth and one by adoption, from Hong Kong. For fifteen years I worked in the midst of clergy networks, church-based community organizing and development, and consulting work that stretched my crosscultural skills. To gain more competencies, I completed a doctorate in international and multicultural education. In connection with International Urban Associates, I also spent time with Asian church leaders in Thailand and the Philippines.

When I was invited by Fuller Theological Seminary to join their faculty in Pasadena, we relocated to this new context. During this transition,

[8]Mark Lau Branson and C. René Padilla, *Conflict and Context: Hermeneutics in the Americas* (Grand Rapids: Eerdmans, 1984).

my Bay Area clergy friends introduced me to Pasadena African American churches. I have been involved in several church-based agencies that are rooted and deeply involved in various urban concerns. My family is active in a multicultural church whose roots are in the Japanese American community, and our sons live in the cultural mix of public schools and urban networks, and the friendships available in that environment. Coauthor Juan Martínez has invited me to teach various bilingual courses in the seminary, and other colleagues help me connect to African American and Asian students and ministries. For six years Juan and I have taught a course concerning ethnic issues relevant to churches, and this book arises from those classes.

Juan. I usually begin my cultural autobiography by looking at the generations of ancestors who formed me. Each of my genealogical lineages has given me something important that shapes who I am today. Through my maternal grandfather I am part of the Guerra clan that came from Spain in the 1600s and settled in what is now south Texas in the late 1700s. The Guerras give me identity and roots. I am part of the twelfth generation that came from Spain and am a sixth-generation U.S. citizen because the United States conquered the land from Mexico and made my Guerra ancestors U.S. citizens.

My maternal grandmother's family ties me to my religious identity, and my *mestizo* (mixed race) reality. Rafaela García, my maternal great, great grandmother, of mixed Native and Spanish background, converted from Roman Catholicism to become a Protestant Christian in south Texas at a time when being a Latino (Mexican) Protestant was a very costly decision. She brought her daughter, Anita, to faith, and they shaped my grandmother Juanita Cáceres. She always prayed that her children would enter ministry. Though Juanita died when I was six, the legacy of these three women influenced me through my mother and gave me a deep sense of God's sovereign shaping of my life.

My father's family formed me in other crucial ways. My father grew up in the Mexican border state of Nuevo León. He went to Texas as an adventurer, where he met my mother. When he married my mother he made no claim to faith. But he later had a profound conversion experience that changed his life completely. He became the only Protestant in his family and was ostracized by some of his siblings, but this conversion led to a call to ministry. My parents studied for ministry and then moved to a small agricultural community in central California (Kettleman City), where they served among migrant workers for over thirty years. They modeled a commitment to work among the poor and marginalized and showed me what a deep commitment to ministry looks like.

This background taught me profound things about faith, identity and church ministry. I learned early on that faith is a costly decision. My ancestors suffered because of their faith, and my parents made great sacrifices because of their faith and call to ministry. As the eldest child of a Latino Protestant pastor I also learned that God's call to ministry demands a willingness to sacrifice all for his service. This sense of call and commitment has shaped each of my ministry decisions.

My identity was greatly shaped by my ancestors. I am part of the United States because the United States "migrated" the border across my ancestors. But I also have a strong Spanish-speaking Latino Protestant identity because I grew up in a Spanish-language Protestant congregation. My commitment to serving the Latino community was shaped by my ancestors, my parents, my church and my community.

As a U.S. Latino committed to ministry in the Latino community I have often faced the questions and confrontations of people who expect me to "assimilate." I have been stopped many times by immigration officers but have also had my identity questioned by people who assume that I should not want to speak Spanish because I was educated in English. Often I have to explain why a U.S.-born and educated Latino chooses to speak Spanish and cast his lot with the poor and marginalized of the Latino community.

My own experience has also reminded me how multicultural the term *Latino* really is. My wife is from Cuba, and we have had to learn to grow together across vast cultural differences. Our children were born in California but raised in Guatemala, where I was the rector of a Mennonite seminary for almost nine years. We are now back in the United States, living in the midst of a broadening Latino multicultural reality. In many ways Guatemala felt more like home than the United States because I did not have to spend my time explaining or justifying who I am. Returning to the United States feels like returning to exile, because the United States is my only home, but one that has often questioned my

Personal Reflection/Group Exercise:
Writing an Ethnic Autobiography

Begin by reflecting on these questions and making notes on each. Then take the time to craft a narrative around experiences and how you interpret their impact on your ethnic identity. In small groups, share selected elements of your autobiography. (For this exercise we use the words *ethnic* and *ethnicity* to refer to cultural and racial elements plus other major sociocultural factors.)

1. What do you know (or can you discover) concerning the ethnicity and national origins of your parents, grandparents and earlier generations? If this is different from the heritage of the household in which you were raised, describe those differences.

2. When were you first aware of ethnic (or racial) categories? When were you first aware of persons who were different?

3. How did your parents and grandparents voice ethnic matters or convey to you what they perceived or what they thought was important? How did other members of the household contribute to your understandings about your own ethnic heritage?

4. Think about phases of your life—childhood, adolescence, early adulthood, middle and perhaps later adulthood. How did your ethnic identity affect you? How has your awareness changed? What difference did it make in relationships, where you lived, what activities you participated in, how you experienced school, and how you experienced your society (city, nation)?

5. How have you experienced societal matters of discrimination, prejudice and inequality among ethnic groups? What do you remember about experiences of being treated unfairly because of cultural identity? Or of treating others unfairly?

6. How have you experienced significant boundary crossing (either in travel, through relationships or in some organization)? What did you learn about others and yourself?

7. What is the relationship between your ethnic identity and your faith? What difference did or does it make in church? In your beliefs or theology?

8. In what ways do the stories, values and practices of your ethnic heritage parallel the gospel or facilitate and nurture being a Christian? What elements of your ethnic heritage make being a Christian difficult?

9. What do you value most in your ethnic heritage? What do you value least?

place here. Yet it is in exile where God wants me to serve.

Because I am a Latino Protestant pastor's son, I learned several important things about the church. It was home when we were rejected by the larger Latino community. It was also the place where my parents demonstrated what it means to serve others and where I confirmed God's call on my life. But it was always also a place with very real broken humans. I suffer few illusions about the church; it is a place full of real humans with real problems. Yet I am happy serving the church even though at times it has been negative. Here my Anabaptist heritage takes over as I believe, practice and continue to struggle in the faith.

My life journey has taken me through small towns in south Texas and central California. As part of my formation I attended a Spanish-language Bible institute, earned an M.Div. at Mennonite Brethren Biblical Seminary (Fresno, California), and a Th.M. and Ph.D. at Fuller Theological Seminary (Pasadena, California). I have served as a pastor in south Texas and central California. For several years I also oversaw Latino ministry for my denomination and started a Spanish-language Bible institute. God's call to leadership development then took our family to Guatemala. Now I am involved in training Latino leaders in ministry at Fuller Seminary. I am a Latino Anabaptist *evangélico* living in exile in the United States. I recognize that "exile" is a theological motif that fits both my Anabaptist theology and my life experience as a Latino. If you ask me where I am from, I will need to respond with a question. Do you want to know about my ancestors, my birth, my family or my life journey? As a Christian I believe God is in the midst of shaping me to cross cultural boundaries; to have an awareness concerning persons who are culturally, socially or economically different; and to teach others who want to be servants of the gospel of reconciliation. And so I continue walking from my Latino roots toward God's future.

AN OVERVIEW OF THE BOOK

We have been teaching a seminary course concerning churches and ethnicities for several years. The chapters of this textbook are structured
around the outline of that course. We are especially indebted to Edward
Stewart and Milton Bennett for their book *American Cultural Patterns: A
Cross-Cultural Perspective.*[9] In that classic book, they have employed the
resources of cultural anthropology, the psychology of perception and communications theory to explain and analyze how crosscultural dynamics
can be understood in the United States. We follow their major categories,
import our resources as framed by theology (especially missiology and ecclesiology) and leadership studies, and provide illustrations from U.S.
churches. One of us provided the initial draft of each chapter, then we
worked together to clarify, illustrate and provide instructional materials.

Part one focuses on the relationship between theology, society and ethnicity. Mark drafted chapter one in order to frame the textbook as a work
in practical theology and to introduce a basic framework on leadership.
Praxis is the term we use to describe the ongoing life of a church that
moves between "study/reflection" and "engagement/action." Each movement informs the other. Chapter two, also shaped by Mark, places our
work into the current conversations about missional ecclesiology. In chapter three we explain various concepts concerning social contexts, race and
ethnicity, and our concern for intercultural life.

Part two uses the resources of cultural anthropology to provide insights
into human dynamics that vary among cultures. In chapter four, "Worldviews, Reality and Assumptions," Mark describes how a culture's worldview is always in the background. We carry with us, usually unconsciously,
a vast array of assumptions about what is visible or invisible, about time
and cause and effect, and about values. Juan, in chapter five, explains how
"Language, Gestures and Power" are actively shaping every social encounter. Then in chapter six, Juan shows how different societies make different
assumptions about social relations. These variants have to do with class,

---

[9]Edward Stewart and Milton Bennett, *American Cultural Patterns: A Cross-Cultural Perspective*,
   rev. ed. (Yarmouth, Maine: Intercultural Press, 1991). Steward and Bennett note their debts to
   the theoretical frameworks and research of Florence Kluckhohn and Fred Strodtbeck, *Variations in Value Orientation* (Evanston, Ill.: Row, Peterson, 1961); George Foster, *Traditional Cultures and the Impact of Technological Change* (New York: Harper & Row, 1962); and Robin Wil-
   liams Jr., *American Society: A Sociological Interpretation*, 3rd ed. (New York: Knopf, 1970).

status, social networks, formal or informal relations, obligation and reciprocity, how problems are addressed, and the role of relations. Juan also drafted chapter seven, "Self-Perception and Individuality," in which he shows that any person's concept of the self is rooted in his or her culture. The concept of individualism in mainstream America leads to a "mythic" individualism that creates a type of antistructuralism, which complicates any attempt to create community in the church. Chapter eight, "Perception and Thinking," which we coauthored, builds on the worldview framework to show that even what we perceive, and how we interpret and think about what we perceive, is shaped by our cultures. In churches our capacities to understand each other and work together can be strengthened when we "get behind" each other's eyes and pay attention to how others think.

Part three of the book focuses on how leaders need to work in the context of these challenges. Mark drafted chapter nine, "Intercultural Communication," which provides a framework for sorting out the communication dynamics of a group. As a church seeks integrity in its communication, this framework offers tools that clarify appropriate ways to discuss our world, ourselves and the common life we have as a church. Then in chapter ten, "Leading Change," Mark works with an extended case study to show how a pastor can form leadership teams and how the church continually invests in discernment and experiments. In chapter eleven, "Practices for the Calling," Juan describes a set of skills and practices that can aid intercultural relations and church ministry. As a resource for practical theology, the appendix provides a collection of quotations that connect theological topics with the theme of congregational intercultural life. An annotated bibliography follows the appendix.

We both have worked in church leadership for decades, and we continue to be active members in congregations and regular consultants with other churches. These experiences, along with numerous conversations with other church leaders, provide the illustrations for this book. While all of the stories and examples in this book are based on real people and events, some illustrations merge stories from various sources, and, except for describing our own roles in some experiences, we alter names and identifying details to protect the privacy of those involved.

Throughout the book we provide Bible studies that are relevant to each chapter's specific topic and to the larger agenda of intercultural life. These are not parenthetical—rather they are essential to our writing. The Bible verses are usually provided alongside the discussion questions, but if the selected passage is longer, readers need to refer to their own Bibles in order to understand the study and its implications. While the book is designed for groups and classes that can work on these studies together, we strongly recommend that individual readers also work with these studies. We have not written this book as a biblical defense of intercultural churches (something that other writers have done quite well),[10] but these Bible studies do provide important texts and interpretive guidance, and they shape our theological and missional commitments.

We have also included exercises that are appropriate for both personal reflection and group discussion. We do not believe that the substance of this book can be adequately understood by a reader who keeps a safe distance from the subject matter. By encouraging reflection and discussion on personal stories and various concepts, we hope to deepen understanding and even prod personal commitments.

Each chapter provides a list of suggested movies. This is an attempt to move beyond the classroom (or personal study) and gain at least a mediated experience of other cultures. We also encourage readers to engage other cultures in personal conversations and through churches, neighborhoods and historic sites. We have also provided a website with additional resources and opportunities for discussions—www.churchescultureslead ership.com. We hope professors, students and church leaders benefit from and contribute to this site.

We are grateful to the congregations, students and colleagues who have engaged us for many years concerning matters of intercultural life in churches. Fuller Theological Seminary supported us with sabbatical time and the expert help of Susan Wood. InterVarsity Press, and especially Gary Deddo, embraced the project and provided important feedback and guidance. Our friends at Dayspring Technologies contributed design and hosting services for the book's website. We also thank several graduate students who worked with us: Craig Hendrickson, Arnaldo Soto, Douglas Abel and Agnes Lee.

In addition to the Stewart and Bennet book already mentioned, we

---

[10]See the suggested reading in chapter one.

At the Movies

These movies show the complexities of ethnic diversity and cultural encounters. Some work with specific historical events; others depict the types of experiences that ethnic groups face in the United States. The last three indicate narratives and characteristics in white America.

Rosewood (1997). The 1922 massacre of black citizens in Rosewood, Florida, by a white mob from a nearby town.

My Family (1995). Traces over three generations of a Latino immigrant family's trials, tribulations, tragedies and triumphs in Los Angeles.

Letters from Iwo Jima (2006). The battle of Iwo Jima seen through the eyes of the Japanese soldiers.

Birth of a Nation (1915). Civil War–era saga in which abolitionists are seen as the destructive force and the Ku Klux Klan are the heroes.

Lakota Woman (1994). The 1960s are the setting for cultural sensitizing and protests that lead to a standoff with government forces.

Who Killed Vincent Chin (1987). One autoworker blames the competitive Japanese automakers for the threats to his job, and he kills a Chinese autoworker in the mistaken belief that he is a Japanese American.

Kite Runner (2007). An Afghani boy struggles with complex family dynamics and his own cowardice and deception, flees the Soviet invasion, and eventually makes a life in Fremont, California, only to receive an unexpected phone call that leads him on a journey of surprising revelation and redemption.

To Kill a Mockingbird (1962). A white lawyer in the Depression-era South defends a black man against an undeserved rape charge. The story line also attends to the segregated town's reactions, the lawyer's relationship with his children and prejudice against a mentally disabled neighbor.

Grapes of Wrath (1940). Based on the John Steinbeck novel in which a Depression-era Oklahoma family faces failure during the dust bowl and leaves for California, where hardships continue. The plot involves bank foreclosures, landowners suppressing labor wages and three generations of the family struggling to survive.

Extraordinary Measures (2010). A family seeks medical treatment for their children's rare disease. Competitive scientific research, diverse personalities, corporate and personal finances, relationships with other families, and the threatening timeline contribute to this drama.

have always used Ronald Takaki's books (either *A Different Mirror* or *A Larger Memory*), the study by Michael Emerson and Christian Smith *(Divided by Faith)* and Emerson's later study of multiracial churches *(People of the Dream)* in our classes. They have all informed and shaped this book. The thrust of this book is not a small matter to us—we believe that God's glory is experienced in the context and mission of faithful churches. And we believe that God's love for the world, a love in which we are to participate, is always calling us to intercultural life. In most U.S. locations intercultural dynamics are already on the ground. This is a gift from God and a task to be embraced by God's churches.

PART I

THEOLOGY
AND CONTEXT

1

PRACTICAL THEOLOGY AND
MULTICULTURAL INITIATIVES

Mark Lau Branson

*This [Azusa Street] congregation was different from most black congrega-
tions in Los Angeles. From the beginning, Pastor Seymour envisioned it
becoming a multiracial, multiethnic congregation. In keeping with that
vision, the mission quickly attracted—and for an extended period of time,
it welcomed and maintained—a membership that was broadly represen-
tative of various racial and ethnic groups: blacks, whites, Latinos, Asians,
and Native Americans. . . . It included people from all classes. It held the
attention of the highly educated alongside the illiterate. . . . Even so, worship at the mission was undoubtedly heavily flavored by the dominantly
African American character of its founding core membership. . . . [Also] the
revivalist camp meeting tradition so prevalent among whites (as well as
blacks) on the American frontier clearly contributed much to the missions,
music, preaching, and prayer life.*

*While the mission was a congregation of ordinary people, they were
people who were hungry for God. . . . They were willing, if necessary, to
violate social strictures—especially on the mixing of races. For roughly
three years, in the teeth of a howling secular and religious press, the people
of Azusa Street Mission demonstrated that they could cross these social
lines, and bear great fruit as they did so.[1]*

This account of the 1906 Azusa Street Mission recalls a church whose life

---

[1]Cecil M. Robeck, *The Azusa Street Mission and Revival* (Nashville: Thomas Nelson, 2006), pp.
88, 138, 314.

was in stark contrast to society and other churches. This multicultural experiment was short-lived, lasting perhaps three years, but the message of the Holy Spirit's radical inclusiveness continued to be an irregular but notable aspect of the Pentecostal movement around the world. There are complex social, theological, organizational and personal factors in the Azusa narrative, as is documented by historian Cecil Robeck. This complexity places demands on any church that wants to attend to the relationship between theological and cultural issues in its own on-the-ground life; that is why we propose that churches develop more thorough ways of doing what is called "practical theology." This chapter provides a glimpse into some biblical narratives that are relevant to our topic, then sets out a method for our work.

BIBLE NARRATIVES AND BORDER CROSSING

Seek the shalom of Babylon where I have sent you into exile,
and pray to the LORD on its behalf, for in its shalom
you will find your shalom. (Jer 29:7, paraphrased)

Is the shalom of Babylon relevant for Los Angeles or Chicago or Charlotte in the twenty-first century?[2] What happens when we read biblical stories about cultural boundary crossing and place those stories alongside our own? Though the Bible does not provide us a strategic plan for action, it does provide us with a crucial understanding of what God is doing in the world. As we read about the exodus, the exile or the earliest churches, we can place these stories alongside our own in order to reconsider our perceptions, convictions, habits and imaginations. We work with the Bible as an authoritative text, and we see God's enduring love expressed in initiatives to shape a people as a community for worship and mission. Through the following chapters we will attend to various biblical narratives. When students, leaders and churches linger in these stories—study them, discuss them, meditate on them, allowing the Spirit to speak—we can see our world and our agency differently.

Jeremiah's narrative is not unique—other Old Testament narratives also provide grounding for multicultural life: Israel was to bless the nations

---

[2]The Hebrew word *shalom* encompasses a whole set of traits: peace, righteousness, justice, welfare, health and social harmony.

Bible Study: Jeremiah 29—Exiles Seek Shalom

[1]These are the words of the letter that the prophet Jeremiah sent from Jerusalem to the remaining elders among the exiles, and to the priests, the prophets, and all the people, whom Nebuchadnezzar had taken into exile from Jerusalem to Babylon. [2]This was after King Jeconiah, and the queen mother, the court officials, the leaders of Judah and Jerusalem, the artisans, and the smiths had departed from Jerusalem. . . . [3]It said: [4]Thus says the LORD of hosts, the God of Israel, to all the exiles whom I have sent into exile from Jerusalem to Babylon: [5]Build houses and live in them; plant gardens and eat what they produce. [6]Take wives and have sons and daughters; take wives for your sons, and give your daughters in marriage, that they may bear sons and daughters; multiply there, and do not decrease. [7]But seek the welfare [shalom] of the city where I have sent you into exile, and pray to the Lord on its behalf, for in its welfare you will find your welfare.

In the early sixth century B.C., when Babylon was continuing its conquest of Judah and forced thousands of Jews to relocate to Babylon, some prophets predicted a quick rescue by Yahweh. They claimed this political and military setback was temporary. Jeremiah had taken a risky and unpopular position in preaching that Judah's kings (Jehoiakim and Zedekiah) should not resist Babylon. He sent a letter to the exiled Jewish population and countered the prophets who spoke for resistance to Babylon in expectation of an immediate return, "Do not listen to the dreams that they [the prophets] dream, for it is a lie that they are prophesying to you in my name; I did not send them, says the LORD" (Jer 29:8-9). As quoted, he commended them to seek the shalom of Babylon. The word *shalom*, here translated as "welfare," is a comprehensive concept of well-being.

Jeremiah's letter provides a radically different perspective on what it meant to live in the capital city of the enemy. Even though the Jews have been traumatized—by warfare, by a forced march out of their Promise Land and by profound challenges to their theology—they are to settle into a strange neighborhood and seek the shalom of their new neighbors.

1. What might be ways to describe the state of the exiled community—their hopes and fears, their situation, their options?

2. What *theological* challenges did they face? That is, what beliefs about God and their relationship with God needed to be reconsidered?

3. Jeremiah provided specific instructions about the practices the exiles were to engage in. (These were in opposition to idle waiting or rebellion.) Why might these activities have been important?

4. How does Jeremiah envision the ways the exiles should live among their neighbors? What challenges and what benefits might arise for the exiles and for the Babylonians?

5. Does this inform us concerning how we look at each other across cultural boundaries? Does this give us different perspectives concerning what God cares about? What specific activities, based in this text, can change relationships among neighbors?

(Gen 12); the law insisted on welcoming immigrants (Deut 10:19; Lev 19:33-34); God sent Jonah to give witness to Nineveh; other prophets reminded Israel of their obligations. The New Testament draws on the narratives of Israel to emphasize that God's inclusive love does not have cultural boundaries. For example, in the early years of the Christian church there were significant debates concerning whether God intended the gospel to be a gift exclusively for Jews (Acts 15). The Holy Spirit's visual and linguistic gifts during the Pentecost festival (Acts 2) had already made it clear that bicultural Hellenistic Jews and Jewish converts were included— but what about Gentiles? Scripture names bicultural persons who played key roles (Moses, Ruth, Paul, Timothy) and Gentiles who are included in the Jewish lineage (Tamar, Rahab, Bathsheba). But how is the church to understand its own social composition?

Antioch, the third largest city in the Roman Empire, would be the first setting for this question. After Hellenist Jewish believers fled Jerusalem because of persecution, some came to Antioch and spoke with Gentiles, who also became believers (Acts 11). The genuineness of their faith was confirmed, and the community began to benefit from extensive teaching. What kind of cultural issues did they encounter? Was there any tendency toward cultural homogeneity in gatherings? Did the Gentiles establish a separate church, hoping to attract more Gentiles by avoiding the discomforts of a mixed congregation? The New Testament only notes the tendency of Jews to segregate, but this was clearly condemned.

Among numerous stories, these episodes indicate that God wants shalom to be known across cultural boundaries. The eschatological images of the book of Revelation reinforce this trajectory: "There was a great multitude that no one could count, from every nation, from all tribes and peoples and languages, standing before the throne and before the Lamb" (Rev 7:9). Does this help us know the shape of any gathering called "church"? What did Jesus envision when he taught the disciples to pray, "Your kingdom come. Your will be done on earth as it is in heaven" (Mt 6:10)? Are these mere ideals, while circumstances and reason tell us that homogeneous congregations have too many advantages to forgo?

Selected Books on Biblical Narratives

DeYoung, Curtiss. *Coming Together in the 21st Century: The Bible's Message in an Age of Diversity*. Valley Forge, Penn.: Judson, 2009.

Hays, J. Daniel. *From Every People and Nation: A Biblical Theology of Race*. Downers Grove, Ill.: InterVarsity Press, 2003.

McKenzie, Steven. *All God's Children: A Biblical Critique of Racism*. Louisville: Westminster John Knox, 1997.

Study Bibles with Annotations Regarding Ethnicity and Culture

The Peoples' Bible. Minneapolis: Fortress, 2008.

The Word in Life Study Bible. Nashville: Thomas Nelson, 1993.

In the ethnic and cultural diversity of the Mediterranean, the church repudiated any attempts to create culture-based fellowships. Even when Paul had a direct word concerning class distinctions in Corinth, his solution was not to form different worshiping groups but to minimize the effect of their differing habits (1 Cor 11). In Ephesians the churches of the region are instructed to be culturally inclusive in ways that are visible to outsiders—including rulers and authorities of all kinds (Eph 4); texts here and elsewhere indicate that this inclusivity was not previously a norm. In addition to theological rationale there is a practical matter—the witness provided by this visibility would be undercut if persons of differing cultures were in segregated gatherings. As the church spread, the topic of fellowship around food received significant attention. Cultural practices concerning meals indicate inclusion and exclusion: Who is allowed into the fellowship at a table? What food is allowed or forbidden? Paul tends to answer these questions with a priority on shaping relationships for trust and inclusion. Rather than endorse occasional events of intercultural life, the church was to live daily life as a new people whose identity bore witness to the new creation. Through the following chapters we will continue to explore biblical texts, asking if they change how we see ourselves and our contexts.

A church's missional life is at the core of God's gospel engagement with the world. There are numerous ways that congregations shape their relationships and activities to care for strangers, migrants and those who are excluded by a dominant culture. Pentecost made this obvious: the poorer immigrants living around Jerusalem and Hellenists from throughout the Mediterranean and further east were the focus of the Holy Spirit, who ministered through their languages and social networks. The Holy Spirit guides and empowers the church to break out of the homogeneous social units of that era. The narratives and writings of the New Testament show an attentiveness to these social realities, including languages, oppression, access to resources, and how leaders are identified, called and commissioned. In the suburbs of Jerusalem many early believers sold their houses and pooled their money for the benefit of the church's life and mission (Acts 2:43-47). In Corinth, where the church met in the home of a wealthier family, the economic diversity of the church created significant social distress, which led to new practices that initially lessened social awkwardness (1 Cor 11:17-34), while a later, more profound teaching about money sought to prompt significant generosity (2 Cor 8:8-15). In Thessalonica Paul and his team took day jobs so they could pay for all the food they needed (2 Thess 3:6-13), while he encourages the Galatians to share their resources with teachers (Gal 6:6). There is no one plan for all congregations; rather, the Holy Spirit instructs and empowers churches to pay attention to their own formation in their cultural contexts as they embody the gospel in a specific place.

How can churches discern faithful ways of intercultural life? Jesus often used fiction; much of the Bible provides poetry; Paul and the prophets often used metaphors. Missiologist and bishop Lesslie Newbigin uses a cluster of metaphors to describe the church as a "sign, foretaste, and instrument" of the reign of God.[3] If that great eschatological, multicultural congregation of Revelation is one image of God's reign, in what ways might each current congregation be a sign that points to this reality? How can a church's relationships and ministries offer participants and visitors a foretaste of the redemption and reconciliation that is God's full salvation? And how can God shape and empower churches as agents (instruments) for reconciliation and shalom? We believe we are invited into new ways of discovery, imagination and discernment—this is called "practical theology."

PRAXIS, PRACTICAL THEOLOGY AND CULTURES

If there is no one ideal strategy or model for all churches, then each particular church, usually in local networks and other associations, must gain competencies and capacities that are specific to its own time and place. In order to do this the leaders of a church need to gain skills in theological reflection—this is what is called practical theology. This is not an approach that selects a theory and then applies it, which is called "theory to practice." The process we propose is messier, and better, than that. If a church is to live in responsiveness to and dependence on God, reflective discernment is a continuous practice, rooted in the current environment and experiences of the church.

During seminary I (Mark) was working as an intern for a nearby university chaplain's office. Because of the ethnic diversity on the campus, I was on the fast-track for learning about various ways Christians expressed their faith. My Midwestern, Scotch-Irish background shaped me as fairly "plain-spoken." That is, words had basic literal meanings, conversations were ordered logically and sequentially, and prayer was also to be within these orderly, plain-spoken norms. Then Keith, an African American student and ordained Pentecostal preacher, invited me to a student prayer meeting. After energetic singing and a devotional (brief Bible exposition), the prayers began—and it was neither orderly nor plain-spoken. Because I knew and trusted Keith, and many of these students were also becoming

---

[3]Lesslie Newbigin, *A Word in Season* (Grand Rapids: Eerdmans, 1994), pp. 60-63.

my friends, I was able to bracket my discomfort and reservations—but my mind kept yelling, She can't mean that. . . . That's not true. . . . He's not serious! With numerous voices praying loudly simultaneously, I could see Keith's hands on a student's head as he loudly instructed her, "Pray every day; your prayers block the gates of hell. Don't fail! Don't fail on a single day or those gates will fail!" This was in the midst of numerous other loud prayers, "Help her, Lord." "Don't fail!" As I remember, there were other prayers that did not match my theology—but I did not doubt that these Christian brothers and sisters were genuinely experiencing prayer with our God.

Over the next few days my theological brain argued with Keith: "If her prayers continue or fail, they don't change the gates of hell. That's God's territory." But something else also happened. I began to remember that Jesus, and many other biblical persons, used language that was similar to Keith's. Conversations, instruction and prayers often included metaphors and analogies. Prophets and apostles spoke of sun, moon and stars falling when empires were being rearranged. Jesus indicated that removing one's eyeballs would eliminate lust. With these reflections I was able to hear and understand better how this African American group was participating with each other and God in prayer. I was also able to begin a much longer path of changes in my prayer life and how I participate in shaping group prayer.

This approach to practical theology, a continual movement from experience to reflection and study, and then on to new actions and experiences, is what we call *praxis*. This term is often misunderstood as "practice," referring to how a concept or theory is first understood mentally then applied in a real-life situation. But praxis is actually the whole cycle of reflection and study on one hand and engagement and action on the other. In my experience of Pentecostal prayer, my previous concepts about prayer, based in earlier study and experiences, were inadequate for this new experience. As I listened and observed, having already participated in friendship, my "knowledge" was being changed. So in further reflection and study I was able to see Scripture differently, and even see and reshape my own personal and ministry practices.

Brazilian educator Paulo Freire envisioned praxis as the way to bring

PRAXIS

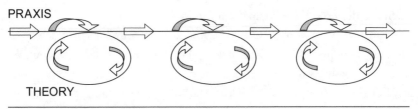

THEORY

Figure 1.1. Praxis cycle

significant social change to people.[4] He contrasted praxis with what he called the "banking" approach to education, in which the teacher simply pours information into the student, and the student's role is to receive the information and act on it or pass it on to another person. Thus, for students education is passive (they are not supposed to be creative thinkers), and it only perpetuates the cultural norms of those who determine what is to be passed on. Instead, Freire wanted men and women to become "culture-creators"—persons who actually shape their own culture and context—by gaining, through praxis, a more thorough and more meaningful relationship with the world. He wanted knowledge to be more than banked information; he wanted knowledge to serve a life-giving role in nurturing persons and communities to change their contexts as they themselves were being changed through the reflection-action cycle.[5] Freire saw the need to counter the hegemony of larger social structures, and he believed that a community of persons could gain the capacities to create the knowledge they needed to bring change. He knew that education could either be directed at conformity to the powerful or it could help everyone become participants in creating the culture they live in. This concept of praxis can help church leaders frame ways for churches to not only understand their ministry context but also to bring about changes in their congregations and in their social contexts.

So in a church, praxis is the constant rhythm that includes study and reflection (including working with theology and other theoretical material) in continual interaction with engagement and action. A church's ca-

---

[4]Paulo Freire, *Education for Critical Consciousness* (New York: Continuum, 2005).

[5]See ibid., pp. 100-101. While conceptually different, Freire's work is consistent with Aristotle's emphasis that praxis includes the true ends or meanings in an action. My emphasis is that praxis is a way of life that allows the texts of our past, our current experiences and the substance of our eschatological hope to be brought to bear, by the work of the Holy Spirit, in our ongoing church life.

pacity to discern and participate in God's will is increased whenever this rhythm is well resourced and intentional. So a church's current way of worship is a praxis, whether or not the theories are talked about. A church's worship probably reflects historic traditions and how they convey Scripture. Also, worship reflects the cultural heritage and the current setting. It also reflects the priorities and skills of the worship leaders who have been present over the decades (or most recently), and the aesthetics of leaders and worshipers. So worship is a bundle of practices in which theology, culture and experiences are already embedded. Every church also has a praxis concerning how they as a whole view and interact with their geographic neighbors or with persons from different ethnic backgrounds. In what ways do they embody a social existence that emphasizes "Keep together. Take care of ourselves. Be cautious of anything strange"? Or in what ways do they believe and act as if initiating hospitality and graciousness, especially to those who are new or different or needy, is the joy and challenge of the gospel? Churches are shaped by habits, which are shaped over decades and centuries by the interaction of reflection and action. Our individual habits and biases are shaped by the habits and biases of the group, whether the group is our church or some other identifiable social influence.

Theologian Pat Keifert often reminds students and pastors, "Experience teaches us nothing!" Then, as questioning looks appear among those who are listening, he continues, "No one learns from experience. One learns only from experience one reflects upon and articulates."[6] We believe churches benefit when they intentionally reflect theologically on a church's life and ministry. We can learn that some of our habits are full of grace and faithfulness, but other habits show that we need to be converted. This is not a matter of finding new rules or strategies and applying them. Nor do we need primarily to clarify our doctrines in hope that any problems will then be fixed. Instead, we need to look carefully at various factors, converse with a genuine care about the voices around us, gain new skills at thinking and attend to the Spirit's initiatives.

In order to shape an appropriate praxis for leaders and congregations, we propose five interactive steps for theological reflection.[7] (1) *Name* and

---

[6]Pat Keifert, confirmed in personal e-mail November 27, 2008.
[7]This method, shaped by Mark Lau Branson, is based on Thomas Groome, *Sharing Faith: A*

describe your current praxis concerning some aspect of church life. This work of observation and description, focused on a selected topic, sets some kind of boundaries for the process. It also makes you aware that you are beginning with a set of experiences, that you don't engage study as an empty slate. When possible, include multiple voices in the description and welcome divergent perspectives. (2) *Analyze* your praxis, seeking to understand all of the influences and consequences, by using resources from your culture. This work includes using the perspectives of the social sciences, history, the humanities and philosophy. We also learn from studies in organizational and communication theories. (3) *Study* and *reflect* on Scripture, theology and Christian history concerning your praxis and analysis. We believe the Scriptures are uniquely authoritative for churches—that these narratives, prayers, prophecies and letters show us how God has already spoken to and worked in specific places. Further, we believe that Scripture, when attended to prayerfully, will help us understand our contexts and what God wants to do among us and through us.[8] For many centuries other believers have read these biblical texts, prayed to God and worked together in their own locations. From their lives we have creeds, historical accounts and theological traditions, all available to help us in our own discernment and practices. Churches need to draw on their own heritage as well as the biblical interpreters and theological resources from outside their culture. (4) *Recall* and *discuss* stories from your church's history

---

Comprehensive Approach to Religious Education and Pastoral Ministry (Eugene, Ore.: Wipf & Stock, 1999), with significant influence from Ray Anderson, *The Shape of Practical Theology: Empowering Ministry with Theological Praxis* (Downers Grove, Ill.: InterVarsity Press, 2001); Alan Roxburgh and Fred Romanuk, *The Missional Leader: Equipping Your Church to Reach a Changing World* (San Francisco: Jossey-Bass, 2006); and Gerhard Heitink, *Practical Theology: History, Theory, Action Domains* (Grand Rapids: Eerdmans, 1999).

[8]Throughout this book we provide biblical texts along with questions and comments, and we have seen how such texts have been used by God in our own churches. We do not read the Bible as a strategic plan that specifies tactics, but we do believe it creates a consciousness, a way to see and interpret our situations, and sometimes commends practices that help us perceive and act faithfully. We cannot offer here a full account of methods for interpretation or a formula for knowing what to do with a text when we use the practical theology cycle, but we can note books that have informed us. In addition to those we recommend throughout the book that specifically address matters of culture and boundary crossing, we have benefited from Joel Green, *Seized by Truth: Reading the Bible as Scripture* (Nashville: Abingdon, 2007); Richard Hays, *The Moral Vision of the New Testament* (San Francisco: HarperSanFrancisco, 1996); Stephen Mott, *Biblical Ethics and Social Change* (New York: Oxford University Press, 1982); and Glen Stassen and David Gushee, *Kingdom Ethics: Following Jesus in Contemporary Context* (Downers Grove, Ill.: InterVarsity Press, 2003).

and your own personal lives that are related to the topic under discussion. These may be stories that note your own misunderstandings and way-wardness, or you may find narratives that are full of wisdom and faith. (5) Corporately *discern* and *shape* your new praxis by working with the results of steps one through four and then prayerfully naming what you believe to be your priorities. Focus on what you believe God is doing in your lives and in your context, and experiment with alternatives, which will lead you to-ward commitments to new praxes.

There are some assumptions behind this method of practical theology. The metaphor cluster by Newbigin that we already noted, that the church is a sign, foretaste and instrument of God's reign, provides a way for us to understand each local church and to envision the role of the worldwide church. Because most of our attention in this textbook will concern local churches, we believe Newbigin's metaphors are helpful. We believe that the Holy Spirit is present and active in the churches and in the world. God's love for the world is expressed in the ongoing initiatives of the Spirit as one who loves, heals, teaches, reconciles, convicts and persuades. Be-cause the church is to participate in the life and activities of God, we be-lieve our work is to discern ways we are to actively enter into God's initia-tives in the world. What is God doing in us and around us? What does God want to do?[9] The purpose of theological reflection is to help us be wiser and more faithful in our discernment and participation.

The biblical and theological work of practical theology (step 3) is espe-cially challenging. In addition to the amount and diversity of biblical ma-terials, there is a massive corpus of commentary and theological writings, from past centuries through contemporary works, and it is impossible for all of it to be taken into account. It is important to realize that no church enters this work as a blank slate. As is emphasized by the practical theol-ogy cycle, a church already has experiences and traditions that have shaped how they read (or misread) Scripture, what theological perspectives they claim, and how those affirmations shape (or fail to shape) their current practices. That is, what they access (the Bible and various theological doc-uments) and how they interpret those resources are influenced by their own situation and habits. This contextual approach to materials is also

---

[9]This framework is explained well in Craig Van Gelder, *The Ministry of the Missional Church* (Grand Rapids: Eerdmans, 2007).

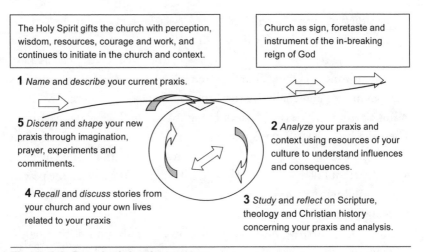

The Holy Spirit gifts the church with perception, wisdom, resources, courage and work, and continues to initiate in the church and context.

Church as sign, foretaste and instrument of the in-breaking reign of God

1 *Name* and *describe* your current praxis.

5 *Discern* and *shape* your new praxis through imagination, prayer, experiments and commitments.

2 *Analyze* your praxis and context using resources of your culture to understand influences and consequences.

4 *Recall* and *discuss* stories from your church and your own lives related to your praxis

3 *Study* and *reflect* on Scripture, theology and Christian history concerning your praxis and analysis.

Figure 1.2. Practical theology steps

true on the inside of those very materials—the works of Moses and Jeremiah, Luke and Paul—were formed inside historical situations, and the creeds and other documents of church history (including systematic theology) are always situated in specific places and times, among particular people and in the midst of concrete events. This does not make them less valuable; rather, it shows how God is more invested in the world and its real situations rather than in timeless ideals.

This state of affairs can provide guidance for a church's work in practical theology. When a thematic frame is named (step 1), and as the social setting is better understood (step 2), then biblical and theological materials can be found and explored as they pertain not just to the theme but also to their own situation. For example, Jesus' focus on reaching Jews may have had a temporary, contextual purpose, but his explicit connections with Gentiles and his later teaching (Mt 28; Acts 1) are more akin to the situations our churches face. So a church would ask, how do these texts help us understand God's priorities, especially for us? The study of theology also needs to attend to the contexts of its formulation, so theological expositions that were shaped in homogeneous environments would tend to differ from those formed in heterogeneous situations. That is, if those writing theology were attentive to and in conversation with social diversity, their reading of Scripture and their awareness of God's initiatives would lead them to write theology that speaks to that reality. So a church would ask,

What situations were these church leaders facing? How did these theological presentations help or hinder the church's life and mission? What would help us see and act as God's people in our context? Leaders have important work in helping churches find biblical and theological resources that can inform and challenge their churches' practices, and that work requires a resourcefulness with both literature and with collegial networks. Then the narratives of the situation, of biblical texts and of theological statements can be brought into the church's conversations. This is done with expectant prayers that the Holy Spirit will give the church the power, courage and wisdom to see what God sees and to care about what God cares about.

In the appendix, we have provided a diverse collection of theological statements from a variety of contemporary writers. These brief paragraphs show how these writers work with theology as it speaks to our American context of cultural diversity. Theological topics include the Holy Spirit, eschatology, ecclesiology, the cross, forgiveness, as well as other themes. We have already written of our conviction that the Holy Spirit engages contemporary churches in discernment and mission. In chapter two we will provide our own theological comments concerning the interface of ecclesiology, reconciliation, the Trinity and missiology. In addition, the Bible studies in each chapter are selected for their relevance to congregational life and mission in the contexts of social diversity.

Even though we have described a sequence for these steps for engaging practical theology, the process is more like a spiral that has multiple entry points and loops. The process may be engaged when a Bible study leads some church members to ask new questions. Or perhaps someone had an experience in the neighborhood, and this experience motivated new conversations and questions in the church. When a number of persons realize the importance of the situation, more intentionality (and time) is given to the process. In the middle of the spiral, the process may require a return to an earlier step. For example, if I am talking about my own Scotch-Irish roots, I may then need to return to analysis (step two) in order to learn about the influence of the Scotch-Irish, and to study (step three) concerning my church's Presbyterian history. So I was recalling my ethnic heritage (step four), then I engaged steps two and three. If God wants to use my pondering for the life of my church, I

Questions for Practical Theology

1. What is our current praxis and situation? Start by describing the activities and context concerning a theme or aspect of life and ministry.

2. What cultural resources can help us understand and interpret our situation and God's presence to and call on us? This includes social sciences, philosophy, cultural studies, critical theory, media and social history.

3. What Christian resources, from our own cultural heritage and from other cultures, can help us understand and interpret our situation and God's presence to and call on us? Reflect on related biblical narratives, episodes in church history, theology and creeds.

4. What do we know about our church and ourselves that can help us understand and interpret our situation and God's presence to and call on us? Tell the stories from our personal lives and our church's history that are relevant, and listen for insights that change how we understand the topic.

5. How do we discern and participate in what the Trinity initiates in our context? In light of what we are learning, and attending to what we are hearing in listening prayer, what can we imagine as a future shape for this praxis? Shape experiments that adapt current activities or initiate new ones, and decide on criteria for evaluating potential longer-term commitments.

would engage some other members, probably by going to step one so we can describe how our church lives with its own ethnic heritage as it engages its own context. Other loops are created when a Bible study shows us that we need to do better local analysis or when a discernment process prompts us to reengage previous steps. All of these resources—these stories and any gathered information—interact as we attempt to see differently, to ask holy and thoughtful questions, and to discern the way forward. It is important to emphasize that this process of practical theology has the goal of faithfully engaging our world; these activities are not praxis unless we are continually reshaped by our engagement with God in our context.

Personal Reflection/Group Exercise:
Researching Congregational Cultural History

Small teams of participants can each select nearby churches for research. Churches, chosen with attention to ethnic variety, should be at least thirty years old. Various resources are possible: websites, publications (archived newspaper articles or denominational materials), church archives, judicatory records, or interviews with staff, other leaders, older members and neighbors who may have information even though they are not participants. Some possible questions:

1. What are the ethnic and cultural roots of the church in the United States and, possibly, in other countries?

2. Were there changes in the congregation's ethnic makeup? If so, why?

3. Were there changes in the ethnicity of pastors?

4. What demographic changes have affected the neighborhood? Did the church ever relocate? If so, were demographic changes considered in the move?

5. Is there a relationship between the church's cultural roots and its theological tradition (like Swedish Lutheran or Latino Baptist)?

6. Ask questions about particular ways that activities or relationships or organizational structures exhibit the cultural identity.

7. What is the relationship between the culture (or cultures) in the church and the culture(s) of the local context?

8. During this work, reflect on how you are similar or dissimilar to the people of the church and its context. Were you aware of how your were well-suited or unprepared to understand what you were researching?

PRACTICAL THEOLOGY AND INTERCULTURAL LIFE

How can practical theology serve this book's concern for intercultural life in churches? Here is a brief overview of the five steps as they might provide a focus on a specific church's question. Later chapters provide specific resources for each step.

1. The church describes its current circumstances concerning ethnic ho-

mogeneity or heterogeneity and their relationships and practices among themselves, in their neighborhood and regarding their larger context.

2. They analyze their environment, including demographics, history, world-views, cultural resources like the arts and the sociopolitical forces that shaped them and their context. (Later chapters expand on this analysis.)

3. Then as they study the texts of Scripture, church history, and their theological traditions and beliefs (concerning the incarnation, the Trinity, the gospel, God's love for the world and the meaning of being a church), they lay these narratives and beliefs alongside their current praxis and analysis. This allows a rethinking of practices as questions are raised, traditions are reconsidered and biblical voices are heard.

4. They tell their personal ethnic autobiographies, the ethnic and cultural story of their congregation, and stories of boundary crossing and of being engaged by persons who are different. The insights of the previous steps often create more clarity concerning these narratives.

5. The church prayerfully enters into discernment, asking God, "What are you doing?" and "What do you want?" They shape a new praxis through imagination, planning, experiments, evaluations and commitment.

This illustration indicates the kinds of resources a church needs in order to engage the complexities of intercultural life. Initially there needs to be willingness, at least among some leaders and members, to talk about the interrelationship of Christian faith and ethnicity. Even though a church can enter the method at any point, they eventually need to engage each step. In their initial conversations about the church's current praxis, there needs to be a basic honesty about their situation, their practices, their beliefs. This is all subject to analysis and change, but it does provide a snapshot of their on-the-ground realities.

Then, when participants begin to do a more thorough analysis (step 2), they have the benefits of numerous resources. In addition to basic statistics about the church and its context, there are other cultural resources that deepen understanding.

As an Oakland, California, church was beginning to deepen its ministry connections with its neighborhoods, members became more aware that they needed to give new attention to their own ethnic diversity as well as the diversity of their context. Through conversations with neighbors and in research at libraries and museums they learned how their city had been reshaped by World War II. After the bombing of Pearl Harbor, the U.S. government began a massive plan to create facilities for building a naval fleet large enough to win the war in the Pacific. This plan required the recruitment of thousands of persons, mainly from the South, including large number of African Americans, which changed the ethnic makeup of these cities.

But the longer-term change was also economic. At the end of the war, thousands of workers were unemployed, many of them African American, and while the United States put millions of dollars into efforts to rebuild Japan and Europe, these western port communities were largely left on their own without adequate manufacturing alternatives or civic resources. As members of the church learned about this history, they gained new perspectives on the relationship between ethnic diversity and economic disparity. They gained new respect for those involved in the decades-long efforts to, in Jeremiah's words, "seek the welfare of the city." They deepened their own participation with various urban organizations that engaged urban challenges, such as Habitat for Humanity, the Pacific Institute for Community Organizations and nearby African American churches.

Any church that wants to learn about and be shaped by God's agenda of gospel reconciliation will need to study its historical context. The intercultural relationships inside and among Oakland churches can be strengthened as cultural histories are studied. To deepen our understanding of each other's cultures, churches can also engage movies, novels and poetry. They can visit museums and cultural sites. These resources are all ways of studying and reflecting on the church's life, context and situation. Many of this book's chapters are developed to deal with the complexities of this analysis. The lessons of cultural anthropology can help us understand each other; the perspectives of organizational and leadership theory can clarify the dynamics we experience. Like the other steps of this practical theology method, analysis is not just done once; it is a continual work or the church.

As an example of step three, this chapter included a brief exploration into the book of Jeremiah. If a church were using the method we have outlined, then this biblical narrative, among many others, should receive study and reflection. Even though we will engage some additional passages, churches will need more extensive resources. What kind of boundary crossing is embedded in the Gospels, Acts or Paul's letters?

Step three also includes the study of theology and church history. Our concern for creating relationships and organizations that exhibit intercultural life is related to numerous topics of Christian theology, most notably anthropology, soteriology, the Trinity, ecclesiology, eschatology and missiology. There are also specific matters of Christian discipleship that arise from our theology of sanctification, such as reconciliation, forgiveness, love, justice, truth, self-sacrifice, peace, hospitality and generosity. Additionally, the narratives of church history and the continuing developments in historical theology are included in the studies of step three. Matters of boundary crossing, encountering cultural differences, and dealing with issues of inclusion and prejudice are always present in the stories of the missional expansion of the church. In the modern historical notes provided in the introduction, we referred to the long record of prejudice and discrimination in churches of North America. There are important stories of inclusion—like those Pennsylvania Mennonites—but they are scarce. In recent years an increasing number of U.S. congregations is experiencing various forms of multicultural life (see the section "Forming Multiethnic Congregations" in the bibliography). Theological explorations concerning the Trinity, ecclesiology and the missional essence of the church are especially noteworthy (see "Selected Books on Theological Topics" in chapter 2). If churches leaders intend to seriously engage our responsibilities in a multicultural environment, these resources cannot be ignored.

Step four is that of recall and storytelling. The activities of self-reflection, which are very important for individual Christians and for congregations as a whole, make it more likely that we can gain new knowledge, discern God's promptings and become more faithful in our habits and activities. We are already shaped before we encounter new experiences and information—and that shaping can hinder or help our faithfulness. As emphasized by Freire, a consciousness about ourselves and our situation contributes to the possibility that we can be creative subjects instead of just objects. If we are aware of the stories and habits behind us, we may be more capable of building on strengths and finding alternatives to our

Selected Books on Theological Topics

DeYoung, Curtiss. *Reconciliation: Our Greatest Challenge—Our Only Hope.* Valley Forge, Penn.: Judson, 1997.

Fong, Bruce. *Racial Equality in the Church: A Critique of the Homogeneous Unit Principle in Light of a Practical Theology Perspective.* Lanham, Md.: University Press of America, 2002.

González, Justo. *For the Healing of the Nations: The Book of Revelation in an Age of Cultural Conflict.* Maryknoll, N.Y.: Orbis, 1999.

Hines, Samuel George, and Curtiss DeYoung. *Beyond Rhetoric: Reconciliation as a Way of Life.* Valley Forge, Penn.: Judson, 2000.

Jones, L. Gregory. *Embodying Forgiveness: A Theological Analysis.* Grand Rapids: Eerdmans, 1995.

Katongole, Emmanuel, and Chris Rice. *Reconciling All Things: A Christian Vision for Justice, Peace and Healing.* Downers Grove, Ill.: InterVarsity Press, 2008.

Schreiter, Robert. *The Ministry of Reconciliation: Spirituality and Strategies.* Maryknoll, N.Y.: Orbis, 1998.

Volf, Miroslav. *The End of Memory: Remembering Rightly in a Violent World.* Grand Rapids: Eerdmans, 2006.

———. *Free of Charge: Giving and Forgiving in a Culture Stripped of Grace.* Grand Rapids: Zondervan, 2006.

See also the appendix.

weaknesses. In the introduction, we both provided a brief personal narrative. Readers need to know that we, as authors, also have perspectives and priorities that arise from our histories. Our knowledge and motivations, our blind spots and our wisdom, are rooted into our autobiographies (see "Writing an Ethnic Autobiography" on p. 24). Research into a church's cultural roots may include work with church records, judicatory recourses, other local publications and interviews.[10]

Several years after the Oakland church began studying the history of its city, they tried two other means for deepening their cultural awareness. Most

---

[10]Concerning interviews, see Robert Weiss, *Learning From Strangers: The Art and Method of Qualitative Interview Studies* (New York: Free Press, 1995).

members were in small groups, each one formed to pursue a particular missional engagement in their context. They decided to use some of their weekly gatherings to share what they called their personal "cultural autobiographies." Some members were already very adept at such stories, but others had to connect with parents and relatives to learn more. At times they were struck by similarities, such as the stories of two young adults, one Mexican and the other Vietnamese, whose families had fled different types of oppression (economic and political) to get to the United States. At other times they became more conscious of the cultural roots behind their differences.

In order to expand these initial cultural understandings, the church decided to connect personal stories with movies. (This links with the analysis noted in step two concerning our need to use all kinds of cultural resources to understand current and future praxis.) Any group of persons with a shared ethnic identity could select a movie for everyone to watch. After the movie, those who chose the movie were in a "fishbowl"; they were to discuss some questions while everyone else was listening. First, to connect autobiographies with the movie, they talked about how they identified with characters or events in the movie. Then they discussed two other questions: What elements in your culture make it difficult to engage Christian faith? And what elements in your culture are parallel to Christian teachings and undergird your faith? The substance of these discussions flowed into numerous informal conversations throughout the church.

The Oakland church's historical records told the stories of several times when the church relocated. In each situation the reasons cited for the move had to do with a changing neighborhood. It was never specified that this Euro-American congregation did not know how to engage African American neighbors. As the city continued to diversify, more members moved to the suburbs. Eventually there were few members still living in the church's neighborhood. After a couple of decades of declining membership, a small, diverse group of adults and families began to revision a future in the church. As they studied the history, met neighbors and studied Scripture, they realized that any hope for being sustained as a multicultural church would require attention to lament. They needed to know the errors of the past; they engaged liturgical rites concerning confession and intercession; they celebrated the hope of friendships and networks that gave them access to a different future.

As part of step four, congregations also need to reflect on their corporate autobiographies—and such reflections can lead to liturgical activities like confession and lament as well as to praise and celebration.

Without this church's ongoing analysis and self-reflection they would not have been capable of welcoming the challenges they would face. This approach to discernment was to become a new praxis, noted in step five.

Step five is a prayerful, creative mix of elements that moves a church to new praxis. In chapter ten we will provide more details concerning leading profound changes in an organization. Practical theology emphasizes that new initiatives are not primarily just new programs or strategic steps. Rather, all of the interactive learning from the other steps comes into prayerful discernment. In step five, a church genuinely seeks to understand God's grace (which is the theological word for what we usually call "initiatives") concerning themselves and their context. This discernment is possible only with an ongoing engagement with the context, in confidence that the Holy Spirit is already at work. Various chapters of this book, concerning the cultural differences we have in matters such as relationships, worldviews and perceptions, are all important as we engage those who are culturally different. These topics are relevant whether difference is inside a congregation or with neighbors. So as a congregation experiments with activities, ministries and relationships, all of the resources of practical theology are continually employed. A church's basic commitment to discipleship and ministry in a multicultural context, through experiments and discernment, becomes a cluster of commitments and practices that bear the marks of intercultural life.

Leadership Triad

Some approaches to leadership, especially in organizations shaped by hierarchies or by modern management theories, focus on experts who have answers and who can manage and control outcomes. According to these frameworks, direction is set by the a CEO-style pastor, sometimes with the involvement of a board, then those goals are announced to the church and then marketed and structured into organizational life. We believe church leadership requires another approach; we will introduce a basic framework here and provide more details in chapter ten.[11] Those

---

[11]See Mark Lau Branson, "Ecclesiology and Leadership for the Missional Church," in *Missional Churches in Context*, ed. Craig Van Gelder (Grand Rapids: Eerdmans, 2007); and Mark Lau

in leadership need to attend to three spheres of activities. Each sphere requires that we perceive, interpret and act concerning on-the-ground situations. *Interpretive leadership* is about meanings: it provides the resources and guidance needed to shape a community of learners that pays attention to and interprets both texts and contexts. *Relational leadership* shapes all of the human connections (internal and external) and attends to the health and synergism of those relationships. *Imple-*

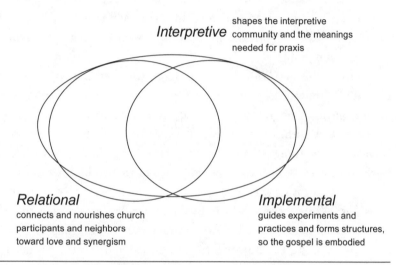

Figure 1.3. Leadership triad

mental leadership guides and initiates activities and structures so that a church embodies gospel meanings and relationships. Even though this description notes separate spheres, they overlap and they must remain vitally connected. If they lose their cohesion, then organizational dysfunction results.

Interpretive leadership. Interpretive leadership is about understanding and shaping meanings. What does it mean to believe the gospel? How do the particulars of our theological heritage help us listen to God and participate in how the Spirit is leading? What do we need to know about our context? Interpretive leadership shapes environments and provides resources so a church can engage the practical theology pro-

Branson, "Forming God's People," in *Leadership in Congregations*, ed. Richard Bass (Herndon, Va.: Alban Institute, 2007).

cess. At each step there is work concerning observations, conversations and interpretations—all in service of constructing the meanings needed for new imagination, communal discernment and the shaping of new praxes. For example, in step two, leaders guide research and analysis that brings new knowledge, new conversations and new meanings. Leaders help participants use their own knowledge and skills, or to seek additional resources, to see their current praxis in light of sociocultural perspectives, media studies, organizational perspectives, psychological insights and communication theory. Interpretive leadership is needed in formal and informal settings, in conversations, preaching and teaching, writing and praying.

Relational leadership. Relational leadership attends to all of the human dynamics among a church's participants and with the world around them. A church is connected to existing social groups among members and within the context: families (immediate and extended), friendships, working teams, prayer partners, neighbors, schoolmates, work colleagues and civic associations. All of the work of practical theology—the repeating cycle of praxis-theory-praxis—is processed in relationships. While there may be individual tasks, leaders are engaging the church in numerous social configurations that require behaviors that serve the goals of faithful discernment and action. So leaders need to identify important relationships, create new connections, enlist existing groups, nourish conversations and give courage for new actions. There will be hard work in facing conflicts and intransigence; social habits will surface that create resistance to the Spirit's promptings. Relational leadership provides awareness, initiatives and resources to shape the church and its contextual connections so that God's life among us is tangible, expressive and redemptive.

Implemental leadership. Implemental leadership concerns reforming and initiating activities and structures that are consistent with the interpretive and relational work. The organizational structures of a church come from various sources—the norms of its sociocultural context and ethnic heritage, the inheritance from a denominational or theological tradition, the ideas of members over the years, and the numerous resources offered in books and seminars. This implemental work concerns regular practices like worship, governance and education; it deals with everything from schedules to signage to authority. Implemental leadership draws attention to activities and structures, discovers the sources of those ways of life, helps to discover the fruit and consequences, and encourages experiments with new approaches that lead to commitments to the modes that serve the church's life and mission.

Leadership is not about an individual or even a small group having great ideas and pulling a church into their vision. Leadership is about shaping an environment in which the people of God participate in the action-reflection cycle as they gain new capacities to discern what God is doing among and around them. Each participant of leadership teams, those who carry titles and those without such recognition, have specific strengths that serve this triad. As they work together they can commend and nourish each others' gifts, gain new perspectives and abilities, discover a social imaginary[12] that is specific to them and their setting, and engage in the redemptive life of the gospel.

ENGAGING PRACTICAL THEOLOGY

The purpose of our writing is to help church leaders to see differently, to gain the skills and competencies needed for multicultural contexts, and to create environments that make God's reconciling initiatives visible and powerful. Leaders can encourage and guide a church to attend to biblical narratives and to ask the Holy Spirit to create new life among us through these texts. We need skills for seeing our churches accurately as the complex and changing systems they are. In order to do this we provided a basic method—practical theology—to connect the various aspects of church praxis. Chapter two will provide some specific theological resources, followed by a chapter concerning sociocultural frameworks plus perspectives on the fluid terms of racial and cultural diversity. Then each of the following chapters provides a particular perspective on this ministry—some way to see and act that is particularly important for intercultural life.

---

[12]A group's social imaginary is that set of self-understandings, practices and expectations that provide their identity and give them a sense of being a group. See Charles Taylor, *Modern Social Imaginaries* (Durham, N.C.: Duke University Press, 2004). These matters of group identity will receive more attention in chapter three.

At the Movies

In these movies, how do you see people trying to understand their context, what God (or various forces) intend, and how they are to respond?

Entertaining Angels: The Dorothy Day Story (1996). Dorothy Day does not appear to be a "saint," but her personal pilgrimage and the social realities of Depression-era New York ignite a passion that create controversy for the church about how faith is to be lived.

The Lord of the Rings trilogy (2001, 2002, 2003). J. R. R. Tolkien's story of a dangerous quest to destroy a powerful ring, including diverse participants (hobbits, humans, elves, dwarves), evil forces and reflections on power, goodness, individual meaning and the fate of the world.

The Gods Must Be Crazy (1980). A native discovers a Coke bottle and brings it back to his people, where it increasingly provokes conflict until he decides to return it to the god he believes sent it, resulting in an encounter with Western civilization, including a clumsy biologist and a despotic revolutionary.

2

MISSIONAL ECCLESIOLOGY AND CHURCH CONTEXT

Mark Lau Branson

*In a book of case studies on churches, the authors describe the transforma-
tion of a small church as it faced a set of decisions: "Instead of a primary
ministry of compassion for the few surviving members, they would need to
focus on telling the good news of Jesus Christ in their community. Instead
of preaching the Scriptures as a source of comfort to the faithful remnant,
they would need to proclaim God's call for the remnant to spread the gospel
to those in their community who were poor in spirit as well as in fact. Instead of taking care of their own, they would need to reach out to others.
Instead of seeking consolation for themselves, they would need to make a
radical commitment to live faithfully as missionaries in a hurting world
that needed desperately to experience God's love and salvation." Over the
next few years the church reorganized its life around small groups that
were committed to an "inward journey" of spiritual practices and an "outward journey" of a specific missional engagement. "The focus isn't on success as much as it is on building up and reaching out, inward and outward
spiritual growth, lives lived in faithfulness to Jesus Christ in the midst of
a non-Christian culture."[1]*

When the word *mission* is used in a U.S. church, the hearers will likely
think of foreign nations or distressed U.S. urban or rural locations. The

---

[1]Lois Barrett et al., *Treasure in Clay Jars: Patterns in Missional Faithfulness* (Grand Rapids: Eerdmans, 2004), pp. 16, 22. Branson was on the pastoral team of this church.

work of mission is often delegated to a committee or staff person, and most congregational life takes place without reference to those ministries. The primary participation of a church member with such activities may be limited to special donations, brief projects and perhaps short-term mission trips. At times members are asked to volunteer for activities, and leaders invest time in creating programs and publicity to increase such volunteerism. This recent understanding has significant theological and ministry flaws.

This means that there is important *theological* work to do here. In this chapter we will describe an ecclesiology that requires attention to God, to each other and to the world that God loves. These spheres of attention and practices cannot be pulled apart; God's initiatives instruct us that these overlapping spheres must be connected.

CHURCH FORMATION

As we provide frameworks for understanding ethnicities and cultures, we also need to provide frameworks for understanding the church. Our focus here is on a local congregation—a real, embodied, located social group that the apostle Paul calls "the body of Christ." Such a church is always part of networks and part of the worldwide church, but our emphasis on a group of people who regularly, face-to-face, come together for worship, learning and caregiving, and live in their own context with concerns for witness and good works.[2] In describing a people who are called "church," we need to consider the interplay of their corporate identity (who they are) and their corporate agency (what they do). Our identity and agency are interactive: what we do shapes our identity, and who we are shapes our activities.

Our work shows a commitment to a particular understanding of ecclesiology as it is rooted in the incarnation and the cross. As Paul wrote to the Colossians, "For in [our Lord Jesus Christ] all the fullness of God was pleased to dwell, and through him God was pleased to reconcile to himself all things, whether on earth or in heaven, by making peace through the

---

[2]Our focus on this concept of church—a congregation in a network of other churches and larger organizational structures—is not the only meaning of the word. The word *church* is also used to name the worldwide presence of believers or to designate particular systems of believers, like denominations. Because our topic is that of intercultural life in a congregation, we foreground this concept of church.

blood of his cross" (Col 1:19-20). In numerous places throughout the New Testament, and perhaps also most notably in 2 Corinthians 5:17-21 and in Ephesians 1:7-10, 2:14, 4:1, God's "one item agenda" of reconciliation is made explicit.[3] That reconciliation of "things in heaven and things on earth" (Eph 1:10), which is defined and won in the life, death and resurrection of Jesus Christ, is to be embodied and voiced by the church in the power of the Holy Spirit. This reconciliation is foremost an initiative of

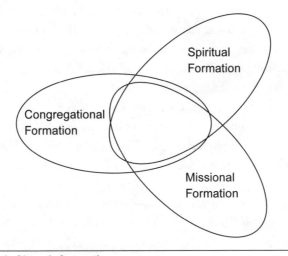

Figure 2.1. Church formation

God's (which is what the word *grace* means), and it addresses the numerous forms of sin and evil that we know. The Ephesians letter calls the church "to lead a life worthy of the calling to which you have been called" (Eph 4:1).[4] While there are numerous personal and societal forces that work against God's initiatives, we believe that the primary call on churches, as we worship and study and serve and witness, is to live into that call as "sign, foretaste, and instrument" of God's reconciling love.

So a church's identity and agency are shaped by how we attend to God, to each other and to the world we live in, in light of our vocation to be

---

[3]Samuel George Hines and Curtiss Paul DeYoung, *Beyond Rhetoric: Reconciliation as a Way of Life* (Valley Forge, Penn.: Judson, 2000), p. 24.

[4]It is worth noting that "you" is plural, that this "call" is to the body, and Ephesians 4 continues to deal with how gifts and character traits are enlivened in the interactions of individual persons in the context of a community.

reconciled and reconcilers. Leaders have the work of focusing attention on the interaction of meanings, relationships and practices that form such a people as a church of reconciliation. As exhibited in this chapter's opening illustration, this life of paying attention is not passive—it requires commitment, constant learning and being engaged actively in all three arenas. We use the terms *spiritual formation, congregational formation* and *missional formation* to describe this continuing and complex set of perspectives and activities.

Spiritual formation is about attending to God, learning about God's activities and character, and participating in God's life and initiatives. We are formed spiritually as we engage the narratives of Scripture, study the church's histories and traditions, worship, welcome God's grace and forgiveness into our lives, describe our lives and longings in prayer, listen to God's voice, and act in congruence with God's grace. Spirituality is not just a few specific practices or a demeanor; it is not an ethereal sphere that is disengaged from the physical world. God not only created but also engages the world, and any way we receive and participate in God's engagement is "spiritual." Theologically, our spiritual formation is in the context of the Trinity—God's self-revelation and continuing presence with us as Father, Son and Holy Spirit, exhibiting unity and diversity. Christian theology calls our attention to the inner life of the Trinity (a *perichoresis* or mutual indwelling and dance of intimacy, unity and submission that does not negate difference)[5] and to the Trinity's external expressions (dwelling in and engaging the world, notably the Father sending the Son, the Father and Son sending the Spirit). Further, God is in us and we are in God. Our receptivity to and participation in the Trinity's initiatives is what we refer to as "spirituality," and it is always both corporate and personal—it is never just a matter of private perspectives and practices. Our commitment to intercultural life is rooted here: God (Father, Son and Holy Spirit) embodies and initiates love that embraces difference and crosses boundaries, and calls us to a gospel of reconciliation and love.

Congregational formation concerns how we attend to each other in our churches. Another appropriate term is "social formation." We have numer-

---

[5]Perhaps initiated by Pseudo-Cyril; see Colin Gunton, *The One, the Three, and the Many* (Cambridge: Cambridge University Press, 1993), pp. 163-79 and 214-31; and Miroslav Volf, *After Our Likeness: The Church as the Image of the Trinity* (Grand Rapids: Eerdmans), pp. 208-20.

ous narratives in Scripture, church history and in our own lives concerning how God's grace becomes visible and available through those around us. The Law and the Prophets teach us about God's priorities concerning relationships, time, money, justice and mercy. Paul gives regular counsel about how we treat each other and how righteousness is embodied in a church. New Testament metaphors are abundant and informative: body of Christ, temple of the Holy Spirit, household, civic assembly, new race, royal priesthood, living sacrifice. All of our friendships, groups, arguments, bonds, births and deaths are embedded in a church's relational life. The affections and activities of a group are altered by Jesus' call to love each other, to attend to anyone who is marginalized by assumptions and routines, and to be especially aware when we import a society's prejudices into our church life. Congregational life is often the crucible in which we face ourselves, name those beliefs and behavioral patterns that harm others, and experience the grace of God that makes us a new creation. Reconciliation with God is always linked to social reconciliation—this is the grace and work of congregational formation, and it requires competent relational leadership.

Missional formation refers to how God shapes a church to participate in God's love for the world. Ever since Abraham, God has been shaping a people whose life reflects the goodness and love of this God who creates and redeems. Every congregation is both called and sent; the call gathers us to hear, understand and accept our vocation, which is that we are sent into the world for the sake of the gospel. As agents of God's reign, churches engage the people and powers of their context. This engagement is one of mutual shaping—any church is changed by its context (in appropriate ways and often in ways that counter the gospel)—and a church embodies and initiates the graces of God in love, justice, healing, peace, witness, invitation and proclamation. We will give more attention to missional formation in the following section.

This framework—the triad of spiritual, congregational and missional formation—provides a basic way for us to examine a church's identity and agency. The leaders of a church need to guide and nourish the church concerning these ways of paying attention (to God, to each other and to the world), and to engaging activities that express the grace of God. Our ethnic heritage brings narratives, habits, vocabulary and mental frameworks to our spiritual formation as we seek personally and corporately to pay attention to God. Our social (congregational) formation is influenced by the relational, organizational and caregiving modes of our ethnic and cultural background. And our missional formation draws on the strengths and weaknesses of how our cultural narratives have shaped the ways we interact with strangers or seek peace and justice.

Personal Reflection/Group Exercise:
Personal Mission Experiences

List various experiences you have had in which you were engaging people outside the church toward gospel purposes. These may have been works of mercy and justice, service projects, evangelism, mission trips, conversations with friends or neighbors, partnering with others to make a neighborhood more humane and so on. First in silence, then in groups, reflect on these questions:

1. What were the goals, theological assumptions and outcomes of these activities?

2. Were there times when outreach was a programmed activity, perhaps requiring staff and significant planning?

3. Did some experiences arise in settings apart from programmed activities?

4. Did you experience new partnerships or meaningful conversations?

5. Were you aware that God was ahead of you?

6. How were you changed?

MISSIONAL CHURCHES

The missional church conversation was shaped and energized by Bishop Lesslie Newbigin, who, after decades of work with the Church of South India, returned to England and found a church that was profoundly out of touch with its cultural context. In India he had practiced key missiological priorities: participate in and understand a culture, engage the culture with appropriate activities and words, and partner new believers in shaping a faith community (church) that is appropriate for God's missional presence in that environment. Now he saw that the churches in England needed those missional priorities—and he also brought that challenge to the United States.[6]

In one of the core textbooks of the missional church movement, Darrell Guder connects our beliefs about God with our understanding of ecclesiology (our beliefs about church):

> We have learned to speak of God as a "missionary God." Thus we have learned to understand the church as "sent people." "As the Father has sent me, so I send you" (John 20:21). This missional reorientation of our theology is the result of a broad biblical and theological awakening that has begun to hear the gospel in fresh ways. God's character and purpose as a sending or missionary God redefines our understanding of the Trinity. . . . This Trinitarian point of entry into our theology of the church necessarily shifts all the accents in our ecclesiology.[7]

As noted by Guder, this missional ecclesiology is grounded in the doctrine of the Trinity, where we see the sending nature of God. The Father sends Israel and prophets; then the Father sends the Son; the Son breathes the Spirit onto the disciples; and the Father and Son send the Spirit to the church. Jesus prays to the Father concerning the disciples, "As you have sent me into the world, so I have sent them into the world" (Jn 17:18). The new emphasis in the missional church framework is that mission is not one activity among many, much less an option for some Christians who are especially dedicated. Rather, God's essence is missional; mission is at the very heart of the Trinity; we (as churches) are "in God," and God (as Trinity) is in God's world and in God's churches. The Latin term *missio Dei* captures this understanding—God is a missional God who acts missionally by preceding and then by shaping and sending the church into the world. So by definition (theologically speaking) a church is to be missional at its core. Mission is part of a church's essence.

From the earliest stories about the disciples, and in the beginning years of the church, this *sentness* is assumed. By our very nature as followers of Jesus, we are a sent people. This does not mean we are all itinerate—moving about from place to place—but that wherever we are, we know

---

[6]For an update on how this is playing out in England, see *Mission-Shaped Church* at www.cofe.anglican.org/info/papers/mission_shaped_church.pdf.

[7]Darrell Guder, ed., *Missional Church: A Vision for the Sending of the Church in North America* (Grand Rapids: Eerdmans, 1998), pp. 4-5.

ourselves to be sent into the world as a church of God for the sake of the gospel. The Ephesian letter calls this our vocation: "I . . . beg you to lead a life worthy of the calling to which you have been called" (Eph 4:1). As that chapter of Ephesians proceeds, this call is connected to Jesus' being sent into the world and the provision of gifts to the church so we are equipped for continual growth (quantity and maturity). The New Testament has few mandates concerning missional activities because throughout the texts this missional *character* and the specified *vocation* are assumed.[8]

Perhaps some claims of the missional church conversation, from the primary books listed earlier, can clarify the distinctives:

- A church is to be a sign, foretaste and instrument of the reign of God.

- God is a missional God who shapes the church in God's image.

- It is not that a church has a mission but rather God's mission has a church.

- A church is sent to be a witness in its location.

- *Missio Dei*, flowing from the sending Trinity, implies a missional church.

- A missional church asks, "What is God already doing in our context, and how do we participate?" A church then also asks, what does God want to do in this context?[9]

Even though historic creeds and these more recent theological affirmations help us frame our understandings, ecclesiology needs to be understood in reference to a specific place, in reference to the specifics of God-on-the-ground in that particular location. All of our New Testament texts are of this kind—always in reference to specific churches, their people and their sociocultural contexts. Theologian Craig Van Gelder emphasizes the importance of a church's context:

> Just as congregations are always contextual, their ministries are also always contextual: The Spirit leads congregations within particular contexts. Ministry can take place only in relationship to a particular context, and, as

---

[8]This theme is developed well by Darrell Guder in lectures on iTunesU: <http://deimos3.apple.com/WebObjects/Core.woa/Browse/fuller.edu.1302926166>.

[9]These questions, and the theology behind them, are well developed in Craig Van Gelder, *The Ministry of the Missional Church* (Grand Rapids: Baker, 2007).

ministry takes place, congregations develop specific practices for that context. This means that all forms of ministry are going to bear the patterns and shape of the culture in which a congregation is ministering.[10]

The missional church framework requires that we deepen our knowledge of our contexts, including ethnicities and cultures, so we can become more capable of wise and effective leadership in our churches. These matters of social characteristics are the stuff of human community and identity. They are the context of sin and redemption, of goodness and evil, of wounds and healing. For a church in which participants engage each other and their neighbors, specific cultural traits and narratives form the pathways for conversations. God sends us and empowers us for this engagement.

SOCIAL FORCES

This conversation about missional ecclesiology has mainly addressed churches that have been shaped in Christendom. *Christendom* is the historic situation in which national structures and church structures are interwoven and participants assume that government, churches and citizens share a broad agenda. Many churches that were planted in the United States had roots in Protestant European Christendom. This Protestant framework is a historic remnant of the merged Roman Empire–Roman Catholic Church, which passed on this understanding to European Protestant churches in which national rulers were often church rulers.[11] Even though official state churches are largely gone, the result of a historic phase called the "disestablishment" of the church, it is not uncommon even now for leaders and members of churches to believe they occupy a privileged position in society. In other words, many of the *structures* of establishment are gone, but the *ethos* of establishment remains. The confused relationship between churches and society's governing structures has often led to misunderstandings concerning the church's nature and purpose. The missional church framework explicitly emphasizes the values of disestablish-

---

[10]Craig Van Gelder, "Missiology and the Missional Church in Context," in *The Missional Church in Context*, ed. Craig Van Gelder (Grand Rapids: Eerdmans, 2007), p. 41.

[11]The history of Roman Catholicism in Latin America also features both establishment and disestablishment, but the contexts and results are different. These variations have influenced the perspectives of Latino immigrants. Also the Roman Catholic Church in the United States was never in a privileged position parallel to Protestantism. But the ethos of Protestantism has influence beyond its own borders.

ment so that our ecclesial role in society can be redefined and our theology and our missional purpose can be clarified.

Understanding the church as a "contrast society" helps reorient the assumptions of Christendom. Numerous metaphors of the New Testament indicate ways the church made claims about its role in God's presence and mission: Jesus (not Caesar) is Light, Savior, Bread and Lord; the church is a kingdom of priests, an army, a company of aliens, a civic gathering (ekklesia), city on a hill—all descriptors that contrast the church with the religio-political claims of imperial Rome. As theologian Barry Harvey writes:

> When the church adopted this term [ekklesia] for their association, rather than that of the ancient guilds or civic clubs, it was claiming the status of a public assembly of the social whole. The goods and activities of this particular body politic, however, were not those of the Greek polis or the Roman imperium. On the contrary the assembly of God's messianic regime ordered the life of its members in ways that called into question virtually every social, political, and economic convention of its time.[12]

This is the challenge of context—how is a church to be aware and engaged in a context while not defined by the authorities and assumptions of that setting? If we do not understand ourselves as privileged within governing structures (the ethos of Christendom) but rather as voice and embodiment of God's priorities for men and women and our communal well-being, what kind of people do we need to become? In what ways will we be a contrast to the forces of our societal and cultural settings, and in what ways might those social realities cohere with gospel living? Like the exiled Jews we studied in Jeremiah 29, when we are without the prerogatives of privilege we gain capacities for seeing our world through the biblical narratives of being "strangers and aliens" who attend with the eyes of justice, compassion and neighborliness.

The missional church conversations challenge another major historic force. During the last century, U.S. churches have often thought of their structures and activities in terms shaped by Western corporations. This framework emphasizes hierarchy, expert leaders and departments fragmented by functional specializations. Corporations are focused on defin-

---

[12]Barry Harvey, Can These Bones Live? (Grand Rapids: Brazos, 2008) p. 102; see also Barry Harvey, Another City: An Ecclesiological Primer for a Post-Christian World (Valley Forge, Penn.: Trinity Press International, 1999).

ing commodities (consumer goods) and services (programs for consumers), and then marketing those products and activities. While this influence has been most notable among Euro-American churches, others have also adopted aspects of these organizational modes.[13] Those planting new churches may mistakenly believe they escape the societal forces that shape older churches, but thoughtful observation will show this to be naive. There will be significant differences in how diverse churches express societal norms, but for now it is only necessary to realize that major societal forces have shaped our churches and undercut our missional identity.

These two societal forces—the remnants of Christendom and the framework of American corporations—are among many other influences that have shaped U.S. churches. The missional church discussion seeks to surface these issues and find a faithful and theologically grounded reframing for the U.S. church.[14]

Many nations of the world never experienced Christendom, nor have they been as strongly influenced by modern corporate structures, so immigrants from those countries arrive in the United States with varied assumptions about the relationship between religions and the sociopolitical environment. Some have experienced various kinds of deference or antipathy to Roman Catholicism or other Christian churches; others lived with diverse kinds of religious alignment, perhaps among Islamic or Hindu cultures. Churches in the United States among non-Euro-Americans, such as African American and Hispanic churches, have no history of assuming that governing structures are aligned with their churches. There is great diversity in how they have attempted to avoid entanglement or to seek influence in social and political structure. So cultural differences and immigrant narratives shape how churches understand and practice their relationships with their neighbors and neighborhoods. Theological convictions

---

[13]Globalization has brought Western influences to churches worldwide, including some operational modes (see Mark Noll, *The New Shape of World Christianity* [Downers Grove, Ill.: InterVarsity Press, 2009]). In the United States, members of a minority group often interact with a dominant culture in two directions at the same time—they might resist certain dominant norms and simultaneously imitate certain aspects of those norms.

[14]For an introduction, see Alan Roxburgh and M. Scott Boren, *Introducing the Missional Church* (Grand Rapids: Baker, 2009). Other important voices have informed the missional church discussion, including missiologists Lesslie Newbigin and David Bosch, and theologians Karl Barth and Jürgen Moltmann. In more recent decades, and focusing specifically on U.S. Euro-American churches, Darrell Guder, Craig Van Gelder, Lois Barrett, George Hunsburger and Pat Keifert have served the conversation.

and ministry priorities also vary concerning boundary crossing—the level of importance given to connecting with persons of other cultures, and the value placed on shaping or participating in a multicultural church. Our embrace of missional ecclesiology is an affirmation of the basic tenants we have noted—that we are to participate in the *missio Dei* and that a church needs to attend to and engage the peoples and structures of its context. We are aware that some ethnic churches have a longer history of missional practices, but we are also aware that cultural boundary crossing has seldom been a priority for U.S. churches.[15]

Even with these distinctives among diverse churches, U.S. society has a cultural impact on all groups. For example, as a society we pay less attention to "place"—so even when churches assemble their members in a building, there may be no significant connection with other people in that place. These societal norms, which in varying ways affect all ethnicities, often shape our understanding of "church" more that the theological resources we claim. Our perceptions, formed in this societal setting, affect how we engage gospel priorities concerning our neighbors.

IMAGINATION AND LEADERSHIP

The *ways* a church embodies this character trait will vary depending on the makeup of that particular church and the context in which they find themselves. But we are making some fundamental assumptions that are both theological and practical. The first assumption concerns the source of a church's missional imagination. The approach to church life previously noted, based in the U.S. style of corporations, emphasizes professional leadership that is responsible for a company's vision and how it implements that vision; everyone else in the company is employed to carry

---

[15]For example, the concerns of Latino churches for engaging neighborhoods and for attending to cultural diversity have been expressed in books like Manuel Ortiz, *The Hispanic Challenge: Opportunities Confronting the Church* (Downers Grove, Ill.: InterVarsity Press, 1994); and C. Rene Padilla and Tetsunao Yamamori, eds., *The Local Church, Agent of Transformation: An Ecclesiology for Integral Mission* (Buenos Aires: Ediciones Kairos, 2004). From an African American perspective, numerous books deal with engaging a neighborhood. Concerning racial reconciliation, see Samuel George Hines and Curtiss Paul DeYoung, *Beyond Rhetoric: Reconciliation as a Way of Life* (Valley Forge, Penn.: Judson, 2000); Howard Thurman, *With Head and Heart: The Autobiography of Howard Thurman* (New York: Harcourt Brace, 1979); Korie Edwards, *The Elusive Dream: The Power of Race in Interracial Churches* (New York: Oxford University Press, 2008); and Spencer Perkins and Chris Rice, *More Than Equals: Racial Healing for the Sake of the Gospel*, rev. ed. (Downers Grove, Ill.: InterVarsity Press, 2000).

out that vision. It is not uncommon in churches for the clergy, sometimes with a small group of leaders, to decide on a vision that members (or a smaller group of volunteers) are to implement. This often leads to a more passive or nominal response among many of the church's members; the work of ministry is for a few, while everyone else is in support roles, often participating like consumers who choose activities based on personal preferences. This also results in a high turnover of members.

A core belief of missional churches is that God's missional imagination is among the people of God. That means that, as stated by Roxburgh and Romanuk, "God's future is among the regular, ordinary people of God."[16] The Holy Spirit resides in churches, in the midst of those, young and old, who have entered a covenant with God. According to Roxburgh and Romanuk, this implies that

> at its core, missional church is how we cultivate a congregational environment where God is the center of conversation and God shapes the focus and work of the people. We believe this is a shift in imagination for most congregations; it is a change in the culture of congregational life. Missional leadership is about shaping cultural imagination within a congregation wherein people discern what God might be about among them and in their community.[17]

What would change in a church if they believed that the missional imagination of God was among the common, everyday members of the church? How would participants respond if they engaged Scripture, neighbors and the Spirit with an expectation that God would reveal a missional life right in their context? Imagine clusters of church members continually

---

[16]Alan Roxburgh and Fred Romanuk, *The Missional Leader* (San Francisco: Jossey-Bass, 2006), p. 20. There are other authors and speakers who claim a missional agenda but are nonbelievers concerning whether existing congregations can be transformed. In our own priorities for missional ecclesiology and toward intercultural life, we obviously believe that churches can experience profound and lasting change in their own identity and agency. See also Alan Roxburgh, *Missional Map-Making: Skills for Leading in Times of Transition* (San Francisco: Jossey-Bass, 2010).

[17]Roxburgh and Romanuk, *Missional Leader*, p. 26. "Missional communities . . . are learning they need to listen and discern again what is happening to people in the congregation and in the community, and then ask these questions: What is happening to people? What might God be saying in the stories and narratives of the people in a congregation, if we would listen to them and give them voice? In what ways might God already be ahead of us and present among people in our community? How might we join with God in what is already happening?" (ibid., p. 24).

Bible Study: Luke 10:1-11—
Sending Seventy Disciples

[1]After this the Lord appointed seventy others and sent them on ahead of him in pairs to every town and place where he himself intended to go. [2]He said to them, "The harvest is plentiful, but the laborers are few; therefore ask the Lord of the harvest to send out laborers into his harvest. [3]Go on your way. See, I am sending you out like lambs into the midst of wolves. [4]Carry no purse, no bag, no sandals; and greet no one on the road. [5]Whatever house you enter, first say, 'Peace to this house!' [6]And if anyone is there who shares in peace, your peace will rest on that person; but if not, it will return to you. [7]Remain in the same house, eating and drinking whatever they provide, for the laborer deserves to be paid. Do not move about from house to house. [8]Whenever you enter a town and its people welcome you, eat what is set before you; [9]cure the sick who are there, and say to them, 'The kingdom of God has come near to you.' [10]But whenever you enter a town and they do not welcome you, go out into its streets and say, [11]'Even the dust of your town that clings to our feet, we wipe off in protest against you. Yet know this: the kingdom of God has come near.'"

This is a *lectio* exercise, often called "dwelling in the Word," which combines reading aloud, reading silently and listening carefully to each other with an expectation that the Holy Spirit is an active teacher among us.[a] Two persons will read the passage aloud for the whole class (or a small group). This is followed by 5-15 minutes for personal reading and meditation. Participants should read the whole passage again, 2-3 times, picturing the story's narrative. As you read, be aware when one verse or a few words seem to call for your attention. You may experience this out of simple curiosity or because your brain is trying to find meaning or because the Holy Spirit wants your attention. Go back to that part of the passage, reread it several times, and meditate on what may be important or attention-getting. When you regather for discussion, first hear from those who had something draw their attention

[a]For additional instructions and stories about *lectio* see Pat Taylor Ellison and Patrick Keifert, *Dwelling in the Word* (St. Paul, Minn.: Church Innovations Institute, 2008), and their Web resources at www.churchinnovations.org/06_about/dwelling.html.

and see if there are common experiences or related observations. Spend time talking about how your experiences relate to your or your church's relationships with your context (neighborhood, networks, etc.).

In addition to Bible studies that we have included in each chapter, we recommend that this exercise, with this passage, be repeated on several occasions as this book is read. Observations will lead you to explore why the societal context is considered threatening, what kind of steps and exchanges allow the disciples to shape conversational environments in a town, how God's initiatives were ahead of the disciples, whose hospitality is important, and how cultural elements play a role. In prayer and discussion begin to suggest analogies with your own church and context. (Also consider using the Jeremiah passage from chapter one for this *lectio* approach.)

organized around missional opportunities—in the neighborhood and along the church's relational networks. Consider what would happen if a church's members came to believe that they are not only supporters but also that they are at the very heart of God's missional presence—that the Holy Spirit can give them sight and passion and gifts to be agents of God's gospel. This is a key assumption: that God's missional imagination is among the people of God.

Francis is almost ninety years old. In a church Bible study, in which significant time and attention was given to asking God to show participants how the church was to live missionally in its town, she noted the emphasis in the passages on the importance of homes and meals. When Jesus was leading his disciples around Palestine, and when he sent disciples as ministers, they often conversed with others in homes and during meals. As a second-generation Japanese American, Francis thought of friends who were not Christians or who had not been active in churches. She decided to invite them to tea, and she asked another (younger) church friend to join her. Among other topics, Francis described how she experienced her church as a place of engaging worship, deep friendships and healing prayer. Her friends were very engaged in the conversation. A few weeks later, a couple of them volunteered to help in the church kitchen during an annual festival (a fairly safe way to spend time with friends); then they began to visit worship services. They connected with some other members. The Bible class prayed, with joy, as Francis told these accounts. Other participants in the class were hosting barbecues for their neighbors and deepened relationships along their block by organizing a block-long garage sale.

The missional church needs a different vision of leadership, and we will develop that more fully in chapter ten. As a matter of introduction, we only want to emphasize what Roxburgh and Romanuk wrote, that the work of church leaders is to shape an environment in which God's missional imagination, which is available to the members, can be discerned and entered into. How can a church's leaders help people throughout the congregation see Scripture, their context and themselves in a way that is congruent with God's love for them and for the world around them? When our common life (in worship, meals, study, prayer and caregiving) helps each member pay attention to the Spirit's missional imagination, they gain the capacities to discern concrete and specific practices for their neighborhoods and networks. What can members talk about, pray about, experiment with and innovate so they find themselves shaped by a missional Spirit? All of these questions engage the practical theology method we developed in chapter one. Everything we are presenting in this textbook is intended to guide and strengthen church leaders so they are more capable of this work.

GEOGRAPHY AND NETWORKS

What is the relationship of a church to its location? Is geography a malleable and somewhat incidental factor in a church's life? Do digital networks eliminate the importance of place? As we explain throughout the book, the society in which a church is embedded has a powerful influence on how that church understands itself. In U.S. society there are numerous influences that militate against the value of place: technologies of communication and transportation, the priority of having a mobile workforce, and the expendability of creation (nature) for capital. How do societal forces and resources contribute to or detract from a church's faithful life and mission? In particular, what influences a church to disengage from a local context or to pay attention to its geographic location? Churches are also connected to their environment through relational networks—the people we see regularly as family and friends, in civic life, at work and in school. Sometimes relationships are strictly functional, perhaps allowing for basic cooperation or courtesies, but without much chance for conversations. But other social connections, perhaps by God's initiatives, make room for a deeper engagement.

How can biblical narratives inform a church's understanding of these missional connections? We want to emphasize two answers: neighborhoods and networks. The exiled community (noted in our Jeremiah study) was specifically called to attend to their new location. In the study of Luke 10 in this chapter, Jesus sent disciples into villages to be agents of healing and witness in those specific locations. He was taking advantage of the built-in connections of a place in which word could spread because of proximity. When a church places its communal activities (meetings, worship, classes) in a neighborhood, it enters into God's missional love for that place and its people. There are similar implications concerning the residential locations and movements of members when they are significantly dispersed from each other. Perhaps focused attention and prayer can reveal opportunities when several households are in proximity to each other. They may have the vocation of living out God's care for their neighborhood and neighbors.

In addition to being located (dwelling among neighbors) a church is also networked. By *networked* we mean that they have relationships through families, friendships, colleagues and other associations. Sometimes those networks even cross national boundaries. For example, the gifts and witness of Pentecost, initially spreading through Jerusalem's neighborhoods, seem to have made their way along Hellenist relational lines. These stories of Jesus continued to spread as they were told among artisans and laborers in the alleys and streets of cities and towns and throughout a network of synagogues around the Mediterranean. Perhaps traveling businesspersons, like Lydia in Philippi and Priscilla and Aquila, brought the benefits of their trade-route connections. Notice how these two approaches (neighborhoods and networks) interfaced—the growing number of churches brought witness to communities, leading to more network connections, which led to more churches in more neighborhoods.

Table 2.1. Church Emphases: The Shift to Missional

Spirituality focuses on my intimacy with God.	Spirituality is our attentiveness to and participation in God's initiatives
The church sends missionaries elsewhere—into other places.	Churches are sent by God to exhibit and proclaim the gospel in places where they live.
Church leaders create plans for outreach and recruit volunteers to help.	Church leaders create an environment in which the people discern and participate in God's initiatives.

CONCLUSION: CHURCHES IN CONTEXT

We believe that neither a church's location nor its networks are accidental or incidental—but that the church needs to engage in person, in prayer and in imagination. There will be variations in energy expended, opportunities available and innovations attempted. As the missional church assumptions already emphasized, the leadership of a church can create an environment in which the hearts and minds and imagination of the church come more fully into God's love for the world, and that leads to a gospel embodiment that reaches out to friends and strangers. Of special interest to us are those opportunities within the church's own relational networks and in a church's neighborhood that require cultural boundary crossing.

For Further Reading: Primary Books on Missional Church

Guder, Darrell. *The Missional Church: A Vision for the Sending of the Church in North America*. Grand Rapids: Eerdmans, 1998.

Newbigin, Lesslie. *The Gospel in a Pluralist Society*. Grand Rapids: Eerdmans, 1989.

Van Gelder, Craig. *The Essence of the Church*. Grand Rapids: Baker, 2000.

———. *The Ministry of the Missional Church*. Grand Rapids: Baker, 2007.

Roxburgh, Alan, and Fred Romanuk. *The Missional Leader*. San Francisco: Jossey-Bass, 2006.

Roxburgh, Alan, and M. Scott Boren. *Introducing the Missional Church: What It Is, Why It Matters, How to Become One*. Grand Rapids: Baker, 2009.

At the Movies

Be attentive to how both of these movies query what God is doing in the world and how we are supposed to be a part with God in that task.

The Mission (1986). Eighteenth-century Spanish Jesuit missionaries successfully convert South American natives and help inaugurate radical cultural change in their tribe, only to then face protecting them when Spain sells their territory to proslavery Portugal.

Avatar (2009). Earthlings, having established a base on another planet, are at odds when commercial and military priorities are challenged by social anthropologists and an untrained paraplegic rookie who bonds with the natives.

3

Sociocultural Structures, Ethnicity and Churches

Mark Lau Branson and Juan Francisco Martínez

When William and Nadine Wilson arrived as the new pastors, the small inner-suburb African American church was composed of elderly, saintly men and women who knew that faithfulness would require change. William was aware that the neighborhood was now predominantly Latino immigrants, so he began to study Spanish. Sharon, a deaconess in the church, talked with Nadine about the homeless people in the community. She and her husband, Thomas, wanted to at least provide an occasional meal. Soon they gathered other cooks, including some from nearby churches, and a weekly meal was served.

If the church were only an invisible, amorphous entity, then history, culture, ethnicity and social context would be secondary or even irrelevant. But churches are real, physical, located groups that are influenced by their countries, societies, cultures and neighborhoods. The gospel deals with humans with bodies and belongings, and salvation is about physical realities now, and later with our resurrected bodies and a new heaven and earth.

Any understanding of intercultural life needs to make sense in our U.S. context—the very real, and changing, physical and social settings of our churches. When the gospel shapes people, it is within their social and cultural contexts. In this chapter we want to consider how social context and our definitions of ethnicity, culture and race affect a missional ecclesiology that seeks to develop intercultural life.

OUR SOCIAL CONTEXTS: SOCIETY, CULTURE, COMMUNITY

Churches exist in the midst of other social structures—like ethnic groups, nations, local neighborhoods or global migratory movements. There are several common terms used to describe and delineate these social structures. The terms are malleable, and writers differ on their exact definitions, but it important to explain how we will frame concepts and use these terms throughout the book.

Sociologists Talcott Parsons and Edward Shils conceptualized a social framework with the triad of the *individual* living in relationship to a *society* and to a *culture*.[1] We are especially interested in their description of a society as a system of structured relationships, like those embodied in various middle-sized systems such as regional economies and cities, and in macro-systems such as corporations and nations (and, for us, globalized entities, like multinational corporations and financial networks). These structures exist to organize people toward the society's goals—even if cultural and personal matters need to be diminished. Parsons and Shils examined four dimensions of a society: social dimensions (the ways a society defines, allocates and uses social relationships); economic dimensions (the manner of defining, allocating and using resources); political dimensions (the norms for defining, allocating and using power); and legal dimensions (the structural approaches to individual and institutional legitimacy). This means that different societies have particular ways of defining jobs and careers, money and banking, governance and authority, and laws and enforcement.

In the midst of societies, according to Parsons and Shils, culture is the patterned and interconnected system of ideas and beliefs, symbols and feelings, and values. Missiologist Paul Hiebert draws on this work and includes mental maps, worldviews, synchronicity and diachronicity.[2] A culture (usually shaped by an ethnic heritage and perhaps a geographic setting over a period of time) can be identified by how a group of people

---

[1]Talcott Parsons and Edward Shils, eds., *Toward a General Theory of Action* (Cambridge, Mass.: Harvard University Press, 1951).

[2]Paul Hiebert, "The Gospel in Our Culture: Methods of Social and Cultural Analysis," in *The Church Between Gospel and Culture: Emerging Mission in North America*, ed. George Hunsberger and Craig Van Gelder (Grand Rapids: Eerdmans, 1996). *Synchronicity* is related to the categories and logic embedded in our understandings of reality; *diachronicity* is related to the large narratives or sequenced events that are primary concerning how we make meanings about our own lives.

envisions and lives out what it means to be human, how they relate to beliefs about the supernatural, or what they assume about creation and their relationship with it. Such beliefs are embodied—so ideas about owning land or stewarding land as a gift will shape how the culture interacts with creation. Cultures also create and are shaped by symbols—whether language or coins or what is called the "built environment" (such as buildings and infrastructures). Many of these topics will be examined more thoroughly in the following chapters. So *society* has more to do with institutionalizing means for serving the goals of large social entities; *culture* embodies patterned meanings that have been developed over time and are transmissible to a culture's children or to others who cross into the culture.

But we also need another social category when we speak of churches because a congregation is neither a society nor a culture, and it needs to relate to the societal and cultural realities of its context. A congregation in the United States may be composed of persons from several cultures: Chinese Americans (of various generations), African Americans (whether recent immigrants or descendants of persons forced to immigrate as slaves), or people of one or various northern European heritages. Such churches are in the midst of the U.S. society and the realities of globalization, while also shaped (in various ways) by ethnic cultures.

To Parson and Shils's triad we propose positing a fourth social entity—*community*—to add conceptual clarity. Community has come to mean many things—from a network of professionals (the medical community) to a neighborhood, to a very temporary group of college students in a dorm. As noted earlier, the explanations here are intended to explain how the terms are used in this book. But this is not a minor issue—the concepts here are so important for understanding churches that, for example, even if the word *community* is not preferred, we still need something that communicates this cluster of meanings. A community can be composed of persons from one culture or from several cultures. A community is usually located in the midst of several societies. For example, a community in U.S. society is also usually within the social structures of a city and a state while also functioning in the structures of economic globalization.

Historically, churches in the United States often brought together community and culture. Many U.S. denominations were formed by ethnic communities, originally from Europe, who maintained their distinct identities through church and community life together. A group of immigrants with common ethnic roots would cluster in a town or urban neighborhood in which their church had a defining role. Many of today's denominations or Catholic parishes originally had a national or ethnic adjective in front of their names, for example, German Baptists, Swedish Covenant, Ukrainian Catholics. This changed as U.S. society pushed them into new intercultural relationships and interactions that caused these denominations to rethink their role as churches in this country. New social connections also occurred through generational and geographic changes. The diversity of church experiences has further increased because more recent immigration, from various parts of the world, is rooted in contexts that have not experienced various phases of multicultural life in their contexts or churches.

Josiah Royce wrote that the elements of memory, cooperation and hope are essential for community.[3] First, *memories*, arising from the narratives of a specific group of people and their life together, contribute to a group's understandings about itself, its world, its priorities, its ways of doing things and how it envisions the future. Memory comes from a commonly held set of interpretations that were developed over years of experiences and conversations. Some memories can be adopted, like when a church adopts biblical memories ("Were you there when they crucified my Lord?") or continues a tradition (such as those of John Wesley or William Seymour).[4] But in order to be a community, a specific group of persons must also have memories of their own shared lives—births and deaths, joys and sorrows, comings and goings, sin and forgiveness and ministry, and mercy and love. These stories accumulate, and the identity and activities of the community are continually renegotiated in the weaving of such narratives.

Second, Royce specifies that a community of persons live together with a kind of *cooperation* that requires that shared meanings be expressed in common side-by-side tasks. A community has implicit and explicit agreements or covenants that are embodied in how they educate children, communicate, work, eat and dance; it is this overlap of various shared practices

---

[3]Josiah Royce, *The Problem of Christianity* (1913; reprint, Chicago: University of Chicago Press, 1968), p. 262.

[4]Concerning John Wesley, see Richard Heitzenrater, *Wesley and the People Called Methodists* (Nashville: Abingdon, 1994); concerning William Seymour, see Cecil M. Robeck, *The Azusa Street Mission and Revival* (Nashville: Thomas Nelson, 2006), especially chap. 4.

that distinguishes a community from other groups that share occasional or specialized activities. Sociologist Robert Bellah calls these "practices of commitment" because "they define the patterns of loyalty and obligation that keep the community alive."[5] Among churches, for example, the history adopted from William Seymour led to well-known practices like Pentecostal prayer or to lesser-known practices like interracial worship.[6] In some current U.S. contexts, churches share the practices of maintaining transnational lives, especially in Latino communities where a geographic commitment is maintained in two nations.

Third, a group is not a community unless it shares *hope*—which means that they use the pronoun *we* in reference to an imagined and realizable future. A community projects its corporate life into the future; this is its social imaginary. When they develop personal talents or discover illness or imagine new ways of life, they are not alone—they will live into the future with this community.

These community qualities—shared memories, cooperation, hopes—are further clarified by another set of descriptors. Cardinal Avery Dulles draws on the work of sociologist Charles Cooley to note that a community has relative proximity, permanence and intimacy. None of these are absolutes—but in comparison with the practices and loyalties of other associations, a community is significantly more engaged in long-term, face-to-face relationships that are more frequent and less specialized.[7]

Royce distinguishes between "a highly organized social life" of a society and this concept of "the life of the true community." "There is a strong mutual opposition between the social tendencies which secure cooperation on a vast scale, and the very conditions which so interest the individual in the common life of . . . community."[8] In other words, society and community often work against each other; the society's claim to resources and power can militate against the covenants and practices of a community, or a community can claim prerogatives that a society deems to be unjust or

[5]Robert Bellah et al., *Habits of the Heart: Individualism and Commitment in American Life*, rev. ed. (Berkeley: University of California Press, 1996), pp. 153-54.
[6]Robeck, *Azusa Street Mission.*
[7]Avery Dulles, *Models of the Church*, rev. ed. (New York: Doubleday, 1987), p. 47. Dulles references C. H. Cooley, R. C. Angell and L. J. Carr, *Introductory Sociology* (New York: Scribners, 1933), p. 55.
[8]Royce, *Problem of Christianity*, p. 262.

problematic for those outside the community. So a community, such as a church, needs to be attentive to the definitions or meanings it has received from society and from cultures, and it needs to test those meanings in light of the gospel.

Table 3.1. Society, Culture and Community

Society	Culture	Community
Composed of micro- and macrosystems that structure the ways a society, across multiple cultures and communities, sets and pursues goals: • Social structures define, allocate and provide for the use of relationships • Economic structures define, allocate and provide for the use of resources • Political structures define, allocate and provide for the use of power • Legal structures define, allocate and provide for the use of legitimacy	Embodies a matrix of social patterns: • Norms (worldview, beliefs, values and practices) • Traditions (heritage) • Patterned meanings (how values are understood and embodied) • Development (learning among those born into the culture, enculturation for those who come from outside) • Symbolic representation (imaginations, media) • Perception (how sensory input is filtered, received, processed) • Conation (character, tendencies, wisdom) • Extension (styles of encounter with outsiders)	A local group of persons • Memories of shared experiences and narratives inherited from predecessors • Cooperative, side-by-side activities rooted in shared meanings and goals • Shared hope and imagination concerning future life together • Relative intimacy, proximity, and permanence • Unspecialized, face-to-face association • Adapts, resists, embraces, and challenges the influences of societies and cultures

Communities are becoming a less common occurrence in U.S. society. Numerous societal forces have other priorities that shape us: the economy wants a mobile workforce; self-realization pushes toward choices related to individual careers and tastes; consumerism as the prioritizing of choices leads us to see location as a consumer preference. Under these societal forces, tasks formerly embraced by communities (raising children, caring for the elderly, employing persons toward personal and community sustenance) are accomplished (or not) by society and its institutions. Without introducing a full set of arguments, we simply want to note that many characteristics of Christian discipleship and mission require something akin to these traits that describe a community. While there are always reasons that God calls persons to relocate (permanently or temporarily) there is always the need for "resident disciples"—people who are stable enough to be shaped in love and to be a visible presence as the "body of Christ" in a specific location. In many U.S. settings, the only facets of a "church" that are long-lasting are buildings and organizational rules ("polity"). Pastors and people move in and out, but a building and the polity are somewhat more stable. So human community is seen as one lifestyle

---

Personal Reflection/Group Exercise:
Personal Traits and Social Influences

This exercise is based on your cultural autobiography, as explained in the introduction.

1. Based in your cultural autobiography, list 3-4 characteristics, values or activity patterns rooted in your culture that you exhibit. Discuss how your list compares with others in your group.

2. Consider the shaping influence of U.S. society (and globalization) on your values, ways of thinking and activities. List 3-4 such traits. Compare your lists and consider adding items from each other. Then talk about how these societal patterns interact with your cultural characteristics—especially noting how culture gets "squeezed" by society.

3. Working with this chapter's definition of *community*, describe the most significant such group you have been associated with. (You may have considered yourself a member of the community, or someone involved but not a full member.) What influences did U.S. society and any specified cultures have on the group?

choice, but societal forces get priority and the deeper qualities of human relationships are discarded. In order for our priority on ethnic boundary crossing to make any sense, congregations need to assume basic character- istics described here under this social concept called a community. With- out churches that embody these traits, intercultural life becomes one more temporary consumer choice.

IDENTITY MARKERS: RACE AND ETHNICITY

Even though we use terms to name racial and ethnic groups, and we as- sume everyone knows what these terms mean, these terms have been fluid and lack solid foundations. Within U.S. society congregational life is in the context of socially constructed understandings about race and ethnic- ity. In particular, race is a construct that has varied over the years. Debates have long been inconclusive concerning biological definitions of race. During the decades prior to the founding of the nation, Benjamin Frank- lin explained his way of classifying the races:

> The Number of purely White People in the World is proportionally very small. All Africa is black or tawny. Asia chiefly tawny. America (exclusive of the new Comers) wholly so. And in Europe, the Spaniards, Italians, French, Russians and Swedes, are generally of what we call a swarthy Com- plexion; as are the Germans also, the Saxons only excepted, who with the English, make the principal Body of White People on the Face of the Earth. I could wish their Numbers were increased.[9]

The New World society, as an economic structure prior to the U.S. gov- ernment's independence, had already constructed race as an economic mat- ter—a means for distinguishing natives from Europeans or for clarifying which humans could own other humans. For example, states created laws that codified what percentage of African American blood would be needed for a person to be classified as Negroid; it was common for a person with one-eighth African ancestry to be classified as Negroid. Using the same logic, but reversing the categories, Papa Doc Duvalier, the former ruler of Haiti, insisted the Haitian population was 98 percent white because the vast majority of Haitians were at least one-eighth white.[10] Race classifica-

[9]Benjamin Franklin, "Observations Concerning the Increase in Mankind" (1751), *The Papers of Benjamin Franklin*, Yale University Press <www.franklinpapers.org>.
[10]Barbara Fields, "Ideology and Race in American History," in *Region, Race, and Reconstruction:*

tions are "folk taxonomies"—socially shaped methods of classifying persons. There are numerous physical differences among humans, and no specific trait or cluster is adequate for a biological system of identification.

But just because race is a "folk taxonomy" does not mean it is not meaningful or powerful—it just complicates research and conversation. These classifications shape all persons of a culture or society—and our norms and imaginations and behaviors become aligned with the myths that define and shape these classifications. In the United States our language, the national census and many researchers use five categories of race classification: white, black, Asian/Pacific, Native American and Hispanic. (Hispanic is considered a multiracial culture in the U.S. census but is more often treated as a fifth racial category.) There is significant social pressure for anyone in the United States to identify with one of these races. That means that other important social concepts, like ethnicity or national origin, are frequently minimized in favor of this simple race classification system.

While the five-category classification is widely used, sociologist Michael Emerson posits that the United States recognizes two "indigenous cultures/races/ethnicities"—white and black. The earlier nations of Native Americans and the Hispanic or French peoples that arrived before the other European settlers are not treated as indigenous to the society called the "United States." Though they had a prior life here, they do not have a central role in how the United States has historically defined itself. All other ethnic groups are immigrants (outsiders) who have to learn to adapt to the two dominant races.

Emerson's framework may help explain why churches that are racially diverse are least likely to have both whites and blacks in significant percentages—churches that Emerson calls "Mixed American Culture congregations."[11] (This is specific to U.S. blacks, not to African and Caribbean immigrants.) This brings a unique focus to the complexities of shaping churches toward this kind of inclusion.

People of both indigenous U.S. cultures believe they have, at the very least,

Essays in Honor of C. Vann Woodward, ed. J. M. Kousser and J. M. McPherson (New York: Oxford University Press, 1982), p. 26.
[11]Michael Emerson, *People of the Dream: Multiracial Congregations in the United States* (Princeton, N.J.: Princeton University Press, 2006), p. 138.

an equal right to practice their culture; have little interest in giving it up; have oppositional cultures, so that adopting one may be seen as denying the other; have cultures that have been institutionalized; . . . have centuries of racial wounds. Conversely, those in immigrant cultures typically come to the United States expecting to adapt to an American culture.[12]

Because of this historical distinction there are unique and complex challenges for multiracial churches that include significant percentages of whites and blacks. It is unclear how this framework applies to the deeply rooted presence of Hispanic culture in this country.[13] All of this undergirds our main point—that even though race is a factor without sustainable physiological definitions, it is a powerful factor because of *cultural* differences.[14]

Ethnicity, also a social construct, usually refers to a cultural group with common links such as biology, heritage, language, religion, and geography or migration patterns. In the United States the term can refer to groups that have been identifiable for centuries, such as Chinese, or to those that have been named more recently, such as Hispanics.[15] As an ethnic group, Latinos/Hispanics are identified through their linguistic heritage, Spanish and some heritage connections through the geography of the Americas; because this category includes people from many "racial" backgrounds, it is not always clear how it is being used in the United States. Other ethnic groups, such as Scotch-Irish, are identified by geography of immigration patterns and some less identifiable patterned behaviors. Jews are mainly identified by the religious beliefs and practices of their ancestors. Perhaps the most important trait is that persons of an ethnic group can tell a particular narrative or learn a narrative that encompasses them. This narrative is shaped in ways that are identifiable to each person in the group and (perhaps in other ways) to outsiders. Such stories might include the geography of ancestors, the causes of migration, the experiences of life in North

---

[12]Ibid., p. 139.

[13]Emerson's statistical analysis is thorough, and indicates the unique difficulties he claims. However, if the Roman Catholic churches were bracketed, because there are other influences that create inclusion in those settings, white-Latino churches would likely be almost as rare.

[14]In his research on multiracial churches, the most extensive to date, we believe that Emerson needs to move beyond social analysis and work extensively with *cultural* factors to explain his data. It is this interdisciplinary work that needs continued research among those of us interested in shaping intercultural life in churches.

[15]The current usage of "Hispanic" in the United States was begun by the Census Bureau in the 1960s and was first used in the 1970 census.

America, and any related matters of language, oppression, opportunity, foods, habits and the characteristics of relationships.

Throughout this work we will seldom use race as a primary construct—though it is necessary in some narratives of oppression or in reference to commonly available statistics. At times we use the term *racism* to describe the abuse of power of one ethnic group over another, particularly perpetrated by the Euro-American culture to maintain dominance.[16] We also recognize that we live in a racialized society, one in which the category of race is used as a defining framework for many aspects of our context: politics, economics, law, education. This means that it is difficult to provide a complete discourse about these topics, in descriptive or prescriptive terms, without referring to race. Sometimes other interethnic conflicts are described as racism, but we will not use the term in that manner. Racism also extends itself to intraethnic perspectives, in which the prejudices of the dominant culture become embedded in minority groups, and they then measure grades of whiteness. People who are not considered "white" will nonetheless consider themselves better than those they perceive as darker than themselves. Among both Latinos and African Americans lighter-skinned people sometimes try to "pass" (to have themselves considered as whites or at least whiter). Instead of becoming proof that race is not an objective category, the lighter-skinned people who accept these categories reinforce the concept of race.

We will use *ethnicities* in references to *cultures,* as explained earlier, and we will use these two terms almost interchangeably. We assume the best access we have for understanding the relationships between congregations and ethnicities is through narratives—personal, societal, cultural. Sometimes demographic data can help, like information about population or income or housing, but only if that data is narrated. In other words, it is in finding and telling and adjusting our stories, in listening and asking and receiving the narratives of others, and in creating new narratives together, that we gain understanding and new opportunities.

In the development of the United States as a country, and within its dominant society, there have historically been a number of narratives that define how the various ethnic and racial groups should relate to each other.

---

[16]See especially Michael Emerson and Christian Smith, *Divided by Faith: Evangelical Religion and the Problem of Race in America* (New York: Oxford University Press, 2000).

Historically, only people defined as white could participate in dominant society. The definition has changed to include most people of European descent. But until recently, people not defined as white were not welcome in the process. Each narrative defines a social "ideal," the way its proponents assume should occur. The *Anglo-conformity* model assumes that since the dominant culture in the United States is Anglo based, then all new immigrants should conform to that culture. A variation of that concept, the *melting pot*, assumes that the various ethnic groups in the United States should conform to a common model, but one in which each group contributes something to the new culture being created. The third major model assumes that U.S. society is best served by *cultural pluralism*, a situation in which each group maintains many of its distinctives, even as it identifies with a common society. Milton Gordon argued in the 1960s that each of these models was an ideal with a long history in the United States, but that none fully described reality.[17]

The issue of intercultural relations also has to deal with the issue of language. Each of the narratives has a different response; the first two assume that there is a common language, English, specifically American English. But there have always been other languages spoken in the country, and currently the United States is the fourth-largest Spanish-speaking country in the world. It is unclear whether languages other than English will be given a space in the social structure of the United States.

INTERCULTURAL LIFE

Since this is a work in practical theology (as explained in chapter one), we draw on personal and group narratives, intellectual and cultural resources, biblical and theological texts, and perspectives on communication and leadership in order to promote intercultural life. We believe that whenever possible churches should pursue cultural boundary crossing with neighbors and intercultural life within their congregations. The frameworks we develop and the skills we promote can serve the readers not only in congregational life but also in relationships with other churches, organizations and neighbors. We believe that matters of culture and ethnicity are important and that we can shape intercultural community in churches not

---

[17]Milton Gordon, *Assimilation in American Life: The Role of Race, Religion, and National Origins* (New York: Oxford University Press, 1964).

Bible Study: Galatians 3:23-29—
Dealing with Our Differences

[23]Now before faith came, we were imprisoned and guarded under the law until faith would be revealed. [24]Therefore the law was our disciplinarian until Christ came, so that we might be justified by faith. [25]But now that faith has come, we are no longer subject to a disciplinarian, [26]for in Christ Jesus you are all children of God through faith. [27]As many of you as were baptized into Christ have clothed yourselves with Christ. [28]There is no longer Jew or Greek, there is no longer slave or free, there is no longer male and female; for all of you are one in Christ Jesus. [29]And if you belong to Christ, then you are Abraham's offspring, heirs according to the promise.

In Galatians 3:23-29 Paul describes the new relationships that exist because of Jesus Christ. Our relationship with God has changed, and this has implications for our human relationships. To make that point clear, in verse 28 Paul mentions the principal divisions among humans in his day and ours: ethnic, socioeconomic and gender. These are very real divisions that create real disparities in our world. But Paul invites us to recognize that if the gospel has in fact created change, these differences can no longer define us or our relationships in the church. These differences are real, yet they are being transformed by the gospel. The passage invites us to live out the implications of the transformation in our day-to-day interactions as believers in Jesus Christ.

1. According to this chapter, what are some of the principal differences and divisions in U.S. society? How are these similar or different to those Paul describes from the first century?

2. The differences described by Paul are very real. How do we both recognize the reality of the differences and also affirm that the gospel transforms those differences?

3. As you think about your own identity, what parts of it do you consider fundamental and what parts are secondary? How does this difference affect how you read this passage?

by ignoring particulars but by affirming our polycenteredness, by engaging our own stories and by creating new stories of mutual accountability and shared missional life.[18]

Several years ago Manuel Ortiz described various ways for churches and communities to relate to each other. He spoke of two major types of intercultural church life. The first is *multicongregational churches*, where various ethnic and/or linguistic congregations maintain separate body life but work together and celebrate their common identity in Jesus Christ through worship and ministry activities. The second is the *multiethnic church*, in which those of various ethnic and cultural backgrounds work together to form one congregation. Ortiz describes variations on each one of these models and the implications for ministry of each.[19] The issues of intercultural life apply in both of these models, though the nuances will often be different. At times the reader may notice that our (Juan's and Mark's) different experiences show through in how we address specific issues.

We have benefited greatly from recent research and analysis concerning multi*racial* congregations. For sociologists who are leading this research, two assumptions shape their analysis: (1) they use race, the five-category classification system, for most of their research and discussions, and (2) they commonly use 80 percent as a marker, so "a multiracial congregation is one in which no one racial group comprises 80 percent or more of the people."[20] While there is some evidence that such churches are at a tipping point,[21] there are significant cultural factors that can make this 20-percent marker either significant or meaningless. For example, in a Euro-American church that has been shaped by the dominant culture for decades, even if 20 percent of those involved are persons of other ethnicities, the *culture* of the church is likely to remain unchanged. That is, the perceptions, habits, structures and practices are assumed and powerful. If there is a presence of ethnic diversity, especially if that diversity is distributed among

---

[18]Similarly, David Hollinger, among others, called for a social framework that was more than naming our ethnic identities and claming our rights: *Postethnic America* (New York: Basic Books, 2005).

[19]Manuel Ortiz, *One New People: Models for Developing Multiethnic Church* (Downers Grove, Ill.: InterVarsity Press, 1996).

[20]Emerson, *People of the Dream*, p. 35.

[21] Ibid., p. 35 n. 3.

several groups, it is less likely that the cultural stability will shift. So even though *race* provides a way for sociologists to categorize and observe church life, we believe *culture* and *ethnicity* are the keys to human and systemic realities that resist or potentially embrace the intercultural life we promote. In general, we do not believe that a cultural shift becomes defining when one ethnic group still has 80 percent of the active participants. However, we do believe that fairly small groups in a church, with even less than 20 percent, can provide significant experiments that begin to shift attention and experiences and commitments.

So we have taken on a more complex and therefore less exact project than the sociologists whose work we build on. We share an agenda with those who want churches to be models and agents of racial reconciliation and authentic diversity.[22] However, we are choosing to focus on ethnicity and culture for several reasons: (1) The racial categories, as an assumed classification system, can have an oppressive affect on ethnic groups. Among Asian Americans there are significant cultural differences between Filipino Americans and Korean Americans, just as there are differences between African Americans of slavery heritage, who have been in the United States for generations, and African Americans with recent Caribbean or African roots. But the race categories are often forced onto us, whether because of the convenience of physical appearance or because of institutional needs for quantifying people and because we live in a racialized society. We believe that it is important for churches to value and work on ethnic diversity. (2) The race categories are too simple for the on-the-ground experiences where cultural traits are the principal issue. A major factor is that cultures are not static but malleable as experiences and narratives change. So the complexities of multicultural life can benefit from several other academic disciplines (such as cultural anthropology, hermeneutics and social construction, and leadership/organizational change theory). (3) While we wish to promote multiracial churches, we also want to serve churches that are doing the very difficult work of shaping multiethnic churches even when racial boundaries are not being crossed. There are significant challenges in pan-Latino, pan-

---

[22]We are especially indebted to Michael Emerson, Christian Smith, Curtiss DeYoung, George Yancey and Karen Chai Kim, who lead with scholarly research and thoughtful analysis that serve U.S. churches.

Asian and pan-African churches, and the topics we explore are significant to those efforts.

CONCLUSION: CHURCHES IN CONTEXT

Congregations need to explore the narratives of their own ethnic heritages and those of the surrounding cultures in order to understand their own identity and their role in the world. We believe that the matrix of frameworks we provide can increase the capacities of a church to cross boundaries and to become more inclusive. There are numerous adjectives that are commonly used to describe these goals: integrated, diverse, inclusive, heterogeneous, multiracial, multicultural, multiethnic. Terms can easily become too static or be manipulated for partisan agendas. We prefer the term *intercultural* as a way to emphasize a continual, dynamic relatedness of diverse peoples. We want to pursue an agenda that acknowledges the ever-changing nature of our churches, relationships and contexts; that specifies real engagement and mutuality; and that pays attention to the narratives of large and small similarities and differences. Michael Emerson, in *People of the Dream*, makes a case for what he calls the "sixth Americans," a classification of persons who do not *culturally* fit the five racial categories (sometimes because they are also racially mixed). We believe this is similar to the intercultural goals we advance—the shaping of persons and churches that are fundamentally changed in their encounter with others. Many of the particularities of each ethnic culture are preserved, sometimes altered, as a new culture takes shape in the congregation and new polycentric identities develop. As underscored in Emerson's research, persons in multiracial churches do not tend to lose consciousness of and commitment to important elements of their cultural identity; learning about and experiencing life with persons of other cultures can deepen one's appreciation of one's own culture. There is no clear map toward goals of intercultural life; each church and context is profoundly unique, but we believe there are important ways to pay attention, to experiment, to prompt each other and to benefit from the generative reconciling work of the Holy Spirit.

Our churches do not spring out of nowhere—even church plants are deeply formed by the social environment the participants live in, and that shapes their context before they create a common life. Clarity concerning our covenant life as a community or communities, the societal forces that shape us, and the cultural realities of our context and church can help make intercultural life a visible and tangible expression of the gospel.

At the Movies

Both of these movies invite us to recognize how our ethnic upbringing shapes our relationships with those who have a different ethnic experience than our own.

Babette's Feast (1987). A French woman refugee enters the household of a pastor and his two adult daughters in an isolated Danish village with austere nineteenth-century Puritan values. After serving for many years as maid and cook, circumstances occasion an amazing culinary surprise and an equally shocking revelation, with villagewide impact.

Gran Torino (2008). Disgruntled Korean War vet and recent widower Walt Kowalski grouses about Hmong immigrants next door, but is drawn into family feasts and the complex and dangerous environment of the teenagers.

PART II

SOCIOCULTURAL
PERSPECTIVES

4

WORLDVIEWS, REALITY
AND ASSUMPTIONS

Mark Lau Branson

Paulo Freire, who became the minister of education for Brazil, was shaped by a theological grounding that included beliefs about humans and creation and God. This led him to see education as a mode for reshaping worldviews and thereby serve a culture and its people. Government-sponsored education is usually focused on creating a citizenry that supports and sacrifices for the government and its major partners, such as industry and wealthy dynasties. Freire knew that the worldview of the upper class and the ruling culture was that they could change things—they had real power to shape their world. In his terms they knew they were "culture creators." He also knew that peasants and laborers (mainly indigenous peoples but also the descendents of African slaves) had a worldview in which they were not culture creators; they believed that they could only accept the situation and work within the world that was given to them. They all lived and worked according to their worldview; Freire sought ways to change the worldview of those who thought they were powerless. In his work, especially in northeast Brazil, Freire developed an approach to literacy that began reshaping the worldview of the culture—so that learners began to believe they were subjects rather than passive objects. As subjects they had a vocation to change their world—to be culture creators.[1]

---

[1]Later Freire was arrested and exiled by the Brazilian government because they understood that this literacy work threatened their systems. He continued his work first in Chile, then later for

WORLDVIEWS AND BOUNDARY CROSSING

We are all nurtured in the context of a culture and its worldview. A worldview is a complex and multifaceted fabric of beliefs, often submerged, concerning the world—what it is, how its parts interact and the place of humans. A worldview may shape us as oppressed or oppressor, as capable of certain skills or physical activities or not, as valued by others or disposable. Encompassed in this fabric are matters of birth and death, life after death, biological and psychological health, time and place, luck and fate and agency. Worldview also shapes our understanding of creation, what is visible and invisible and how to relate to it. All of the topics of our other chapters are related to worldview, so this chapter will deal with larger concepts and the interaction of the multiple worldviews in which we live. We will study how a philosopher, Jürgen Habermas, and a missiologist, Louis Luzbetak, explained the role of worldviews. Whenever churches are involved in ethnic border crossing, their leaders need to gain skills for themselves and shape their churches to see and understand worldviews—their own and those they engage.

Habermas on lifeworlds and world concepts. Jürgen Habermas, a German philosopher, proposes a conceptual framework that can assist us in understanding how a culture might be understood and even reshaped. In the context of the large social structures of the market economy and various structures of nations and globalization, he conceives of "lifeworlds," world concepts and communicative competence. A *lifeworld* is the full worldview of a culture; *world concepts* provide conceptual means for understanding a lifeworld; *communicative competence* among persons gives them the abilities to communicate fully and with integrity about their world and how to live in it.[2]

Participants are within a *lifeworld*, constituted by culture and language, and are not able to step outside of it or objectivize it (that is, separate themselves from it and see it from "outside"). A lifeworld is a preconscious social

---

the World Council of Churches. See Paulo Freire, *Education for Critical Consciousness* (New York: Crossroad, 1974).

[2]Jürgen Habermas, *The Theory of Communicative Action*, vol. 2, trans. Thomas McCarthy (Boston: Beacon, 1987). We have chosen to work with Habermas because his framework is less static than others concerning worldviews and because he proposes means for increasing a group's competencies for understanding and cooperative action. We will engage him further in chapter nine, concerning communication.

and personal context, and it has elements that endure and elements that are more fluid. While the lifeworld (with its resources and inadequacies) is in the background, assumed, participants act according to numerous unspoken assumptions concerning their actions, including matters like location, time, goals and words. For example, in a congregation, with the lifeworld (including heritage, theology and other norms) in the background, a group of persons participates in a time of Sunday worship. Some may plan or prepare to lead, others may perform certain tasks like greeters or ushers or musicians. The activities of participants and leaders may simply arise out of centuries of assumptions, or perhaps they have recently determined a newer set of norms. While actions may be from habit or from new planning, the larger framework is preconscious and not discussed. This is the lifeworld—and every large and small culture carries on with daily living while this background is unconscious and assumed.

However, when participants are consciously problematizing a situation (which means they are paying attention to something and conversing about it, often because some challenges are being recognized), they are dealing with some definable segment of their common lifeworld that is thereby moved from preconscious to conscious.

World concepts provide conceptual access to the lifeworld. There are various circumstances and motivations for moving something from our unconscious lifeworld into some kind of discussion so that we can pay attention to it. Concerning our lives as Christians, when we encounter persons or experiences that do not fit our assumptions, we can benefit if we become conscious of our assumptions, and we may be able to work with others on examining our habits and beliefs. We need to move beyond our prior lifeworld, in which everything is already interpreted (assigned meanings), so that we can gain the benefits of new insights, agreements and resulting actions.[3] Shaping a congregation toward mutual understanding is a matter of interpretive leadership—discerning when and how to make visible elements of a congregation's lifeworlds.

For example, circumstances may have brought new persons into worship, or certain participants may decide they want a voice in the formation of worship. This problematizing can give participants access to the usually

---

[3]Ibid., p. 125.

invisible lifeworld. As this set of actions continues, world concepts are at play. In problematizing some aspects of worship—the music, the use of Scripture, the role of the pastor or other leaders, the activities of participants—these elements are brought to consciousness by a group of persons who begin to explore their world concepts. In other words, what was previously unconscious, part of the lifeworld, now needs to be conceptualized. Leaders have a significant work in guiding relational dynamics and implementing meetings and activities in service of deeper understanding and perhaps experiments toward new praxis.

Table 4.1. World Concepts

	Objective World	Subjective World	Social World
Subject matter	Generally available propositional knowledge	Personal narratives and affect	Group norms and intentions
Type of speech	Descriptive	Expressive	Regulative

The manner in which this conceptualizing takes place will make a significant difference in the outcome of the group's life. So Habermas conceives of *world concepts* that are specific to three "worlds"—the objective world, the social world and the subjective world. Each world features its own sphere of relevance, its standards for validity claims and its own grammar. We use *descriptive language* to talk about *objective world*, and our goal is to make and validate truth claims. For example, we can say that the theology of a certain song comes from the Reformed tradition and the musical style is from eighteenth-century Germany. We use *expressive speech* to talk about the *subjective world*, and this speech is valid if it is honest. Someone may say that they appreciate the particular theology of a hymn or that the music style creates a depth of reverence in them. Third, we use *regulative speech* because a group needs to determine the norms for their *social world*, which will include their imperatives and intentions.[4] Chapter nine examines more closely how a church can foster communicative competence in such situations.

Daniel and his family decided to visit a church in their new culturally mixed neighborhood. They were Latino (with English as their primary

---

[4]Ibid., p. 120.

home language), and the church was primarily Euro-American. They began to appreciate some friendships, their kids were welcomed into Sunday school classes, and they learned that some members of the church were working with their kids' school as mentors and teacher aids. But after a few months, Daniel found himself becoming less interested in Sunday morning worship. When he voiced this to Sarah, his wife, she asked him what was bothering him. As they talked, he realized that he would often come home from church feeling somewhat tired or even discouraged. The sermons often provided good teaching, and they addressed various important personal and world concerns. The people around them were genuinely friendly. But he did not feel enlivened; he did not sense the Spirit's energy. As they talked, he became more aware of what he expected during a worship service, but he did not know what his new friends expected. How did God touch and guide them? What could he remember from his earlier churches concerning how he anticipated the place of worship in his life?

Participants in a church live in somewhat similar but also differing lifeworlds, which means that they are often not conscious of the numerous factors that shape their practices and priorities. When a church crosses cultural boundaries, either in its internal life or in its missional life, members become increasingly aware of tensions or anxieties, but the issues often remain vague and unspoken. Their lifeworlds are at variance, but their consciousness and communication are limited. Then it is not uncommon for a church to initially problematize some issue like worship solely in the *social* world by voicing opinions concerning "oughts"—"we ought to have contemporary music," or "we should have children stay in the sanctuary during the sermon." Such a conversation gives little attention to the concepts of the *objective* and *subjective* worlds. This limited approach, because it provides so little access to lifeworlds, tends to prevent substantive mutual understanding or significant change. A more complete exploration would discern ways to talk about the subjective world of the participants ("Tell us your autobiography of worship") and the objective world ("What biblical, historic and cultural forces have shaped our practices?" and "What biblical, historic and cultural resources are available for us to experiment with new practices?"). In the context of more complete conversations, the social world—what we might try together—can be more adequately discussed.

Bible Study: Ephesians—Breaking the Dividing Wall

[5][God the Father] destined us for adoption as his children through Jesus Christ. . . . [7]In him we have redemption through his blood, the forgiveness of our trespasses, according to the riches of his grace [8]that he lavished on us. With all wisdom and insight [9]he has made known to us the mystery of his will, according to his good pleasure that he set forth in Christ, [10]as a plan for the fullness of time, to gather up all things in him, things in heaven and things on earth. . . . [22]And [the Father] has put all things under [Christ's] feet and has made him the head over all things for the church, [23]which is his body, the fullness of him who fills all in all. (Eph 1:5, 7-10, 22-23)

[12]Remember that you [Gentiles] were at that time without Christ, being aliens from the commonwealth of Israel, and strangers to the covenants of promise, having no hope and without God in the world. [13]But now in Christ Jesus you who once were far off have been brought near by the blood of Christ. [14]For he is our peace; in his flesh he has made both groups into one and has broken down the dividing wall, that is, the hostility between us. (Eph 2:12-14)

[8]Grace was given to me to bring to the Gentiles the news of the boundless riches of Christ, [9]and to make everyone see what is the plan of the mystery hidden for ages in God who created all things; [10]so that through the church the wisdom of God in its rich variety might now be made known to the rulers and authorities in the heavenly places. (Eph 3:8-10)

[1]I therefore, the prisoner in the Lord, beg you to lead a life worthy of the calling to which you have been called. . . . [11]The gifts he gave were that some would be apostles, some prophets, some evangelists, some pastors and teachers, [12]to equip the saints for the work of ministry, for building up the body of Christ, [13]until all of us come to the unity of the faith and of the knowledge of the Son of God, to maturity, to the measure of the full stature of Christ. (Eph 4:1, 11-13)

As the gospel became known throughout the Mediterranean world of the first century, an old cultural hindrance seemed to challenge the new churches. While there is no evidence that nationality or skin tone created divisions, the social barrier between Jews and "others" persisted. In the churches this was evident in the ways that Jewish Christians were resistant to Christian converts who did not convert to Judaism. The letter to the Ephesians addresses this as a theological, ecclesial and missiological matter.

1. The worldview of the Ephesians includes beliefs about the universe, its purpose, its end and the means that God uses. How are these matters engaged in these Bible passages?

2. Worldview includes expectations that social groups have concerning each other and how permanent or flexible any current arrangements are. How might worldviews in Ephesus have influenced social divisions? How does Ephesians connect God's long-term plans with the life of the church?

3. "The heavenlies" include Christ, the Ephesian church, and other rulers and authorities (Eph 1:20, 2:6, 3:10). Chapter 3 indicates that social reconciliation in the church is a visible witness to God's wisdom. What are the implications of this perspective?

4. If the church's vocation (Eph 4:1) is essentially tied to social reconciliation across cultural barriers (Eph 2:14), then what implications are there for the work of the gifted leaders of chapter 4?

5. Even though the meaning of terms change over time, the gifts described in 4:11 emphasize living outside the church's internal life. For example, *apostle* means "sent," prophets frequently dealt with how Israel and the church are to relate to matters of embodying God's love for the world, and pastors—"shepherds"—are not so much needed inside a corral as with the sheep in the wild. So what are the opportunities of such leaders for shaping and deploying the whole congregation toward intercultural life?

Luzbetak on worldviews. The lifeworld (or worldview) of a culture is composed of numerous facets. Missiologist and anthropologist Louis Luzbetak proposes that a worldview consists of a culture's concepts and practices concerning supernature, nature, humans and time.[5] These matters get expressed in basic questions:

> Who or what am I? Why am I in the world? What is reality? How do humans differ from nonhumans (animals, objects, the invisible beings)? Who belongs to the invisible world and what are the invisible forces in the world? What is the proper orientation to time and space? What about life after death? What in life or the world is desirable or undesirable, and to what degree?[6]

Luzbetak notes that a worldview has dimensions that are cognitive, emotional and motivational. Since our worldviews are often unconscious, these categories can help us surface the elements that need attention. *Cognitive* dimensions deal with whether the world is real or an illusion, whether time is linear or circular, and whether one can best gain knowledge through logic or analogs. (This will be explored further in chapter eight, on perceiving and thinking.) What Luzbetak calls the *emotional dimensions* concern matters of values, attitudes and primary interests. These are complex topics of cultural priorities—like saving face, aggression, beauty, goodness and wisdom. While these matters may trigger deep emotions, they go beyond popular understandings of emotions to specific commitments and ways of life. The *motivational dimensions* of a worldview deal with purpose, ideals and hopes.[7] This includes what is called a "social imaginary"—a culturally held image of the future, why it is important and what is required to participate.[8] In a congregation that is seeking significant intercultural life, Luzbetak's framework raises helpful questions.

In an urban West Coast church, an Asian American congregation, including mainly immigrants and second-generation immigrants, had arranged to use the facilities of a church that was in transition from being mainly

---

[5]Louis Luzbetak, *The Church and Cultures: New Perspectives in Missiological Anthropology* (Maryknoll, N.Y.: Orbis), p. 252.
[6]Ibid., p. 252.
[7]Ibid., pp. 252-55.
[8]See Charles Taylor, *Modern Social Imaginaries* (Durham, N.C.: Duke University Press, 2004).

elderly Euro-American to being younger, local and of several ethnic groups (a multicultural church). The Asian church had a growing number of children who spoke mainly English, and the multicultural church welcomed them into their own activities. While the Asian congregation had previously had frustrations with the more elderly Euro-American congregation concerning the kitchen, these matters were quickly resolved as the multicultural congregation sought a more genuine equality with the Asian congregation. The multicultural congregation began raising questions about co-ownership of the property, deeper relationships and partnership in ministries, but the pastor of the Asian American congregation was hesitant, and various efforts were stalled. Soon the Asian American congregation decided to seek a new location in the suburbs; the multicultural congregation was disappointed. Their initiatives, aimed at creating a way for the Asian American congregation to stay and to begin sharing some aspects of ministry, were not successful.

In Luzbetak's framework the multicultural congregation had not adequately understood the Asian American congregation's worldview. While there were similar approaches to some cognitive matters (theological tradition, organizational polity), the *emotional dimensions* and *motivational dimensions* need to be foregrounded. The *emotional dimensions* of an immigrant group include the goodness of staying cohesive, of maintaining cultural boundaries and of protecting cultural wisdom. The *motivational dimensions* include the goals they have for their children, which were more connected with the images of the suburbs than with the urban environment. Further, the hopes and ideals of the multicultural church (to intentionally develop an intercultural life together and with urban neighbors) were not part of the Asian American church's motivations. Without understanding the facets of each other's worldviews, conversations and shared imaginations are profoundly limited.

SOME ELEMENTS OF WORLDVIEWS

As worldviews develop over many years the numerous factors that compose the worldview are interwoven—even if we are not conscious of the connections. So our understanding of time is tightly bound to our understanding of relationships, and our understanding of nature is connected to how we view God. When we are engaged in crosscultural relationships, we might become aware of a certain factor—like frustrations over meeting times or an appreciation for particular expressions of kindness—but we do not connect the dots to the larger, encompassing worldview. As noted by Habermas, our lifeworld (worldview) is preconscious, and we need to bring certain elements into consciousness in order to stretch our own worldview so that we might genuinely relate to the "other." We will note a few specific elements of our worldviews.

Nature and the "other." Cultures in the United States have various worldviews, shaped through geographic settings, influenced by economics, politics and religion. The Scotch-Irish, whose worldview has significantly shaped Euro-American norms, came from centuries of scraping out a living under oppressive British forays in the harsh environments of Scotland and then northern Ireland. That later chapter, in which the ruling British lured the Scots to push the Irish out of northern Irish lands, fit with the Scot's norms of working in tight clans to battle nature and opponents. They also assumed that they were somewhat at the mercy of larger governing structures (the British), with which they preferred minimal contact. Continued hardships, especially famine, then led many to immigrate to the United States and Canada, and they continued to battle both nature and Native Americans to gain farmland. Sociologist James Leyburn compares Scotch-Irish settlers with their German neighbors:

> It was usual to expect Germans to be orderly, industrious, carefully frugal; they rarely had trouble with Indians; if they interested themselves at all in politics, it was usually on the local level. Scotch-Irish, by contrast, were regarded as quick-tempered, impetuous, inclined to work by fits and starts, reckless, too much given to drinking. No contemporary observer praised them as model farmers. Their interest in politics on the Provincial level was soon to become active, even tempestuous; and their fame as Indian fighters was to become almost as notable as their reputation for causing trouble with the Indians.[9]

The Scotch-Irish, having been shaped over centuries in Scotland and northern Ireland, continued to live with a worldview that required persistent aggression with the land and with neighbors.

---

[9]James Leyburn, *The Scotch-Irish: A Social History* (Chapel Hill: University of North Carolina Press, 1962), pp. 190-91.

By contrast, Native Americans were shaped within a worldview that conceived of themselves as part of nature, and creation as a gift from God. This called for a kind of partnership of respect in which any necessary killing (for food, clothing and shelter) prompted gratefulness to creation and Creator. Richard Twiss writes,

> Natives believe the land was created by God, and, hence, is sacred, while Western culture views land as a natural resource or commodity. . . . I venture to state that the Native American perspective is much closer to the ancient Hebrew understanding of creation and is a much more holistic and integrated view.[10]

This Native American sense of creation is just one element in a worldview that is profoundly integrated. While most Euro-American worldviews since the Enlightenment tend to be more compartmentalized (and often functionalist), Native American life was more seamless. George Tinker notes:

> Thus the social structures and cultural traditions of American Indian peoples are infused with a spirituality that cannot be separated from, say, picking corn or tanning hides, hunting game or making war. Nearly every human act was accompanied by attention to religious details, sometimes out of practiced habit and sometimes with more specific ceremony. In the Northwest, harvesting cedar bark would be accompanied by prayer and ceremony, just as killing a buffalo required ceremonial actions and words dictated by the particularities of tribal nation, language, and culture. Among the Osages the spiritual principle of respect for life dictated that the decision to go to war against another people usually required an eleven-day ceremony-allowing time to reconsider one's decision and to consecrate the lives that might be lost as a result of it.[11]

So, among many Native Americans, there was an assumption that gave priority to the humanity of others. There was a consistency in a worldview that featured the sacredness of creation, which included other persons. There are parallels between the perspectives of some Native worldviews, regarding the sacredness of creation and the spirituality of labor, and Celtic

---

[10]Richard Twiss, *One Church Many Tribes* (Ventura, Calif.: Regal, 2000), p. 96.
[11]George E. Tinker, "Religion," *Encyclopedia of North American Tribes*, cited in Vine Deloria Jr., *God Is Red: A Native View of Religion*, 2nd ed. (Golden, Colo.: Fulcrum, 1994); available at <http://college.hmco.com/history/readerscomp/naind/html/na_032600_religion.htm>.

spirituality that connects the Trinity with everyday activities.[12] In chapter six we will explore varieties of social relationships in different cultures.

Time and progress. Worldview also concerns time. The Euro-American view of time is rooted in Hebrew and Christian understandings—that time is linear (progressing from creation to the eschaton and beyond), and our lives are related to factors in both the past and the future. This linear view was developed in particular ways as a result of the Enlightenment's framework of scientific rationalism. Time is a sequence of causes and effects, and "progress" is a related matter, based on assumptions about a sequence that makes life better. Thus conceived, time is often viewed as a commodity to be segmented and used. The digital era contributes to this worldview: time is managed in variously sized blocks rather than as an analog to the flow of events.

Modernity, as expressed in Western society and Euro-American culture, has continued to separate numerous human activities from biological time (seasons, days, human rhythms). The priorities of industrialization and globalization are efficiency, predictability and control. This social time is not synchronous with nature or human beings, so while some celebrate increased productivity (manufacturing more marketable commodities more quickly with less human labor) there are consequences that tend to not be included in relevant measurements—matters of ecology, stress and relational consequences in families and communities. Jeremy Rifkin notes, "Local times had long been tied to traditional values, to the gods, to the mythic past. The new world time was bound only to abstract numbers. It flowed evenly and remained aloof and detached from parochial interests. The new time expressed only a single dimension: utility."[13] This modern approach to time is tied to belief in progress. Rifkin notes that we are more apt to live into and try to shape the future than to reflect on the past or live in the present.[14]

This Euro-American approach differs from other cultures that emphasize the present or the past or that have a cyclical view. Although the more linear priorities of Communist society in China have pushed against an-

---

[12]See Esther De Waal, *Every Earthly Blessing: Rediscovering the Celtic Tradition* (Harrisburg, Penn.: Morehouse, 1999), esp. chap. 2.
[13]Jeremy Rifkin, *Time Wars* (New York: Simon & Schuster, 1987), p. 134.
[14]Ibid., p. 20.

cient traditions, those older cultures still have tremendous power. Rifkin connects these roots with the cultural worldview:

> All of the great Chinese religions—Taoism, Confucianism, and Buddhism—taught that time and history endlessly repeat themselves in strict obedience to planetary movements. . . . The Chinese, then, perceived time as slow-moving, cyclical, predetermined, and saw themselves as guardians of past glories rather than initiators of new visions.[15]

In contrast, Japanese culture, rooted in Shinto religion, is more linear, more adaptive and more interested in drawing on the past for the sake of the future: "The Japanese temporal orientation was more expedient than that of the Chinese, more pragmatic and instrumental, and more poised to constructing the future rather than protecting the past."[16]

The manner in which a worldview includes concepts of time is related to numerous factors—the role of relationships, the value of the present, the place of social events, the value of imagining and working toward change, ways in which respect is communicated, and concepts of life after death. All of these possibilities affect how one understands a church's life in relationship to time.

Janice and Robert were leading the songs at the close of worship. The congregation was fully participating, and Janice and Robert were enjoying the experience, which seemed to be both peaceful and energized. They led the congregation in repeating verses and the chorus. Jeff, in a pew toward the back, checked his watch—it was after noon and he was ready to move on to his afternoon activities.

■ ■ ■

Denise was new to the church board. She was only the second African American person on the board of a suburban church that had a small but growing number of African American families. She got to the meeting a few minutes early because she had already adapted to the church's norm of starting meetings on time. After a brief opening devotional of Bible study and prayer the meeting proceeded to discussions about various ministries. The last topic concerned adjustments to the budget, which created signifi-

---

[15]Ibid., p. 136.
[16]Ibid., p. 137.

cant energy among some participants. As their discussion continued, De-
nise was surprised to see that the meeting was going well beyond the an-
nounced ending time of 9 p.m.

In some cultures, worship may not start "on time" (according to a clock)
but is flexible and therefore apt to stretch into the future for an extra hour
or so. In other churches worship may start and stop on the clock, but business meetings might be prolonged in order to pursue particular goals.
Some churches might give weight to the past and the future while not paying much attention to the present context, while others live into the present without attending to the resources of the past or future. Leaders have
the work of helping participants to notice differences, to have conversations about the experiences and values behind such diversity, and to shape
experiments that draw on varied strengths of those involved.

Reality: Visible and invisible. My wife, Nina, grew up in Texas as the
second daughter in a Chinese immigrant family. The family had come to
Texas so that her father could fulfill a commitment to work with a family
friend to establish a small grocery. The preceding years in China had been
times of warfare and famine, and this was to be the beginning of a new life
in the United States. But as the store was being prepared, their main sup-
plier informed them that because they were Chinese, he could not sell
goods to them: "Many of my other clients have told me they will cancel
their orders if I supply you." Without supplies, all of their investments of
time and money were lost. They struggled for years to create and sustain
other means of income.

But that was not the only threat that Nina remembers. In the home,
even as a child, she was aware of a darkness that was present because of
her grandmother's practices of traditional Chinese religion. Nina's father
did not allow the traditional altar—even though he did not have other
convictions to offer—but the grandmother still continued her rituals.
Nina's sense as a child was that in her home there were spirits that were
against her. As a child, she was aware of threats in the world and threats
in her home.

In this context a neighbor invited her to a nearby Baptist church. Nina
reports, "In that church I learned that Jesus was a nice white man who
loved children. But the stories I heard there had nothing to do with the

economic and racist forces that worked against us in the world or the dark spiritual forces that threatened me at home."

Many Chinese cultures posit the continuing life of ancestors as spirits who are present and influential. Some African and Afro-Caribbean cultures believe much of nature is spirited. In some South Asian cultures, invisible systems (rather than particular beings) rule matters of moral consequences and reincarnation. Materialist cultures, especially European, deny any sentience or agency to invisible beings but (like in the United States) may still have almost reverential expectations concerning the power of "the market," which "knows everything." There are various worldviews among Christians concerning angels, demons and deceased-yet-active saints. There are also differences concerning the present, active role of the Trinity, and specifically of the Holy Spirit. No one church can make sense of all these differences, but the very real persons in the congregation and in the context deserve respect. Our own stories matter; Bible study will not solve many differences but will help us see the diverse worldviews of an-

---

Personal Reflection/Group Exercise: Considering Elements of Your Worldview

Normally our worldview remains unconscious and in the background. Then some type of experience (or study) brings some element to consciousness. Recall any experiences in which you became aware of elements of your worldview. First, reflect on these questions:

1. When did you become aware that you and another person had different concepts of time or nature or invisible realities? How did you initially respond? Are you aware of the cultural roots of these elements of your worldview?

2. When have you been challenged by your Christian faith to reconsider some element of your worldview? In what ways were other Christians or the Bible or some experience involved as you became aware of this issue and began to reconsider your own assumptions?

After making notes on your personal reflections, talk about these matters with another participant or a small group. Try to articulate what makes you anxious or adventurous.

cient cultures; empathetic listening and mutual pursuit of the shalom and faithfulness of the whole church will lead to appropriate experiments and supportive partnerships.

Worldviews and practical theology. When we gather together in a congregation or connect and work with our neighbors, we always bring our diverse worldviews. Our capacities to understand each other, to share in work, and to hope require an increasing consciousness about our own worldviews and a commitment to listen to and walk under the influence of the worldviews of others. For many in the dominant culture, in which one element of the lifeworld is entitlement, this can be a stressful experience. For those in the minority the need for trust remains a challenge, especially if memories are saturated with wounds. Leaders can use the numerous sociocultural perspectives of this text to gain skills in analyzing cultures, then through conversations they can continually learn about the beliefs and experiences that shaped particular assumptions and habits. The whole cycle of practical theology, as explained in chapter one, is needed so understanding can be deepened in the midst of stories and theology—so as leaders create a learning environment, an increasing number of participants gain the needed praxes of intercultural life. The Ephesians study shows

At the Movies

Look for preconscious (worldview) beliefs and assumptions behind these narratives. What elements of their worldviews are brought to the surface for reflection and conversation?

Joy Luck Club (1993). Through a series of flashbacks, four young Chinese women, born in America, and their respective mothers, born in feudal China, explore their past, helping them understand their difficult mother-daughter relationships.

The Matrix (1999). A computer hacker learns from mysterious rebels about the true nature of his reality, where humans believe they are free but are really slaves to sentient computers and their software, and he is challenged by prophecies concerning his own destiny.

Thunderheart (1992). Based on events in the 1970s; an FBI agent with Sioux ancestry is sent to a South Dakota Indian reservation to help solve a murder. Even as he tries to avoid owning his heritage, he slowly enters tribal relationships and worldview, eventually learning of government participation in a cover-up.

how worldview issues were addressed in the midst of on-the-ground realities. This was a praxis-theory-praxis approach. Church leaders can foster continual experiments in areas of difference, helping the church discern its own unique ways of unity and diversity.

5

LANGUAGE, GESTURES AND POWER

Juan Francisco Martínez

I was asked to work alongside a denominational official who was frustrated with the leaders of a Latino congregation that he oversaw. He wanted the leaders of the church to take concrete steps related to denominational expectations on financial reporting. Every time he met with the leaders they agreed to send the reports on the required dates. But the reports never arrived. When he called to ask about the reports, there was always a reason and an apology. He has gone through this process three times and is now convinced these Latino leaders are lying to him. He recognizes that the local church leaders are highly committed to ministry but senses that they have a weakness with integrity.

The situation presented a series of intercultural complexities, many of which were related to language and communication. The denominational official began from the assumption of a direct relationship between words and meaning and was therefore unable to see that the situation included issues of translation, language and power, indirect forms of communication, and nonverbal communication. Because these other factors were not being taken into account in the interpretation of the situation, it was impossible to know whether the Latino leaders (1) did not intend to send the reports, (2) did not understand the reporting process, (3) did not have the means to comply with the reporting expectation, (4) felt intimidated by the denominational official because he could withhold approval on a loan they had requested, (5) some combination of all of these, or (6) something completely different.

Because the denominational leader did not clarify these communication issues, the frustration level continued to rise and the communication
process became increasingly complicated. Though the communication was
taking place in English, the language the denominational official feels
most comfortable with (though not the Latino leaders), each person's understanding of the role of language is so different that there is more mis-
communication than clarification. By helping churches understand the
different ways we communicate, leaders can make it more likely that effective communication will occur across cultural and linguistic boundaries.

LANGUAGE AND MEANING

According to Edward Stewart and Milton Bennett, most native speakers
of English in the United States, particularly those who are monolingual,
have a mechanistic understanding of language.[1] The assumption is that
words are merely mechanisms that express the essence of meaning and
reasoning, which all people share. There is little sense that specific languages and grammars affect reasoning or perception. In its most basic
form this means that many monolingual people, such as many speakers of
U.S. English, tend to assume that there is a direct relationship between
what they say, what they mean and what they perceive "out there." Little
thought is given to the idea that different languages might affect how
thinking is organized and how what is "out there" is perceived.

But language is much more than a (mechanistic) tool that humans uti-
lize for communication. It is a complex system that weaves perceptions,
meanings and imaginations into a "system of representation." Language is
a means of sorting out reality at the boundary between objects (out there)
and concepts (constructs in our mind). In a sense, languages are "maps"
that have been drawn by very different cartographers using very different
scales, different assumptions about what is being mapped and how the
map is going to be used, different assumptions about the understandings
of the people using the map, and a dynamic sense of needing to change
and adapt the map as new objects are added to the "landscape."

As long as everyone is speaking the same language, in a similar social
context (e.g., U.S. English in a specific region of the United States), all are

---

[1]Edward Stewart and Milton Bennett, *American Cultural Patterns: A Cross-Cultural Perspective*,
rev. ed. (Yarmouth, Maine: Intercultural Press, 1991), p. 46.

using a similar "system of representation" and can anticipate that they are weaving together perceptions, meanings and imaginations in a similar way. But once people change the context or the language, the understanding of the relationship between objects and concepts also changes.

Anthropologist and linguist Benjamin Whorf addresses this issue in what is known as the Whorf hypothesis. He states:

> We dissect nature along lines laid down by our native languages. The categories and types that we isolate from the world of phenomena we do not find there because they stare every observer in the face; on the contrary, the world is presented in a kaleidoscopic flux of impressions which has to be organized by our minds—and this means largely by the linguist systems in our minds.[2]

Whorf developed a "strong hypothesis" in which he stated that language largely determines how we understand our reality. According to the strong hypothesis, if we do not have the language for something, we are significantly limited in our abilities to even perceive that the thing exists. But he also laid out a "weak hypothesis" in which he spoke of the interrelationship between language, thought and perception.[3] This means that interaction between peoples who speak different languages is complicated by the fact that they perceive the world in very different ways. They organize, categorize, analyze and draw different types of conclusions about what they "see out there." This affects basic things like how we define different colors and spatial relationships. But it also affects how we perceive and describe social relations and our relationship to the physical world.

But people will only tend to understand what Whorf is describing if they interact with native speakers of other languages in a multilingual setting. People who are monolingual and usually interact solely with other people who speak only their language seldom have occasion to question their mechanistic assumptions about language. They unconsciously assume that their language map is an accurate representation of what is "out there" and that the maps of other languages are fairly similar to their own. Misunderstandings between native speakers of the language, or even with nonnative speakers, are explained in mechanistic terms, such as lack of knowledge or improper usage of the language. For example, many speakers of U.S. Eng-

---

[2]Benjamin Lee Whorf, *Thought and Reality: Selected Writings of B. L. Whorf*, ed. J. B. Carroll (New York: John Wiley, 1956), p. 213.
[3]Stewart and Bennett, *American Cultural Patterns*, p. 46.

lish seldom interact with nonnative speakers of U.S. English. This is not just a matter of language, but the native speakers probably do not know that this makes them unaware that they all are perceiving the world differently. And because any interaction with nonnative speakers will be in English, it is easy to conclude that any misunderstandings reflects misusage of the language by the nonnative speaker and not something more profound.

Personal Reflection/Group Exercise— Variations on U.S. English

Think about times when you have been among people who do not speak U.S. English:

1. Have you ever had problems understanding a native speaker of English who did not speak U.S. English? Why? How did you react?

2. What about a person who spoke "correct" English but with a non-American accent?

3. How do you feel when you hear people around you speaking a language you do not understand?

4. If you are not a native speaker of English, how do you feel when you speak grammatically correct English, but people say they do not understand you?

After answering these questions personally, talk to others about your experiences and reactions. Be particularly attentive to the responses and perspectives of monolingual speakers of U.S. English, native speakers of non-U.S. English and nonnative speakers of English. How does the issue look different from these various perspectives?

GRAMMAR AND HOW WE ORGANIZE OUR THINKING

One way of perceiving the differences between languages is to study the grammars of those languages. For example, U.S. English has certain characteristics that shape how its users understand their world. These understandings are assumed by native speakers but are often confusing to those whose first language is not English or to those who speak other variants of the English language.

Structure as a model for thinking. English is a language that has a subject-predicate structure. This means that the speaker is predisposed to "interpret as fixed the relationship between subjects or things and their qualities or attributes."[4] It has a binary focus of "is or is not" and is not
well-suited to describe situations where such a polarity does not exist.
Thus it is fairly easy in English to describe a relationship as love-hate, but
it is much more complicated to describe human emotional interactions
that exist along the love-hate continuum.

The subject-predicate structure also reflects the idea of "implied agent."
English requires speakers to assume a subject such as *it* in "it rained last
night." There is no "it" causing the rain (except in a theological sense), but
the language structure insists on having an "it." According to Glen Fisher:

> In its conception of actions and events, English is an actor-action-result
> model, and tends to suggest that perception of this universe and what hap-
> pens in it. The actor-action-result pattern is very useful for conceptualizing
> mechanics, business and much of science. It suggests the question "What
> caused that?" or "What effect will this have on the end result?"[5]

This feature of English predisposes native speakers of the language to
interpret events in a linear cause-and-effect relationship but often creates
difficulty when used to describe complex human interactions. Complex
social problems cannot usually be explained (or solved) by appealing to a
linear cause-and-effect type of interpretation.

Over 40 percent of the languages of the world do not have such a gram-
matical structure, including many Asian languages that place the principal
verb at the end of the sentence. Therefore, the thinking patterns and
worldviews of these people tend to be different because their language
structure does not predispose them to think in terms of linear cause-and-
effect relationships.

Dichotomies and opposites. Anthropologist Paul Hiebert states that we
can learn a lot about a people's worldview by the way they group words and
set up domains (ethnosemantics). Such practices tell us about their systems
of thought but also the "emic order [cultural insider's perspective] that

---

[4]Ibid., p. 50.
[5]Glen Fisher, *Public Diplomacy and the Behavioral Sciences* (Bloomington: Indiana State University Press, 1972), p. 120.

people impose on the world."[6] He draws on the pioneering efforts of Whorf and Edward Sapir and the subsequent work of James Spradley, and others, to show the links between word groupings and underlying worldviews.[7]

For example, adjectives in English tend to be grouped as extreme dichotomies (e.g., tall-short, far-near, good-bad). These pairs seem to complement each other and seem to have the same power in describing positions on a continuum between them. But in most of these polar relationships one of the two has much more value than the other. For example, if a person asks, "How good is that preacher?" one can respond across the good-bad continuum. But if the person asks, "How bad is the preacher?" a value judgment has already been made and the assumed answer can only fit on a bad-worse continuum. In "English precise qualifiers are negative while ambiguous ones are positive."[8] This means that it is much easier to criticize and define what should not be done than to praise and describe desirable behavior.[9] That is why "authority and regulations in American society tend to be exercised from the negative side: the individual is told exactly what not to do, and typically, punishments for infractions are far more precise than rewards for appropriate behavior."[10]

The role of verb conjugation. The verb conjugation patterns of a language point to what native speakers of that language consider important if they want to communicate effectively about the actions of the subject of a sentence. For example, English conjugation distinguishes time and person. Spanish conjugation is much more explicit about time, person, the singularity or plurality of the subject, and the social relationship between the speaker and the listener or the human subject and human object. Ko-

---

[6]Paul Hiebert, *Transforming Worldviews: An Anthropological Understanding of How People Change* (Grand Rapids: Baker Academic, 2008), p. 95. *Emic* and *etic* are terms used by social and behavioral scientists to describe how people describe human behavior. Emic is the perspective of the cultural insiders, how people within a culture explain their actions and experiences. Etic is the description of the outsider, the observer who does not share the cultural interpretation of the insider.

[7]Edward Sapir, *Selected Writings in Language, Culture, and Personality* (Berkeley: University of California Press, 1949); James Spradley, *Participant Observation* (Newbury Park, Calif.: Sage, 1980).

[8]Stewart and Bennett, *American Cultural Patterns*, p. 54.

[9]This example applies to common U.S. English, but not to all forms of English used in the United States. In some forms of English, saying that something is "really bad" means that it is very good.

[10]Stewart and Bennett, *American Cultural Patterns*, p. 55.

rean conjugation considers time but is also very careful to distinguish social relationships between speaker and listener, human subject and human object, and focuses on intentionality and potential results.

In practical terms this means that English, particularly U.S. English, "feels" direct and to the point. The social relationship between the speaker and the listener is not considered directly important to clear communication in English. Because of the subject-predicate nature of the language, a subject is always assumed and so does not have to be explicitly recognized in verb conjugation. Spanish conjugation assumes that many more details are needed before there can be clear communication and that the social relationships between the speaker and the listener affect communication. Korean conjugation is extremely conscious of social relationships and their effect on communication. It also communicates more about the subject's or narrator's perception of the actions being described. The verb form relates the subject's intentions, perception of control over the situation and interpretation of potential results.

Language and the role of the printed word. Many traditional cultures put a great deal of emphasis on the oral word. The wisdom of the people is transmitted from generation to generation through stories and sayings. The orality of this process is crucial because the person telling the story is also the interpreter. That person decides when to tell the story, how to connect it with the current situation and how to interpret it in the new context. The ideas being communicated are intricately linked to the feelings of the person telling the story.

Speakers of languages with strong print traditions, or those with extended formal education, tend to give much more importance to the printed word. There is often an implicit assumption that what is printed (published) has been vetted so that it is more authoritative than an oral communication. Many people also assume that the printed word also allows people to separate ideas from feelings, providing a sense of objectivity to what is being stated. Traditional languages, or oral traditions, are not given the importance or are not considered as objective as what is printed.

A unique version of this tendency is the importance given to the Internet. People quote opinions as facts, and false statements seem to become true if repeated often enough. Because something has been printed it is perceived as more authoritative than statements made only orally.

Nonverbal communication. Because of the assumed directness of language many people find it difficult to understand the importance of nonverbal behaviors in the communication process (paralanguage). Nonverbal behavior is usually treated as a commentary on the verbal communication and not as a fundamental part of the communication process. The tone of voice may modify the verbal communication by providing a context for interpreting the words. But the words are seen as fundamental to the communication process.

> *After expending a great deal of energy, the pastor convinced the church council to vote for the new mission project. There had been hesitation, and some of the members were a bit quiet during the vote. But this was a very important project that would give the church a chance to interact with their community in new and creative ways. Yet, though the vote had been unanimous, the pastor was beginning to wonder. Some people kept their heads down when they voted. Others seemed to be following the lead of some key leaders who spoke about the project with great enthusiasm. Well, a yes was a yes, and it was time to move forward.*

Leaders need to be aware that social situation, physical distance, hand gestures, tone of voice and even actions after the fact are all part of the nonverbal communication process. Physical distance may be expressing fear, hand gestures may be negating the words being spoken, tone or pitch of voice may be completely changing what the words mean, and actions after the fact may be the real response to a face-saving situation. Those who assume that words are the fundamental aspect of communication may recognize that nonverbal behaviors affect the process but are not usually attuned to the messages being given beyond the words.

The example given at the beginning of this chapter reflects the problem that arises when nonverbal communication is not understood. The assumptions made by the denominational official are either that (1) the person had no intention of performing the action; (2) the person was lying; or (3) the person is not trustworthy. He was not sufficiently taking into account the unequal social relations, the nonverbal behaviors in previous communications or the very simple fact that the reports he requested had never been delivered. By not taking these other issues into account he was not able to understand what the Latino leaders were trying to communicate to him (i.e., the denominational leadership had made a major mistake in how the loan for the property had been arranged).[11]

Nonverbal communication has its own grammar and interpretation within different languages and social structures. It is as deeply embedded as language and is a crucial part of the communication process. Because of its nature it takes more work to learn for those who are not used to using it.

Language and social relations. Spoken English in most parts of the United States reinforces the myth that there is no social distinction between peoples. Everyone is "you." Titles are often omitted when talking to each other, and people frequently use each other's first names. But in many languages there are not only different levels of politeness, there are even different words depending on the social relationship between speaker and hearer, or between them and the person one is speaking of. For example, many languages, like Spanish, have formal and informal forms that are used depending on the relationship between the speaker and hearer. Other languages have more complex structures that take into account not only speaker and hearer but also the subject and object of the conversation. People who are learning other languages and who do not grasp the importance of social differences in the communication process are often seen as socially challenged or even as insulting.

People who speak a language that has several levels of politeness, but who were born or educated in the United States, often do not distinguish between the formal and the familiar when they are not speaking English. Because they use the incorrect form of address to elders, they often end up communicating the indirect message that Americans do not respect elders and that an American education encourages that lack of respect.

Language and power differentials. Communication becomes more complicated when there is a power differential and no common social understandings or rituals to use in communicating across that differential. This is a common problem in multicultural church settings in the United States. The working assumption is that we are all sisters and brothers in Jesus Christ. Yet one side has all the power (buildings, finances, access to structures, etc.), and the other is in a dependent relationship. As mentioned in

---

[11]The situation had been so badly handled that both the local church and the denomination ended up losing the property. A former pastor ended up with the title deed.

the introduction to this chapter, this type of relationship complicates communication for several reasons. First, since U.S. English does not provide social conventions for clear communication across social and sociolinguistic divides, there are no clear rules for this situation other than "power rules." Second, power is constantly in the background creating noise that complicates relationships, which makes communication more complex. Third, since different sets of language games (the languages of the various groups, the theological language and denominational structures) are being used simultaneously, people may opt to change to a different set of rules, depending on which provides the most potential advantage.

For example, in the problem from the beginning of the chapter, both sides might appeal to theological language games. The denominational leader might talk about the importance of honesty as a sign of Christian discipleship, indirectly questioning the Christian commitment of the Latino leaders. The Latino leaders might play the same game by mentioning God's love toward the poor and oppressed and trying to "guilt" the denominational leader into helping them, even though they might not really need it. On the other hand, the denominational leader might have wanted to show grace by being flexible with denominational requirements. The Latino church leaders might be trying to submit to spiritual authority by saying yes, even though the denominational bureaucracy confounds them.

Because one of the roles of leadership (see "Leadership triad," fig. 1.3) is to build relationships, it is very important for the leader to understand the role of power in the communication process. In multilingual, multicultural environments the leader needs to be particularly sensitive to the complexities of the communication so that he or she can strengthen relationships across these differences.

Dominant and subordinate languages in the United States. Multilingualism is a common phenomenon in many parts of the world. It is usually the result of the encounter between peoples, be it by trade, migration or conquest. In many situations different languages are used in different domains. If no language is dominant an outside language, like English, is used as a trade language, and people continue to use their native language in all other functions within their own group. When one language is imposed on others by force, the relationship between languages changes. Either the minority language is limited in its domain, or it is

Bible Study: Matthew 5:1-12—
Whose Blessing Do We Want?

[1]When Jesus saw the crowds, he went up the mountain; and after he sat down, his disciples came to him. [2]Then he began to speak, and taught them, saying:

[3]"Blessed are the poor in spirit, for theirs is the kingdom of heaven.

[4]"Blessed are those who mourn, for they will be comforted.

[5]"Blessed are the meek, for they will inherit the earth.

[6]"Blessed are those who hunger and thirst for righteousness, for they will be filled.

[7]"Blessed are the merciful, for they will receive mercy.

[8]"Blessed are the pure in heart, for they will see God.

[9]"Blessed are the peacemakers, for they will be called children of God.

[10]"Blessed are those who are persecuted for righteousness' sake, for theirs is the kingdom of heaven.

[11]"Blessed are you when people revile you and persecute you and utter all kinds of evil against you falsely on my account. [12]Rejoice and be glad, for your reward is great in heaven, for in the same way they persecuted the prophets who were before you."

The Sermon on the Mount (Mt 5–7) is preached in the midst of a reality defined by the Roman Empire. *Pax Romana* offers a blessing to those who become a part of it and accept the empire's "language," its definition and interpretation (hermeneutic) of what is good. In this Roman language (actually Greek), blessing is defined by the goods and services the empire provides. Many Jews had adopted this language and were seeking this blessing, and others resisted in various ways.

It is in this situation that Jesus offers a very different definition of blessing, a different language and hermeneutic. The Beatitudes are hermeneutics, a different way of interpreting reality. All of the Sermon on the Mount challenges the language of Rome, the Jewish establishment and those who turn to violent resistance. In the sermon's reality those suffering under Rome will be comforted (Mt 5:4), and those caught in the legalistic structure of the Jewish piety of the day have a different option.

Jesus offered an alternative language, a different way of interpreting the reality of his day. His challenge is also crucial for us today. We have many "languages" (systems of representation) telling us what a blessed life looks like. The Sermon on the Mount continues to offer us a different narrative, an opportunity to enter into God's reign, if we have "ears to hear."

1. What are the principal "languages" defining reality for us today? How do they shape our definitions (our hermeneutics) of what is real and important? What "blessings" do they offer?

2. How does the Sermon on the Mount challenge the blessings offered by our society?

3. In what ways do we see churches living according to the language of our societal context? And what are churches doing that reflects a different hermeneutic, like that of the Beatitudes and the Sermon on the Mount?[a]

[a]For more work on the Beatitudes from this perspective, see Mark Lau Branson, "Ecclesiology and Leadership in Context," in *The Missional Church in Context*, ed. Craig Van Gelder (Grand Rapid: Eerdmans, 2007).

forced underground. In the worst of circumstances the conquered language is eradicated.

United States English is clearly the formal language of trade and commerce in the United States. But it is also seen as a crucial unifier among peoples of different linguistic backgrounds. Through the public school system, the mass media and the public sphere, it seeks to impose itself in all areas of life. So there are no clearly accepted domains (public or private) for any other language. The working assumption is that U.S. English eventually takes over in all areas of communication among people in the United States.

Languages other than English have always been spoken in the United States. But the popular assumption is that they only have a transitional role, being spoken while people learn English and gradually transition from their native language to the dominant language. These languages may survive in ghettos, where they have extensive public and private domains, but these are either seen as threats to national unity or as quaint tourist attractions. Though many people in the United States lament the lack of multilingual citizens that can interact with people in other parts of the world, little effort is made to strengthening the languages already spoken by linguistic minority groups in the country.

Spanish is currently the one language that might yet find a national role in the United States. Though about 20 percent of the Latino population does not know Spanish, its influence continues to grow. In some regions of the United States, such as Los Angeles, Spanish competes with English in the public domain. Several states have approved laws to limit its public role. But many social and economic factors continue to drive its expanding influence.

This situation is causing concern among some people in the United States. For example, Samuel Huntington of Harvard University was concerned because many Latinos are not forgetting Spanish as they are learning English. From his perspective if Latinos maintain their language and ethnic identity, this will be a challenge to U.S. national identity. Anything that works against the Anglo-conformity model of cultural adaptation is perceived as a threat. Given this understanding among some people in the United States, non-English language usage creates tensions in society.[12]

A group of Latino pastors wanted to expand ministry among Latinos in a growing neighborhood, so we presented a project to leaders of a local church from our own denomination that already served in the area. One of the leaders asked us if we would minister in Spanish. Our response was that we needed to understand the community better, but that very likely some Spanish would be used in our planned outreach. His response: "I am against bilingual education and a bilingual ballot. So I guess I need to be against a bilingual church."

The use of languages other than English becomes even more complicated in the life of the church. Native languages are usually the best tools for effective communication of the gospel and for an understanding of communicating with God. But since speaking English in all domains of life is considered crucial to national unity, American Christians often find their Christian and national assumptions at odds. Should the church encourage the use of languages other than English, or should it adopt an ESL perspective, using other languages only as transitional tools as people

---

[12]See Samuel Huntington's *Who Are We? The Challenges to America's National Identity* (New York: Simon & Schuster, 2004), esp. pp. 221-56.

learn English? If churches use languages other than English, are they not giving a social message in conflict with the national message of the importance of one national language? Churches are social agents, and the way they reach out to people that speak languages other than English has a social impact.

The relationship between languages has other crucial ministry implications. A common problem faced by churches, schools and other social agencies is the lack of sufficient translators. A common "solution" to the problem is to use children, who know or are learning English, to serve as translators for their parents or other elders. This seems like an easy solution, but its impact on family structures is often destructive. Children are given power over their parents, and elders are placed at the mercy of their children. This makes it more difficult for parents to maintain authority in family systems. But this also affects communication because children often do not have adequate language competencies to express the important nuances of theology, relationships or regulations.

All of this linguistic interaction is occurring within the larger U.S. social order. Because of the relative value of languages in the United States, how minority languages are used in ministry gives a clear message as to the relative value given to that language in relationship to English. It also invites Christians to think about the role of languages in ministry.[13]

LANGUAGE AND MINISTRY

Christians confess that the gospel can be proclaimed and lived out in any culture and that God speaks all languages. Yet in the midst of a multilingual environment this confession can be severely challenged. The issues raised in ministry have to do with things like translation of the gospel and the usage of various languages in ministry.

Vocabulary and Bible translation. Missionaries around the world have stories about the complexity of translating the gospel into different languages. The gospel speaks of things that have ultimate meaning. Therefore, the objects of our conversation cannot easily be defined and have very

---

[13]Sociolinguistics studies how languages interact in specific social situations. The relative importance of each language is seen in how they are used in relationship to each other. For example, when a language is used in ministry in ways that are "less" than English, the message given is that the other language is not as important as English.

different connotations in different languages. Many linguistic "systems of meaning" are far removed from first-century Palestine and so create challenges for understanding the cultural framework within which the biblical message was communicated. Translators, who are usually not native speakers of the language to which they are translating, have to seek out "dynamic equivalents" between two languages, the biblical language and the language to which they are translating, both of which are second languages for the translator.

This is one of the reasons why the role of pastor-teacher is so crucial in the life of the church today. One of the tasks of the pastor has to be helping Christians "read" through the various texts and translate, interpret and connect them to life and ministry today. This has always been a challenge for the pastor but now is much more important, given the multilingual environment of much of intercultural church life. This task will not only need to address the different languages in the community but also the different ways that a common language like English is being used by different people.

English usage in a multilingual U.S. environment. Because English has become the international language of the world, the assumption often made in the United States is that people have adopted American "systems of meaning" when they are using U.S. English. Yet we often find that people are using English words but with the thought patterns of their own language or uses framed by their own cultural experiences. English functions well as a trade language or as an academic language, such as Latin did in Europe for many centuries. But it does not easily communicate the depth of meaning presented in the gospel for those whose first language is not English. Using English as a common language among people who do not use it as a first language will also make being church together more challenging. Those who speak more than one language will likely identify the complexities of the task, while monolingual speakers of English will tend to miss it.

The Bible study in the introduction (Acts 2) demonstrates that the encounter between "powerful" and "weak" languages in the preaching of the gospel does not have one solution. On the one hand, the gift of tongues is about people hearing the gospel in their own heart language. But Peter preached in the language the people had in common, Greek, the language of the Roman Empire at the time. And the early multilingual congregations of the first century likely also used Greek as the language of common worship and Bible study.

This tension is particularly complex among people who are bilingual and who constantly negotiate between two systems of representation. Various forms of code-switching, such as Spanglish, are common among many people in the United States. Some use Spanglish as a mixture of both languages or as a dialect of Spanish, while others seem to be negotiating a new system of representation in this encounter between English and Spanish. These phenomena can also be noticed among speakers of other languages in the United States.

This situation presents missional and theological questions about the role of language in the church's mission. The complexities of language choices are often understood as of interest only for ethnic minority churches, but they are increasingly of importance to churches that are serious about multiethnic and multicultural ministry. How can churches celebrate linguistic diversity together even as we live in the midst of the potential development of new systems of representation? How do seminaries and other training systems prepare people to effectively minister in this type of environment?

One of my (Juan's) most joyful experiences was leading a nontranslated bilingual (Spanish-English) Bible study among young adults in Los Angeles. The group included recent immigrants, Latinos who had been in the United States for generations and some non-Latinos who spoke Spanish. One commonality was that all were somewhat bilingual. People were free to communicate in either language, to code switch or to practice their weak language. The people in the group were also able to see how the Bible was translated into each language and how those differences might impact their understanding of Scripture. They lived in a bilingual environment and were free to study the Bible and learn about God in their system of representation.

Even as globalization continues to encourage the usage of English as the language of global communication, it is also creating a situation where more languages come into contact with each other and where those who speak "subordinate" languages take more pride in using and maintaining those languages. It is within this encounter of various systems of representation in which churches need to negotiate between Babel, Pentecost and

God's vision of all peoples, nations and languages worshiping God together. Here the gospel invites leaders to shape congregations that combine creativity, agency, respect and humility to find new ways of both recognizing the influence of English and the role of other languages in the process of being church together.

When First Church saw that the neighborhood around them was changing (step 1 of the practical theology cycle; see fig. 1.2), their leadership was able to draw on the church's best resources to envision a new missional future. They invited a couple that had been missionaries in Latin America but had to return because of health issues, as their pastors. These new pastors drew on the Swedish immigrant background of the congregation as a bridge toward immigrant Latinos (step 2). They led the congregation to see the changes as a mission opportunity by calling them to be faithful to the same impulse that had previously funded the pastors as missionaries in Latin America (step 3). Though the older Swedes did not speak Spanish, they did understand the needs of immigrants because they still remembered the stories of their parents and grandparents (step 4). So they responded by helping people find jobs and housing and by providing transportation to church on Sundays. Often the only common language between the people was God's love (and the bilingual gospel tracts they gave the people).

As the Spanish-language congregation grew, the older congregation worked alongside (step 5). During joint services the joint choir would sing in English, Spanish and Swedish. The new immigrants knew they needed to learn English. But this congregation also showed them that their own language was important as they sought to fit in in their new country.

Over a twenty-year period the old congregation kept calling bilingual pastors to serve both congregations. The old Swedish group also opened their social hall/gym to young Mexican Americans who were trying to break out of a gang lifestyle. The Spanish-language congregation eventually became the largest congregation. But they saw the importance of providing support to the ministry among Mexican American youth and their share of the expenses of supporting one pastor and a building that also was used by a Korean congregation. When the city bought them out because of development plans, the congregations were able to use the proceeds to develop a new church and new ministries that continue to have an impact years later.

At the Movies

Both of these movies address the complexities of language, power and relationships. Though everyone speaks English and assumes they are being understood, the different experiences impact how language is understood.

Long Walk Home (1990). An African American maid working for a white family, despite being well-treated, decides to walk to work as part of the bus boycotts in 1955-1956 Alabama, causing lateness and exhaustion, and forcing not only herself but her white "Misses" to face and respond to the times.

My Big Fat Greek Wedding (2002). A single, thirty-year-old Greek American woman, looking for more in life than her father's family restaurant in Chicago, falls in love with a non-Greek man and struggles to get her family and her fiancé to accept each other, while she comes to terms with her heritage and cultural identity.

For Further Reading

Dillard, J. L. *Black English*. New York: Vintage, 1973.

Geok-lin Lim, Shirley. *Among the White Moon Faces: An Asian-American Memoir of Homelands*. New York: Feminist Press, 1996.

Gudykunst, William. *Asian American Ethnicity and Communication*. Thousand Oaks, Calif.: Sage, 2000.

Morales, Ed. *Living in Spanglish: The Search for Latino Identity in America*. New York: St. Martin's, 2003.

Rodríguez, Richard. *Hunger of Memory: The Education of Richard Rodríguez*. New York: Dial Press, 2004).

Smitherman, Geneva. *Talkin That Talk: African American Language and Culture*. New York: Routledge, 1999.

———. *Word from the Mother: Language and African Americans*. New York: Routledge, 2006.

Stavans, Ilan. *The Hispanic Condition: The Power of a People*. New York: Harper, 2001.

6

Defining Social Relations

Juan Francisco Martínez

Before becoming a church planter in Los Angeles, I had pastored fairly homogeneous Latino congregations in south Texas and central California. Most of the members of these churches shared a common history and culture from the border regions of south Texas and northern Mexico. But in Los Angeles I was now planting a church with Latinos from places as varied as northern New Mexico, El Salvador and Peru. We all spoke Spanish but were "separated" by our common language and significant cultural differences. For example, how should the pastor greet the women of the church? Some expected a hug and a kiss. Others assumed that men and women should maintain a certain distance, even in greetings.

The first time I got in trouble was when a new woman visited our church. When in doubt I always greeted "from a distance." Our visitor got the message that the pastor was "cold." A female member of the church, who was her friend, had to apologize for me. From then on, I was always grateful when a new woman visited the church with someone from the church. At least I could guess that both had a similar cultural background and that I could treat the new woman the way I would normally treat the church member.

Language not only affects communication, as noted in the last chapter, but it also affects social relations. For example, one of the most difficult things for me is defining social relations when I speak Spanish in the United States. Spanish has a formal, an informal and, in some parts of the Spanish-speaking world, an intimate level of speech. The use of each varies in different parts of the world. When I speak Spanish, my vocabulary and grammar will depend on whether the situation is formal or informal, and on the linguistic background of the person I am talking with. The way each level of formality is used reflects class, education and racial differences, and these differences are not consistent from country to country. As a mestizo Latino born in the United States, who directs Spanish-language masters and doctoral level theological programs in the United States, I have to recognize that formal and informal language use means different things in different settings, depending also on who is using them. This all has to do with interpretive leadership—how I work with language and meanings, how I interact with students who need these skills—and how this affects our work in churches. But it is also explicitly about relational leadership, which requires that we attend to the cultural differences and commonalities regarding human dynamics.

Concerning the use of Spanish in seminary, some students use the formal when speaking to professors. These students understand that respect is crucial in the student-professor relationship. Other students are accustomed to informal language with theological professors because they see themselves as ministry colleagues. From their perspective the key issues are affective qualities of the relationship, commonality of ministry and theological understandings. Some students may use the formal to maintain difference and distance, or the informal to indirectly state that a U.S. mestizo Latino, by definition, is not at their social level. So I often need to use both formal and informal Spanish in a school situation because the students bring different understandings about the language and different expectations concerning the student-professor relationship.

This connection between Spanish and relationships becomes especially complicated for Latino and Latina students who were born or educated in the United States. They are trying to define a relationship that tends to be informal in English but potentially formal in Spanish. Should the professor-student relationship be defined by U.S. standards or by Latin American standards? Should the relationship be defined one way in English and a different way in Spanish? How should Latino and Latina students relate to the large number of Latino and Latina employees at the school, with whom they interact in Spanish?

Table 6.1. Comparison of Social Relations[a]

Egalitarian Assumption	Hierarchical Assumption
• Assume equality	• Assume class
• Status changes	• Status endures
• Multiple networks	• Prescribed networks
• Informal	• Formal
• Avoid obligations	• Required reciprocity
• Confront problems	• Problems mediated
• Relations instrumental	• Relations for group
• Need to be liked	• Popularity not priority

[a]See Edward Stewart and Milton Bennett, *American Cultural Patterns: A Cross-Cultural Perspective*, rev. ed. (Yarmouth, Maine: Intercultural Press, 1991), pp. 89-112.

Social relations in the United States follow certain characteristics that influence how people of different ethnic and national backgrounds relate to each other. Most majority-culture people in the United States assume an egalitarian understanding of social relations. This is different from many other parts of the world, where hierarchical relations are assumed and are often embedded in the languages and social protocols.

Throughout this chapter we will be looking at some of the common social assumptions of U.S. egalitarian culture and how these affect social relations when others do not make the same assumptions. We are aware that social relations in the United States are not fully egalitarian. Rather, in our founding narratives, as immigrants constructed a society that featured specific contrasts with those cultures they left, many traditional hierarchies were significantly altered. By comparing and contrasting various types of social assumptions we will be able to address how these influence intercultural ministry efforts and how to work together in ways that recognize these differences and their implications. In the practical-theology cycle, this is mainly step 2: we are learning from sociocultural studies that we need to attend to cultural diversity regarding relationships. In our work with Scripture, we also demonstrate interaction between step 3 and step 2.

Bible Study: Acts 10—Peter's Slow Conversion

[1]In Caesarea there was a man named Cornelius, a centurion of the Italian Cohort, as it was called. [2]He was a devout man who feared God with all his household; he gave alms generously to the people and prayed constantly to God. [3]One afternoon at about three o'clock he had a vision in which he clearly saw an angel of God coming in and saying to him, "Cornelius." [4]He stared at him in terror and said, "What is it, Lord?" He answered, "Your prayers and your alms have ascended as a memorial before God. [5]Now send men to Joppa for a certain Simon who is called Peter; [6]he is lodging with Simon, a tanner, whose house is by the seaside." . . .

[9]About noon the next day, as they were on their journey and approaching the city, Peter went up on the roof to pray. [10]He became hungry and wanted something to eat; and while it was being prepared, he fell into a trance. [11]He saw the heaven opened and something like a large sheet coming down, being lowered to the ground by its four corners. [12]In it were all kinds of four-footed creatures and reptiles and birds of the air. [13]Then he heard a voice saying, "Get up, Peter; kill and eat." [14]But Peter said, "By no means, Lord; for I have never eaten anything that is profane or unclean." [15]The voice said to him again, a second time, "What God has made clean, you must not call profane." [16]This happened three times, and the thing was suddenly taken up to heaven. . . .

[19]While Peter was still thinking about the vision, the Spirit said to him, "Look, three men are searching for you. [20]Now get up, go down, and go with them without hesitation; for I have sent them." . . . [23]So Peter invited them in and gave them lodging.

The next day he got up and went with them, and some of the believers from Joppa accompanied him. [24]The following day they came to Caesarea. Cornelius was expecting them and had called together his relatives and close friends. [25]On Peter's arrival Cornelius met him, and falling at his feet, worshiped him. [26]But Peter made him get up, saying, "Stand up; I am only a mortal." [27]And as he talked with him, he went in and found that many had assembled; [28]and he said to them, "You yourselves know that it is unlawful for a Jew to associate with or to visit a Gentile; but God has shown me that I should not call anyone profane or unclean. . . .

³⁴Then Peter began to speak to them: "I truly understand that God shows no partiality, ³⁵but in every nation anyone who fears him and does what is right is acceptable to him.

Peter was a "good" Jew who had a certain understanding of how God worked in the world and what the proper relationship between Jew and Gentile should be. Because of his understanding he found it very difficult to share the good news with Gentiles. Even after receiving a vision from God (Acts 10) it was difficult for Peter to treat Gentiles as equal before God. According to Paul (Gal 2:11-14) this would be a problem for Peter for a long time.

1. What was Peter's understanding of the relationship between Jews and Gentiles? Where did he learn this?

2. Why was this understanding so important to Jewish identity?

3. Why does it take Peter so long to understand what God is doing and its implications for social relations?

4. What does this story tell us about the relationship between culture, social relations and the gospel?

5. What are your own slow conversions? What are some of the slow conversions in your church and community? What are the signs of conversion and the signs of hesitation?

THE ASSUMPTION OF SOCIAL EQUALITY

As mentioned in chapter five, U.S. English, with a few exceptions, mostly in the South, treats everyone as an "equal." This theme of equality runs through all interpersonal relations; it is a fundamental assumption in U.S. society. Because of this assumption "interpersonal relationships are typically horizontal, conducted between autonomous individuals who are presumed to be equals."[1] This understanding is applied to all social situations, even those in which there is a clear hierarchical difference in the relationship. Supervisors want to be seen as

---

[1]Paul Hiebert, *Anthropological Insights for Missionaries* (Grand Rapids: Baker, 1985), p. 127.

"regular Joes," and people value political leaders because they sound like "regular people."

This means that most Euro-Americans function best in situations where equality is assumed. Interactions become very confusing when they are in a crosscultural situation in which they have to act in a way that acknowledges that some people clearly have a higher social status, particularly if that status is ascribed, not acquired. How does one listen to an elder who is "clearly" not qualified but who is considered an important leader by those of his cultural community?

The concept of social equality is often tested in the church, particularly when crossing boundaries where there are different assumptions about social relations. Protestant theologies emphasize the "priesthood of all believers," and many U.S. Protestants place a great deal of emphasis on this concept (though many maintain a class division with the way they deal with ordination). But this concept is severely tested both within and beyond U.S. culture. Many of those Protestants who speak strongly about egalitarian leadership admire the large churches in Korea, Latin America or Africa, all of which are "successful," at least in part, because of clearly defined social hierarchies. The members of these churches accept a deferential status for "God's anointed" and those in leadership. Those models of church are admired and set up as examples of successful church growth. But leaders from those countries are often criticized if they establish hierarchically based congregations among minority-culture people or immigrants in the United States.

This leadership issue is also being redefined within the United States. Many large churches have leadership styles that are very hierarchical. They use hierarchical models, such as the pastor as CEO, that are rapidly being accepted within "egalitarian" U.S. society. Because it is a model that fits within U.S. social relations, it is easier to accept than equally hierarchical models that developed in a different social or cultural context.

These differences play out whenever churches and leaders attempt to work together.

When a Midwestern city completed a major low-cost housing development, a multiethnic group of clergy gathered for a time of public prayer. A councilman was going to introduce the pastors, and he noted that some wore robes, one came from work with his carpenter clothes, another wore chinos and another wore her clerical collar. They did not seem to be especially comfortable with each other. When the councilman began asking about appropriate ways to introduce each person, some gave him instructions for formal recognition of degrees and church hierarchy, others simply provided first names.

Though the councilperson did not understand what was happening, he was interacting with both theological and social assumptions about appropriate demeanor for pastors in public situations and also assumptions about how social hierarchies were defined among pastors. These differences not only made his work more difficult but also created tensions among the clergy present.

Nonetheless, social equality is restricted in its application in the United States. Historically, it has not applied to African Americans, Latinos, Asians, Native Americans and other ethnic minorities. When Europeans first came to the Americas they seriously questioned the full humanity of black Africans and Native Americans.[2] Throughout the nineteenth century many "scientific" studies "demonstrated" the inferior status of minority groups, particularly those of African descent. These explanations became "common knowledge" and the accepted understanding among those of the dominant culture. They served as basis for legal prescriptions (e.g., Jim Crow laws of late nineteenth- and twentieth-century southern United States, which mandated "separate but equal"—which was separate, but never equal) and for immigration quotas well into the twentieth century. To this day there are many people in the United States who question the ability of people who are not of European background to integrate into the social fabric of the United States.[3]

But this is a subject most people in the United States choose not to recognize publicly. According to sociologist Thomas Kochman, people in polite American society practice a social etiquette in which one does not

---

[2]This is reflected in the original U.S. Constitution, where African slaves were counted as 3/5 of a person for taxation and representation purposes, even though they did not get 3/5 of a vote.
[3]See Samuel Huntington, *Who Are We? The Challenges to America's National Identity* (New York: Simon & Schuster, 2004). Huntington questions whether Hispanics will become a part of the national identity.

address the differences of minority groups in public. This practice developed during the period when the differences between groups were used to "prove" the inferiority of minority group peoples.[4]

Because the subject is not openly addressed, many stigmas persist. Almost no one will publicly admit it, but many majority-culture people in the United States implicitly assume that the social stigmas faced by minority groups are of their own making. The majority seldom thinks about the implications of imposing its social values on the minority (such as forced Americanization of Native Americans and English-only laws). Those that recognize they are imposing something from outside likely consider the imposition a good thing for the minority group. Any differences exhibited by minority groups are often seen as a social deviance or as a sign of unwillingness to fit in the social order of the majority.

Because of such differences in social and familial relations, it is difficult for different ethnic groups to agree on issues of structural racism or social barriers in U.S. society. If someone cannot succeed in a specific institution, then that specific person might have a basis for seeking correction of the situation. There is little ability to recognize how the underlying social assumptions create an environment where no one person discriminates, but where the majority of people from minority groups can never succeed to the level of their capacities.

In *Divided by Faith*, sociologists Michael O. Emerson and Christian Smith address this situation within the life of evangelical churches. The divide between white and African American evangelicals resists healing because each side sees a fundamentally different problem. White evangelicals only see individuals and want to solve the tensions by addressing the situation of individuals. They assume that once the specific issues of a specific person have been addressed, the issue is resolved. African Americans, on the other hand, confront structural problems every day and recognize that they need to address structural issues. But majority-culture evangelicals rebuff them because the latter do not have an interpretative framework to even recognize the existence of social hierarchies and structural inequities, such as poor schools, nonexistent social services, racial profiling and exclusive social networks.

---

[4]Thomas Kochman, *Black and White Styles in Conflict* (Chicago: University of Chicago Press, 1981), p. 11.

Personal Reflection/Group Exercise: Identifying My Privileges

Spend time in personal reflection, then discuss these questions with other participants.

1. As a person who was born or raised in the United States, name five things you have that others might not have (U.S. passport, access to study, income level, legal protections, etc.).

2. Identify someone you know or know about in the United States who does not have these things. What is the basis for the difference?

3. How might your opportunities be different if you had been born in a different country or into a different family (with a different ethnicity or class)?

4. What barriers make it difficult for the other person to obtain the privileges you have?

Emerson and Smith state that majority-culture evangelicals have three religiocultural tools that adversely affect how they understand the complexities of social relations between African Americans and majority-culture whites in the United States. Specifically, they believe in *accountable freewill individualism* (that all individuals are fully free to make their decisions and then are fully responsible for the implications of their decisions), *relationalism* (that interpersonal relations are central to dealing with problems of all kinds) and *antistructuralism* (the inability or unwillingness to recognize the impact of social structural influences). It is difficult if not impossible for majority-culture evangelicals to recognize that social *structures* may have a negative influence on social relations. So while many African Americans try to address the social structures that adversely affect them, most majority-culture evangelicals assume that the problem is personal and can be solved with better personal interaction and greater personal accountability.[5]

SOCIAL EQUALITY AND SOCIAL GROUPINGS

A related issue is that of how people form social groups. In egalitarian-

---

[5]See Michael Emerson and Christian Smith, *Divided by Faith: Evangelical Religion and the Problem of Race in America* (New York: Oxford University Press, 2000).

oriented societies the assumption is that people relate with others because of common interests, not because of group or family commitments or social ranking. According to missiologist Paul Hiebert, "We [Americans] tend to participate in group activities as separate individuals united in a common activity, rather than as a corporate body in which our personal rights and interests are subordinate to those of the group."[6]

This means that for the dominant U.S. culture, social relations tend to be tied to self-interest and not primarily to a commitment to family or to the group or organization. Most people in the United States assume that the individual will tend to separate from family and enter into new social groupings such as professions, voluntary networks, associations or clubs.[7] There are all types of clubs, some of which endure over time. But in these groups "relationships are often superficial and confined to such specific areas of life as work, sports and politics, and individuals have a right to leave if they wish."[8]

This understanding affects intercultural relationships. On an individual level people assume that they are not racist because they have social acquaintances that are from ethnic minority groups. Since they work together, served together in the military and some even attend the same church, they assume that they have done the hard work of dealing with racism. The harder questions of structural injustice or privilege are not addressed (or even recognized as issues to be addressed). This is a major challenge for relational leadership—how can we create environments and shape conversations so that this complexity receives attention?

RELATIONS AND OBLIGATIONS

When I (Juan) returned from a trip to South America, I brought gifts for most of the people in my church. Because of my pastoral role, I am expected to bring a small gift, but any gift I give becomes part of the larger web of relationships in the church. When members of my congregation traveled, they often brought a small gift to me as well as to close friends, and they would bring a small memento to the church. I always try to include the

---

[6]Hiebert, *Anthropological Insights for Missionaries*, p. 125.
[7]See Francis Hsu, *Clan, Caste, and Club* (Princeton, N.J.: D. Van Nostrand, 1963), esp. chap. 9, specifically p. 204.
[8]Hiebert, *Anthropological Insights for Missionaries*, p. 125.

poor and marginalized in the gift giving, but do not want to create a social obligation that is beyond their financial means. I want them to know that they are special in our church, but I do not want to make them feel bad because they cannot reciprocate. This usually seems to work well, except when I get a gift bought with a "widow's mite." These have usually been the most difficult gifts for me to receive, but also those that have usually been used by God to develop special ministry opportunities.

In many cultures gifts are part of a structure of social relations. In traditional rural Latin America the rich often have social obligations toward the poor in their communities. This type of social obligation is also assumed between richer and poorer relatives and between older and younger siblings. Important social celebrations such as weddings, quinceañeras and baptisms are often possible because *padrinos* provide financial support. (Of course, these types of arrangements do not obligate the rich to practice fairness or justice. But they do "share the wealth," at least for this occasion, when the rich take on this obligation.)

In many Asian cultures there are elaborate understandings of gift exchange. Each participant knows that gifts create reciprocal obligations that must be fulfilled to maintain strong social relations. At times, these obligations can be very expensive. A gift that is too large or too small, or one given when gifting is not called for, can create significant social disequilibrium beyond the persons directly involved. But those in the social system accept the importance of maintaining these social obligations. Gift giving is part of a social network where this type of social interchange helps maintain the social fabric.

These types of obligations may go far beyond gift exchange. A person may be expected to help friends or relatives obtain employment or to house them when they immigrate to the United States or move to a new area looking for work. The basis for these obligations may be linked to complex familial relationships or social networks that reveal a web of human relationships and interactions that are not easily understood by an outsider.

According to Stewart and Bennett, most majority-culture people in the United States prefer relationships that do not carry defined social obligations or personal commitments to others. If a person receives a gift they recognize that they should also give that person something, but there is no clear assumption or obligation to reciprocate. Their preference is to develop relationships in way that minimize these types of social obligations.[9]

In much of the rest of the world, relationships and social obligations are closely linked. This leads Stewart and Bennett to conclude that in most of the world, except the United States, "a relationship without obligation is simply not significant."[10] Whereas many people in the United States assume that self-reliance is an important value and they tend to minimize the role of social obligations, many other peoples understand that a good relationship is based on mutual obligation.[11]

This significant difference in understanding the link between relationships and social obligations can create problems when majority-culture and minority-culture people interact in the United States. Many majority-culture people may not realize the social obligation that they are creating for another when they give or receive a gift. They may assume that a "don't worry about it" may suffice. But a person who has been taught the importance of social exchange *will* worry about it. A person who does not "properly" reciprocate may also be seen as rude, stingy or unfriendly if they receive a gift, but do not take care to respond in a socially appropriate way (which they may not understand). Relational leadership develops a church's capacities for interpreting these differences and shaping understanding and practices.

During her second year in a church that is dominantly Asian American, the new pastor wanted to develop small group home Bible studies. Several of the Asian families that had strongly supported her in coming to the church seemed to be reticent about meeting in homes. The new pastor continued talking about how meeting in members' homes helped build community and that hospitality in homes provided opportunities to make contact with neighbors. Even with additional teaching and conversation, the resistance continued. She raised her questions with some younger families who had parents in the church, and learned through these conversations that many of the families were seldom in each other's homes, but they associated with each other in other settings This helped her become aware of

---

[9]Stewart and Bennett, *American Cultural Patterns*, p. 94.
[10]Ibid., p. 95.
[11]Hiebert, *Anthropological Insights for Missionaries*, p. 124.

how cultural issues of obligations and reciprocity were the basis of the reti-
cence. The next August, when members were regathering after vacations,
she asked the men's group to sponsor several cookouts in their homes—and
five volunteered. Since this was an activity of a church group, the issues of
reciprocity were not raised. They shaped the invitation lists so everyone
was invited to one of the cookouts. The pastor preached about how the
biblical festivals were times of food, stories and prayer. She asked the men
to help with a few questions—mainly to create intergenerational conver-
sations about favorite vacations, funniest stories and when they were es-
pecially aware of God's blessings. By experimenting with ways of reducing
obligations and increasing social motivations, this group of church leaders
succeeded in drawing a majority of members into home activities and
deeper relationships.

Egalitarian social structures place a high value on creating and maintaining personal options—and the assumption is that obligations work
against personal freedom. In a church these issues are related to matters of
Christian practices such as the meaning of membership. Is church to be
understood as a primary community (as we defined *community* in chap. 3),
an optional community, or even a dispenser of religious goods and services? How might new obligations be shaped within a congregation as
persons grow in love and commitment to each other? In the United States,
churches become clubs, in the sense that people develop self-interested
relationships and see themselves as free to leave if their interests are not
fulfilled. Discipleship and community are difficult concepts to develop
among people who do not value interpersonal obligations and deep and
long-lasting social commitments.

HOW TO DEFINE FRIENDSHIP AND PERSONAL RELATIONSHIPS

People from egalitarian cultures usually have a number of relationships
with others that are marked by friendliness and informality, but far less
common are relationships with significant mutual personal knowledge
and where mutual dependence is assumed. According to Stewart and Bennett people from the U.S. majority culture tend to develop friendships
based on "spontaneity, mutual attraction, and warm personal feelings."
They feel it is important to "preserve personal initiative in pursuing friend-

ships," something that is very different from societies where friendships and social obligations are closely linked.[12]

This means that social relations are defined very differently across cultures. Many people from the U.S. majority culture can honestly say that they "made a new friend last weekend," while other people might describe the same encounter as having made a new acquaintance. The key differences are the basis for the relationship and the depth of responsibility and commitment assumed in a "friendship."

This type of difference in understanding can be detrimental to intercultural relations. On the one hand, the value of an existing social relationship may be very different when read from one side or the other. A person from the dominant U.S. culture may assume that they have built a friendship with a person from another ethnic group, while the other merely sees a superficial social relationship. On the other hand, a minority person may assume that a person who says they want to be a friend is ready to take on the types of social depth and obligations that would make the other person uncomfortable.

A Presbyterian church of three hundred had become diversified to about 45 percent African American and about 45 percent Euro-American. The board of deacons training on visitation included a discussion on crosscultural care-giving. Difference in spatial comfort, unspoken rules regarding touching and hugging, length of visit, and the use of prayer were all discussed and guidelines given. With just this training, the only new African American male deacon began to make his initial visits to some members who were homebound. He went to the door of the first woman on the list, a Caucasian woman, who greeted him in a very formal matter through a screen door. He became increasingly nervous and began to stammer about who he was and why he was there. After getting the whole explanation out, the voice from behind the door said, "Jeff, thanks for coming to visit me. Come on in." At the next deacon's meeting Jeff reported that while he enjoyed his visit, in the end, he felt she had made a visit on him as well as he on her. The relationship between the two of them has grown over the years.

---

[12]Stewart and Bennett, *American Cultural Patterns*, p. 101.

Because solid intercultural relationships are important for multicultural churches, these congregations will need to address how different cultures define relationships and social concepts such as friendship, commitment, partnership and even "belonging" when it refers to a congregation.

NEEDING TO BE LIKED

According to Paul Hiebert, most people from the U.S. majority culture "place a high value on being liked and see it as a sign of success in social relationships."[13] Because of that value, Americans can find many books and seminars that teach techniques of personal communication and how to be liked by others. "Americans base their esteem of others on being liked by them" and often judge their success "almost literally by the number of people who like them."[14]

This means that interaction and even service toward others is often based on this expectation. Volunteer service is often not only based on need but also on whether people seem grateful for the service. If the external and superficial signs of friendship are not present, many people assume that they are failing in the workplace, in their social circle or in their efforts to help others.

For example, people often choose a church because it feels friendly. In other words people in the church liberally use external signs of friendliness such as ready smiles and glad handshakes. Churches that provide these "seeker-sensitive" types of responses toward new people are more likely to see them return. Majority-culture Christians in the United States are likely to choose a new church based on the relational warmth they receive and on their overall comfort level. Denominational, historical, doctrinal or kinship ties would not likely influence them as much as the feel of the church.

DEALING WITH PROBLEMS

A common assumption among most majority-culture people in the United States is that the best way to deal with problems is to address the issue directly. This does not mean that people do not use avoidance and passive-aggressive modes when dealing with problems, but the ideal problem-

---

[13]Hiebert, *Anthropological Insights for Missionaries*, p. 126.
[14]Stewart and Bennett, *American Cultural Patterns*, p. 108.

solving mode is assumed to be one in which people are faced directly and the priority is "getting the facts." Confrontation is not necessarily seen as an intense emotional event. The ideal is that people will express their feelings, speak honestly about the situation and deal directly with the people involved in the problem.

But in many cultures it is much more important to "save face," to avoid direct confrontations that might cause embarrassment or shame. Problems are dealt with through various indirect means, well understood by those within the culture. People who practice indirect means of problem solving find that Euro-American directness is often "harsh and destructive" to interpersonal relations that depend on subtlety and indirection.[15] On the other hand, Euro-Americans often perceive indirect problem-solving techniques as dishonest or as attempts to cover up problems, instead of "getting to them" and "dealing with them."

An Asian American church hired a Euro-American organist who had retired from teaching. Over several years her musical competencies declined and her attentiveness wavered. There were awkward times during worship as younger members of the worship team tried to assist her. When discussions arose among leaders, the Japanese American voices said that they should do nothing—the organist could have the job for as long as she wished. It was inappropriate to tell a professional that she was not performing adequately. But other leaders, Euro-American and Chinese American, said that it was inappropriate to allow a professional musician to continue in this situation—her own professional standards were not being met, and if she were mentally more competent, she would be embarrassed by this ongoing experience. They said it was more loving and appropriate to have another older, professional person have a conversation with the organist.

This difference concerning cultural approaches to problem solving is crucial in intercultural church relations. Multicultural ministry creates problems merely because people are different. Those problems are complicated because the people affected often have very different ideas about

---

[15]Ibid., p. 99.

how to deal with issues. The direct issue (the organist in the narrative above) almost becomes secondary to the issue of how interpersonal problems are best addressed. A sensitive leader recognizes that the desire to deal with problems directly often makes intercultural relations worse. A person unwilling to address a problem publicly and directly might wrongly be accused of avoiding the issue or even worse, of lying. That person may have other means for addressing the problems. Successful interethnic relations in the life of the church recognize that people have different understandings of problem solving; various approaches are suitable for differing challenges. The key issue for leaders will be to use methods that take people into account as steps and procedures are considered. Because the leader wants to both strengthen relationships and to get things done, he or she will need to interpret what is happening to each group and to help each understand the importance of the position being proposed by the other.

INFORMALITY AND FORMALITY

The concept of equality is closely tied to the informal ways many majority-culture people treat each other. People look directly into each other's eyes, greetings are usually brief and people refer to each other using their first names. The sense among most people in the United States is that it is important to treat everyone informally, whether they are close friends, business associates or servers at a restaurant. This way of treating people is usually considered normal, though it can also risk communicating disrespect in an ambiguous multicultural setting, like the one presented in the introduction to this chapter.

The dominant culture's norm of informality conflicts with the social understanding of most cultures around the world where informality and formality are used to define different types of social relationships. There are clear demarcations of formality between people of different social standing. Formal greetings usually follow a ritualized and often extensive format, even among people who are in conflict. This type of greeting allows people to demonstrate concern for the other, while recognizing that they do not necessarily have a close relationship. The use of titles among people of different social rank is also a way of recognizing and respecting very real differences. In some languages it is almost impossible to refer to someone of a higher status without a title.[16] These cultural differences are also apparent in clothing.

> *An African American Church of God had made cultural diversity an explicit church value, and an increasing number of Euro-American and Latino families were coming on Sundays. The church pastors were quick to increase ethnic diversity in worship leadership and in various church leadership teams. One summer the pastor said, "Our Sunday morning attire is shaped by our own African American traditions—the men are wearing suits, the women are wearing dresses, the (church) mothers are wearing hats, the choir and pastor are wearing robes." He explained that they, like other churches, always say "everyone is welcome—come as you are," but he told them about a conversation he had with someone he had invited. The friend said, "Look—you are in a suit, and everyone else is dressed up. You told me to just come, but this is uncomfortable. I feel duped." And he noted that even persons from other cultures who had been raised in a church "do not have formal dress as a point of reference." So the pastor proposed a summer experiment—"Let's go casual." Later that summer the pastor checked in with older African American members—and learned that their commitment to being welcoming was more important than continuing their own tradition. So the pastor announced that they would continue the casual approach, but "if you like a more formal tradition, that is also appropriate. The diverse dress on Sundays can be a plus for us and for visitors."*

Church leaders who shape processes toward intercultural life will experiment with options that attend to all participants and evaluate how to work with traditions, respect and hospitality. Congregations may not always need to go through the complete praxis cycle, but they will be able to recognize their starting point and how to think through different ways of responding to the challenges of intercultural life.

COOPERATION AND FAIR PLAY

Most majority-culture people in the United States focus on the individual

---

[16]We also understand that titles can be oppressive, a way to maintain injustice or to dehumanize others. Relationships in a church need both empathy and respect as a church works toward new practices.

and are often in competition with each other. But they are able to combine competition and cooperation because their commitments to groups or organizations are often based on perceived personal gain. People accept the rules and goals of a group but do not wholly commit themselves to it. If their needs and expectations are not met, they feel free to leave one group to join a different one that will potentially address the unmet expectation.[17]

This is an important asset because Euro-Americans are often able to get things done with people with whom they strongly disagree because "getting things done" is a more important value than the interpersonal relationships among those who are working together. Groups use agendas and procedures to create a due process that allows individuals to be recognized but also gives them space to compromise while maintaining their principles.[18]

The ability to work with people with whom we disagree is seen as a hallmark of civil society in the United States. But this value can easily be misunderstood as opportunism. People from cultures that value principles over cooperation may assume that this level of working together reflects a willingness to let go of principles to "get things done." There is a need to interpret this practice among minority peoples and peoples of other cultures so that it is not misinterpreted as the unwillingness to stand for what one believes.

Cooperation based on rules and procedures often works in the workplace. But when brought into the life of the church it can create social and theological confusion. Should decisions be based on accepted procedures (such as Robert's Rules of Order) or on relational commitments? How does one or the other affect the level of commitment a person has to a church community? What might rules and procedures look like that address both the importance of formal policies and the importance of relational interaction in decision making?

Related to the issue of cooperation is the majority-culture concept of fair play. The idea is that rules and procedures should be such that the stronger person does not have an unfair advantage. People want to win a game, but they want to be able to say that it was done "fair and square." Most majority-culture people assume that laws, rules and practices in the United States follow this understanding of fair play.

[17]Hiebert, *Anthropological Insights for Missionaries*, p. 130.
[18]Stewart and Bennett, *American Cultural Patterns*, p. 106.

Since the rules are fair, then those with privilege can argue that they earned it "fair and square."

But the concept of fair play makes it difficult to deal with structural inequalities between people groups in the United States. This is because the basic assumption is that the playing field is more or less even for all. For example, affirmative action has been one attempt at fair play designed for people of ethnic minorities who have traditionally been excluded from the benefits of American society. Yet one of the (many) reasons it is not working is because fair play is mediated by an individualized view of the problem. Individual members of the dominant culture might recognize that they have some level of privilege, but any action that can be interpreted as adversely affecting them directly is seen as not being fair play. Under current understandings of affirmative action as a means to overcome prejudice, members of minority groups are given a special "leg up," not because there is a structural problem but because they are personally disadvantaged. But if they accept this help it means they have to accept the interpretation that they as individuals were unable to compete "fairly" and that they have received an opportunity they "really" do not deserve. As a result we see situations in which (1) majority-culture people claim that affirmative action discriminates against them, and (2) people from ethnic minorities who advanced because of affirmative action now work against continuing this policy. In an individualized egalitarian society it is very difficult to recognize and compensate for any structural barriers that are group oriented. Therefore, if minority groups are "staying behind," it must be completely the fault of individuals who are not willing to take the actions necessary to succeed.

PEOPLE AS A FUNCTION OF THEIR ROLES

Majority-culture persons in the United States tend to value people based on their occupational roles. These roles tend to be very specialized, depending on education, experience and place within an institution. These work-related roles are important to the extent that they are seen as contributing to society, particularly to its economic success.

Social roles that do not directly contribute to a corporation or organization's accomplishments are valued to the extent that they provide some other "useful" function. A homemaker has some potential value, of raising children (though a daycare center has trained specialists to do that). A grandparent may also find social value in caring for children.

This means that people who cannot contribute because they are ill, infirm or do not have a specialized occupational role do not have a clear place in the social order. They have *relationships* but not *roles*. In many societies being an elder is an important social *role*. Their role is linked to their position in society, their relationships or history or what they symbolize, not to what they do. People provide social space within family and community structures, not because of what they can contribute, but because of who they are. Traditionally "in most societies old people are viewed positively as wise and experienced."[19]

But because "Americans perceive aging as a progressive loss of function, . . . it is not surprising that social roles based on functionality narrow with age."[20] This understanding has a direct impact on church leadership. To what extent is a pastor chosen because he or she is a wise elder in the community and to what extent is "capacity" (understood as having the skills necessary to lead a church) the principal value in finding a "good" pastor? What is the importance of age in deciding on elders for a church? How is leadership chosen in an intercultural context where there are different perspectives as to the role of elders in the community?

Because church life is about social relations, pastors and other leaders will need to help people walk together, making sure each understands how others interpret their actions. Part of the interpretive and relational work of leadership is taking the time to work toward this type of understanding. This means leaders need to lead the congregation through the praxis cycle so that people understand the assumptions about social relations of those who are in the church community and also those of the people the church wishes to reach. As pastors begin to understand differences in how people interact, and as they help people develop new ways of interacting in the life of the church, they will be involved in the praxis of intercultural church life.

---

[19]Hiebert, *Anthropological Insights for Missionaries*, p. 133.
[20]Stewart and Bennett, *American Cultural Patterns*, p. 112.

At the Movies

The common theme of the three movies is social relations within common cultures, in light of migration to the United States. Observe how the transnational experience changes people, even as they continue to live within their own cultural background.

Quinceañera (2006). Magdalena, anxiously awaiting her fifteenth birthday until she discovers she is pregnant, is abandoned by both her own family and her baby's father, but finds a new family and new life.

A Great Wall (1986). When a Chinese American computer programmer is passed over for a promotion because he is Chinese, he quits and takes his family to mainland China, precipitating a clash of cultures.

Monsoon Wedding (2001). In India, where telecommunications and a Western lifestyle mix with old traditions, young Aditi accepts an arranged marriage with a groom living in Texas. Scattered relatives from both families come to New Delhi during the monsoon season to attend the wedding.

7

Self-Perception
and Individuality

Juan Francisco Martínez

We hold these truths to be self-evident, that all men are created equal, that they are endowed by their Creator with certain unalienable Rights, that among these are Life, Liberty and the pursuit of Happiness.

THE LINE ABOVE, FROM THE Declaration of Independence, is a powerful description of the perception of self in the United States. Human individuals have the right to live their lives, making their own choices, seeking their personal happiness. This perspective is based on a specific view of the individual that developed in the Western world and affects how people view themselves and their place in society and in the world. It affects the dominant culture's understandings of the role of church and community and also how ethnic minorities relate to the majority in the United States.[1]

COLLECTIVISM AND INDIVIDUALISM IN CULTURES

All cultures address the issue of the relationship between the group and the individual. The differences among cultures concern levels of prominence and the spheres in which the differences are most notable. In individualist cultures, like North American middle-class culture, the empha-

---

[1]One can argue that today's interpretation of individualism is much more radical than what was envisioned by those who wrote the Declaration of Independence. The Founding Fathers assumed that people had common duties that bound them together (the law of nature), something that seems to get lost in today's understanding of individualism.

sis is on individuals as "potentially self-sufficient agents endowed with fundamental rights" such as those mentioned in the Declaration of Independence. In contrast, collectivist cultures give priority to the group and underscore the "values of group harmony, cooperation, solidarity, and interdependency."[2] Church leaders need the competencies for observing when these preferences and habits are in play and for guiding processes in their church for guiding intercultural practices.

An Asian American church participated regularly and generously in the annual ecumenical CROP Walk, which raised money for hunger relief. Each year the church set up tables after worship, and members pledged money to support the group that represented them at the walk. This was a group event—those who walked knew they represented the congregation, as did those who donated. But unlike other participating churches, donations were not ascribed to individual walkers—this would have been seen either as inappropriately competitive or too individualistic. But a problem arose when the church's organizers met with the event's record-keepers. All income was to be assigned to some individual—so the church had to create an artificial distribution of the monies among the participants. Even though there were discussions every year that this was not the church's understanding about how funds were raised and donated, the event's organizers insisted that all accounting be done in this manner.

According to the social psychologists Hazel Markus and Shinobu Kitayama, individualist and collectivist cultures create different conceptions of the self. The first focuses on independence, the second on interdependence. This means that the person either defines his or her self as separated from the social context or as connected with the social context. While the individualist seeks to be unique or to express the self, the collectivist seeks to fit in or to find a place in the social order. As a result, individualist cultures seek to help a person to express him- or herself, while collectivist cultures want the individual to learn to adjust and restrain the self to maintain shared benefits and social harmony.[3]

---

[2]Dan McAdams, *The Redemptive Self Stories Americans Live By* (New York: Oxford University Press, 2006), p. 278.
[3]Hazel Markus and Shinobu Kitayama, "Culture and the Self: Implications, for Cognition, Emotion, and Motivation," *Psychological Review* 98 (1991): 224-53.

Bible Study: 1 Corinthians 12—Gifts for the Body

[4]Now there are varieties of gifts, but the same Spirit; [5]and there are varieties of services, but the same Lord; [6]and there are varieties of activities, but it is the same God who activates all of them in everyone. [7]To each is given the manifestation of the Spirit for the common good. . . .

[12]For just as the body is one and has many members, and all the members of the body, though many, are one body, so it is with Christ. [13]For in the one Spirit we were all baptized into one body—Jews or Greeks, slaves or free—and we were all made to drink of one Spirit.

[14]Indeed, the body does not consist of one member but of many. [15]If the foot would say, "Because I am not a hand, I do not belong to the body," that would not make it any less a part of the body. [16]And if the ear would say, "Because I am not an eye, I do not belong to the body," that would not make it any less a part of the body. . . . [21]The eye cannot say to the hand, "I have no need of you," nor again the head to the feet, "I have no need of you." [22]On the contrary, the members of the body that seem to be weaker are indispensable, [23]and those members of the body that we think less honorable we clothe with greater honor, and our less respectable members are treated with greater respect; [24]whereas our more respectable members do not need this. But God has so arranged the body, giving the greater honor to the inferior member, [25]that there may be no dissension within the body, but the members may have the same care for one another. [26]If one member suffers, all suffer together with it; if one member is honored, all rejoice together with it.

[27]Now you are the body of Christ and individually members of it.

Throughout the Gospels we see Jesus calling individuals from within a collectivist culture, but inviting them into a new community, the church (a transformed social group). The New Testament uses many analogies to help us understand the role of the church in God's mission. One of the key analogies is that of the body. This concept provides us with important understanding of the self in relationship to the community. In 1 Corinthians 12 Paul states that the Spirit gives specific and individual gifts to people. He clearly describes the diversity and individuality of the gifts. But he also clearly places the diversity within the unity of the body, under the head, Jesus Christ. The individual has a clear and specific role in the life of the community. But that role only finds purpose in relationship to the body. The gifts are not primarily for "me" and "my" benefit.

1. How might Christians from individualist or collectivist cultures understand the concept of spiritual gifts differently? Why?

2. What are the advantages or disadvantages of reading this passage from an individualist perspective or from a collectivist perspective? What do we learn and what do we lose from each type of reading?

3. How does the concept of body challenge a church in the U.S. individualistic culture? What challenges does this imply in a church that mixes persons from both perspectives?

INDIVIDUALISM IN DOMINANT U.S. CULTURE

The concept of the individual expressed in the Declaration of Independence is largely based on the philosophy of John Locke, particularly as described in the second of his *Two Treatises on Government*.[4] According to Locke the biological individual is the basic unit of nature and society. Humans have a number of natural rights as individuals, and society and civil government are organized to protect those individual rights. The individual, with his or her rights, is the center, the basic building block of society;[5] therefore the function of society and its structures is to provide "space" for the individual.

This perspective affects all social relations in U.S. society. Economically, it is commonly assumed that the "invisible hand" of enlightened self-interest directs capitalism and free enterprise. This framework assumes that when all individuals have the freedom to "pursue happiness" a maximum number will find happiness. When individuals do not find happiness, or financial stability, the assumption is that the person must be at

---

[4]John Locke was born in England in 1632 (d. 1704) and lived during a time of imperial oppression throughout Europe. His works were influential in the changes that later occurred in England and other parts of Europe.

[5]Paul Hiebert, *Anthropological Insights for Missionaries* (Grand Rapids: Baker, 1985), p. 122.

fault. Even obviously structural issues, such as the loss of job opportunities in a specific market, often fall back on the individual. Individuals can relocate to find better opportunities or educate themselves for the changing economy. The fact that some segments or groups, such as young African American males, are more adversely affected by structural changes only means that the individuals in those groups have more work to do. After all, as Benjamin Franklin said, "God helps those who help themselves."

The individual is also a key driver of the consumer economy. We are free to buy the car we want, or clothing, consumer goods, or the vacation to exotic locations. The economic focus tends to be on detachment from social obligations and the "freedom" of consumer choice, driven by commercial advertising. Purchases are not driven by need or larger social goods but by the ability to make an individual choice.

Politically, this means a constant push toward individual rights over the values of family, minority groups or other social structures. Many people in the United States push this concept toward various types of libertarianism, where the role of government is tightly limited and the role of the individual is exalted. But even those committed to a strong role for government in the United States give priority to the language and structures of individual rights.

This individualism also affects concepts of ethics. Personal morality is usually defined by individualistic concepts of right and wrong. A standard framework for what is considered ethical behavior starts from the individual. For the most part, if something is done among consenting adults and no one is "harmed," the action is considered ethically acceptable. Many Americans react strongly against laws that seem to go against these two general rules. This can be seen in the changing mores of acceptable sexual behavior and the use of drugs like marijuana. Even many Christians in the United States appeal first to the "consenting adults" argument when addressing these issues and only later consider how Scripture might speak to the issue.

Of course, individualism does not automatically lead to individuality. Since the individual is considered a free agent, then social control and coercion usually happens much more informally or indirectly. For example, American society has little space for people who do not conform to the accepted social norms in all areas of life. People who do not conform, such as the Amish or Old Order Mennonites, do not receive the esteem and recognition so important in American culture.

This type of individualism often seems to give everyone the freedom to be like everyone else.[6] Children quickly learn that they need to wear clothes that are similar and eat food that everyone else is eating. It is very difficult for a child to take unacceptable ethnic food to school or to speak anything but English on the playground. There is no law or clearly pre-scribed norm against these actions, and some people even celebrate ethnic diversity. But the informal social pressure, such as shaming or branding, is so strong that few are willing to go against common practice.

What is acceptable and what is not varies from time to time. But there are several things over which social pressure is always very strong. Our society, and we personally, want to believe that individuals are free agents as consumers. But mass media and social pressure define "good taste," and everyone who wants to be accepted conforms to those dictates. When sys-temic economics allow, individuals feel pressure to borrow beyond their earning capacities so that their consumption is at a level that conforms. People who choose to limit their consumption or to do without consumer goods that are considered by others to be essential are seen as strange. There is some freedom to develop alternative consumption patterns, such as buying "green" or even "simple living." But living with less is not a so-cially acceptable option, and those who choose to do so are indirectly pres-sured to conform by the mass media and social norms.[7]

DIMENSIONS OF THE SELF

The autonomous self of U.S. individualism is defined by a number of unique characteristics. These frame how that individualism is lived out and reinforce the concept that the self is, and should be, at the center of human action. In churches these traits may be connected to biblical or theological sources, or just to the congregation's norms, so leaders need to shape environments that increase awareness and conversations that draw on the full resources of practical theology.

---

[6]Florence Kluckhohn and Fred Strodtbeck, *Variations in Value Orientation* (Evanston, Ill.: Row, Peterson, 1961), p. 23.

[7]It is currently not known how the recent economic downturn will change these societal habits. However, if historical patterns prevail, consumption driving personal debt will again become common.

Individual actions. The Euro-American concept of self is largely defined by personal actions. Self is not primarily defined by family ties or by our history. Self-definition does not come from who we are, but what we do. "Self-actualization" is dependent on doing.

> The American self-concept is the integral assumption of the culture. Americans naturally assume that each person is not only a separate biological entity, but also a unique psychological being and a singular member of the social order. Deeply ingrained and seldom questioned, the dominant American self, in the form of individualism, pervades action and intrudes into each domain of activity.[8]

The self is the center of action, capable of making good decisions and finding happiness on one's own. This framework assumes that actions are self-motivated and not coerced or limited in any way. Therefore any negative results are the principal responsibility of the acting self. As mentioned in chapter six, Emerson and Smith call this "accountable freewill individualism," the belief common among many Americans, and Euro-American evangelicals in particular, that people have the freedom to make choices that benefit them, and if they make bad choices, they are fully responsible before God and others. This individualistic view of the self does not allow for recognition of social control and of the structures that limit the "choices" of many people, particularly those in ethnic or racial minority groups.[9]

Mythic individualism. This sense of self leads to the belief in self-reliance. The stories of the Old West glorify individuals who went out and "made it on their own." The basic idea is that people can "pull themselves up by their bootstraps." The classic myth of western expansion in the United States presents a rugged self-reliance, one that calls people to break from family, community and culture. This mythic individualism seems to say that one "can be a truly good person, worthy of admiration and love, only if you resist fully joining the group."[10]

---

[8]Edward Stewart and Milton Bennett, *American Cultural Patterns: A Cross-Cultural Perspective*, rev. ed. (Yarmouth, Maine: Intercultural Press, 1991), p. 129.

[9]Michael Emerson and Christian Smith, *Divided by Faith: Evangelical Religion and the Problem of Race in America* (New York: Oxford University Press, 2000), pp. 76-77.

[10]Robert Bellah et al., *Habits of the Heart: Individualism and Commitment in American Life* (Berkeley: University of California Press, 1985), pp. 82, 145.

Personal Reflection/Group Exercise:
Success Narratives and the Self

1. Think through your family's "success" narratives, be they personal or of family members. Do the stories focus more on the hard work of the individual, the role of family or community, the help of outsiders, or something else? How are those stories passed on in the family? When are they told or retold?

2. Talk to 2-3 other people about their success narratives. What is common about your stories? What is unique?

3. What do the stories tell you about the relationship between self and community? What is most valued in your family background, the successful individual or the unity of family and community? If different people in your group have different perceptions, talk about why those differences exist. Is it cultural? Familial? Or something else?

On the one hand, the mythic individual is like Horatio Alger Jr.[11] Throughout the latter part of the nineteenth century, Alger wrote many novels in which he glorified the actions of those who overcame enormous odds and created for themselves successful lives. His heroes were often children that society had abandoned but who had worked hard and made it in U.S. society. The message the author wanted to give was clear: the past may not provide much to draw from, but anyone who is willing to work hard can succeed in the United States. Of course, if we read the stories more carefully, we discover that other people's resources usually played an important part in the success of the "mythic individual." Success was often a matter of being in the right place at the right time and having access to the right people, and was not necessarily because of hard work and self-mastery. These types of narratives invite people "to think of themselves as individuals and to behave as individuals, believing in the efficacy of their own behavior."[12]

Historically, this type of narrative has been very attractive to many im-

---

[11]See "Horatio Alger Jr. Resources," Washburn University <www.washburn.edu/sobu/broach/algerres.html>.

[12]Wuthnow, *American Mythos*, p. 110.

migrants, particularly those who feel stifled by collectivist cultures. The United States provides an attractive opportunity for immigrants to break out of the limitations of their homeland, family and culture, and create their own success. If a person is willing to work hard enough, it is assumed that the future is limitless.

Nevertheless, these types of stories focus on the individual that "made it." They tell the story of the child of immigrants who is an American success story. But they ignore what happened to the rest of the family or to others who worked just as hard but were not chosen for the key scholarship or opportunity. These types of biographies sell the American myth, but they also cover up the fact that many of the hardest-working people in the United States are at the bottom of the socioeconomic ladder, and their chances for moving upward are very limited. They also downplay the role that family and community had in making success possible.

The Lone Ranger, Superman and similar heroes present another side of this mythic individualism. These heroes are people who always have to be on their own. They cannot be a part of the community and submit to interdependent roles. Occasionally they also have to break social conventions or even some laws to protect others. The regular people can continue living in their group innocence because these heroes choose to continue to live by themselves, always on the edge of life in community.

This sense of individualism is seen in the importance traditionally given in the United States to leaving home. Moving far away from parents and living in a dorm are seen as a healthy signs of self-development and crucial for success. If a young person rejects a scholarship to stay near a sick family member, this is seen, at best, as a major sacrifice. Refusing a job promotion for "the sake of the kids" is assumed to be a temporary decision that can be corrected as soon as the children leave home. One of the signs that a person is ready for success is the willingness to make whatever move is necessary for upward mobility. This is reinforced in the immigrant success narratives. They give the message "One must *leave home* in order to earn the benefits America has to offer."[13]

---

[13]Ibid., p. 102.

A large, majority-culture church began offering college scholarships for underrepresented young people in their area. They worked hard to identify promising high school students in their community and tried to connect them to prestigious universities outside of the state. But they often became frustrated when trying to help immigrant Latinos and Latinas. The Latino parents often did not seem to support the church's efforts. Church leaders gave out several scholarships, but one of the Latinos decided to study locally and the two Latinas they sponsored returned home after one semester.

The implicit assumption is that "the way to 'help them' is to draw their most talented young people away from their families and neighborhoods."[14] As a result, individual young people often become estranged from their families and support systems, "succeeding" while damaging their families and themselves. This means that they cut themselves off from those who could help them succeed and from those who could benefit from their academic success. They might succeed as individuals but not benefit their communities, or even worse, have an overall negative impact on their family or social network.

Self-reliance is a crucial social value that is not necessarily valued in other societies. In many societies breaking from family and seeking self-reliance is not seen as a way to develop identity but as a loss of identity. Self exists in relationship to others and finds its place in relationship to others. To break from one's family or social circle is to loose the mooring that gives self a place, a community and a common identity.

The part of the story that does not get told in this process is that people who leave family or community circles do not become autonomous individuals outside of any social network. Most become part of new social systems, such as a mobile workforce at the service of large corporations. They claim to be making their choices freely and do not recognize that they are not self-reliant but are very much dependent on a system that benefits from their mobility. As we noted in chapter three, this usually means they are increasingly dependent on larger societal structures while less connected to cultures and communities.

---

[14]Ibid., p. 183.

Pragmatism and antistructuralism. This view of the individual is also highly pragmatic. If something seems to work, it is often deemed effective, whether or not the idea is consistent with other values. That is why "coherent personal philosophies and systematic ideologies are both rare in American culture."[15] People change political, ideological and religious perspectives based on what seems to work for them and not on a consistent ideology.

This means that political parties in the United States are more about securing and maintaining political power than they are representatives of ideologies. People who have strong ideological differences will join the same political party if it helps them have access to power. Most people from other democracies around the world find it hard to understand the U.S. political process because politics in this country is much more about winning than about convincing people to join our ideological cause. Ideologically, by world standards, there is little consistent difference between most Democrats and most Republicans.

This is also seen in church life. Church-growth theory is based on the social reality that people find it easier to go to church with people like themselves. This is built into our marketing way of life—just as we are attracted to the goods and services of companies, we respond to what attracts us to a particular church. Most "successful" churches in the United States are based on some version of the homogeneity principle or a market-oriented strategy. Few people take the time to ask whether this is consistent with the teachings of the gospel. If homogeneity or the marketing of services brings people to church, it is assumed that such approaches are good.

This pragmatism also tends toward antistructuralism, the inability or unwillingness to recognize how structures shape access or create barriers, no matter what people and societies say they want. The most obvious barrier in the United States is the treatment of African Americans. Historically, the dominant society has explained the situation of African Americans in different ways. Up to 1865 (the end of the U.S. Civil War) slavery was justified because people of African descent were not really human. Studies in the latter part of the nineteenth century "demonstrated" the inferiority of people of African descent. Their lack of success in the United

---

[15]Ibid., p. 140.

States was not because of structural injustice, but because they were not capable of succeeding.

In 1896 the Supreme Court of the United States upheld the constitutionality of "separate, but equal" *(Plessy v. Ferguson)*. African Americans could have their own structures, which would keep them "out of sight and out of mind." This did not significantly change until the civil rights movement of the 1960s, which gave significant new energy and direction to the process of questioning this contradiction between the concept of equal opportunity for all and the lived reality of African Americans and other minority groups. The problem today is that many if not most members of majority culture assume that any structural problems were solved years ago. Therefore, cases of discrimination are seen as issues that need to be solved on an individual basis. Any attempt at addressing structural injustice, such as affirmative action, is seen as providing unfair benefits to individuals, not as a correction of an existing problem. Therefore, "the self-made American is unlikely to perceive any *systemic* ways in which the society might be improved, other than calling for individuals to be better persons. The irony then is not that the poor are overlooked; it is rather that their condition is misunderstood."[16]

The denominational executives gave up on the growing rural Latino congregation using a building that had belonged to a majority-culture church that closed down. The congregation was growing but would likely never grow enough to pay the pastor's full-time salary and benefits that the denomination expected of all member churches, because its members were almost all farm workers. The denomination had certain financial expectations that did not fit the socioeconomic reality of the community, since no Latino pastor there earned a salary that large.

So they sold the denominationally owned building to another thriving Latino congregation from a Pentecostal movement. The first church left the denomination and has continued to grow, though now they need to rent a building. The denomination found it easier to sell the building than to deal with a Latino congregation that was likely never going to meet its criteria for being a full-fledged church. Yet it felt comfortable selling the

---

[16]Ibid., p. 127.

*building to another Latino congregation from another denomination that
was about the same size.*

When majority-culture church leaders are not able to recognize systemic social, cultural and class issues, they are unable to develop structures
that allow congregations to thrive among those that do not share their assumptions. They are also unable to provide the type of support that can
address the large pockets of what seem like permanent underclasses, places
where socioeconomic success seems as far away as ever.

Church and Life Together

Working between individualist and collectivist cultures provides unique
challenges and opportunities for intercultural church life. The worst-
case scenario is one in which there is inadequate reflection among participants in a church that includes a group of individuals who are shaped
mainly by enlightened self-interest and others who have a cohesive
monocultural community shaped by a collectivist perspective. Misunderstandings and tensions arise as some participants begin to move
among the diverse groups. Some persons are attracted to the perspectives
of individual rights and opportunities afforded by the U.S. dominant
culture, and may seek to escape some obligations they grew up with.
Others who have been shaped by individualistic cultures may admire the
social cohesion they see among those of another culture but find that it
is difficult finding entry.

Changes in U.S. individualism. United States individualism has had a
major impact on the church. Many churches have assumed that they have
to reach an autonomous consumer and so have developed church ministries
shaped by research about individual preferences. Worship, preaching, programs and even staff hires often seem to be driven more by market tastes
than by the call of the gospel. People choose or change churches based on
individual interests, and so "successful" churches adapt to the market. This
has often warped common life, since people make choices based on their
own tastes and not the needs of their common life together. Calls to change
or conversion are either played down or completed ignored.

Yet individuals are looking for expressions of common life. Internet
social media and various on-the-ground networks throughout the West-

For Further Reading

Emerson, Michael, and Christian Smith. *Divided by Faith: Evangelical Religion and the Problem of Race in America*. New York: Oxford University Press, 2000.

Hughes, Richard. *Myths America Lives By*. Champaign: University of Illinois Press, 2004.

McAdams, Dan. *The Redemptive Self: Stories Americans Live By*. New York: Oxford University Press, 2006.

Wuthnow, Robert. *The American Mythos: Why Our Best Efforts to Be a Better Nation Fall Short*. Princeton, N.J.: Princeton University Press, 2006.

ern world demonstrate that people want to be connected and do not want to be mere consumers, even of religious goods. They want to be a part of something larger together. The challenge for many churches framed by individualism is to learn new ways of being church that invite people to relativize the self in relationship to the community, in the name of Jesus Christ.

Learning from each other. Earlier in the chapter we described the dimensions of the autonomous self, many of which militate against life together in a church community. One of the opportunities that intercultural church life offers is the possibility that people from both individualist and collectivist cultures can learn from the other and both learn together about following Jesus Christ and being church together. Even as we need to challenge models of church that are based on individual interests and tastes, we also have need to challenge collectivist churches to help individuals see themselves as part of God's mission in a world much larger than their cultural setting.

If we take seriously the understanding of church described in chapter two, reconciliation has to do with our relationship with God and with each other. The metaphor of the body of Christ (Rom 12; 1 Cor 12) challenges both individualist and collectivist cultures. Individuals have gifts that the body needs. But it is the body that recognizes those gifts and builds up the individual. Christian churches from collectivist cultures remind us that we cannot develop a strong church unless individuals are willing to submit to each other in love (Eph 5:21). Market-driven churches can attract many people but find it very difficult to call people to the level of commitment necessary to develop true community. Dominant-culture churches in the United States need to learn from minority churches about group harmony, cooperation and solidarity, recognizing that Western individualism often points us away from the biblical concept of the individual created by God to live in community. But those from individualist cultures can help believers from collectivist churches find the freedom of God's grace in Jesus Christ, something often missing in church's where the self is subsumed under the hierarchy of vertical leadership. They can also help churches whose collectivist cultures draw boundaries along ethnic or other sociocultural markers to recognize that the gospel challenges those boundaries and calls us to loyalties that cross culture, class and generations.

One of the challenges of the gospel is to identity those parts of a culture that are helpful in presenting and living the Christian message and those that must be judged by that same gospel. Pastors and other leaders will need to work in the midst of congregations to shape processes that help the congregations discern when to affirm and when to question their cultural background. As Christians of different cultural backgrounds choose common cause as Christians, then leaders need to help their congregations learn from each other and be challenged in those areas in which specific cultures pull people away from the gospel.

The New Testament clearly points to a redeemed community, a body called by the Father that works together with Christ as its head, in the power of the Holy Spirit (see chap. 2). But that body is composed of individuals who make a commitment to follow Jesus. We need each other to help think through what it means to live in light of this new community. The gospel call is the same, and the church continues to be God's community in the world. But its specific manifestations will vary as people of different cultural backgrounds work together to make it a reality.

The call of the gospel is toward becoming one body, a people redeemed by the Lamb, finding their identity and purpose in relationship to God and others. Our individualistic concepts of self and of self in relationship to others will be constantly challenged by the biblical call of living in unity in the midst of our diversities.

At the Movies

How are narratives of these movies shaped by the self-perceptions of the characters, and how are the characters shaped by individualist or collectivist assumptions?

The Visitor (2008). When a widowed and disillusioned college professor is sent to a conference in New York, he is surprised to find that a young couple, having been scammed, is residing in his New York apartment. An unlikely friendship develops with the Syrian man and Sengalese woman as they face problems concerning justice and immigration documents.

Real Women Have Curves (2002). A first-generation Mexican American teen in a predominately Latino community of East Los Angeles receives a full scholarship to Columbia University, provoking a conflict as she reflects on the solidarity her mother has with work colleagues.

Crouching Tiger, Hidden Dragon (2000). In a mythic tale set in ancient China, two great Zen warriors in pursuit of a stolen sword and a notorious fugitive find themselves intertwined in the life of an impetuous, physically skilled but deeply troubled teenage nobleman's daughter.

8

PERCEPTION AND THINKING

Mark Lau Branson and
Juan Francisco Martínez

As a young pastor in a Latino congregation in central California I (Juan) found myself in hot water with the denominational leadership. I was perceived as too radical in my work on behalf of Latino churches. One leader compared me to César Chávez, assuming that this would help me understand why what I was doing was such a problem for the denomination. Yet he never realized that his "negative" comparison was a compliment to me. He perceived César Chávez as symbolic of a number of "bad" things that were happening in central California, while for me Chávez was a symbol of hope and a model of the type of change I wanted to see happen in my denomination.

Our mental processes are shaped by our worldview, which is shaped within a particular culture, as explained in chapter four. Perception and thinking concern the unique ways people in different cultures receive, filter and interpret data. The data itself is always sensory in some manner—it comes from outside us through our senses—but our modes of perceiving the data have been shaped by the conceptual models of those who formed us culturally. Then the ways we think about the data are also culturally shaped. So while different people experience the same object or event, such as a cloud or a conversation, the way that data is interpreted is culturally specific. So, as Juan looked at his church context and provided pastoral leadership, he was working on the basis of his perceptions and thinking. He had been shaped by his culture and was seeking to be an agent of the gospel in his context. But some denominational leaders looked at the same situation and read the same Bible and concluded that Juan looked like a radical activist rather than like their image of a Christian leader. Was this a purely theological matter, or were cultural modes of cognition at work?

It is not uncommon for church disagreements to be rooted in different ways of perceiving and thinking. Because these words—*perceiving* and *thinking*—are defined in a variety of ways, we will use them more attuned to psychological perspectives rather than the frameworks of anthropology or cultural studies. In this chapter we will use *sensing* for the initial impression made on a person by an outside object or force—through the traditional five senses and (recognized in some cultures more than others) through what can be called "spiritual" senses. By *perceiving* we mean that these sensory experiences create some level of reception, and an initial interpretive process begins. So an eye *senses* light, and then a process of *perceiving* sorts the data concerning shapes, colors, distance and so forth. While some perceptions lead to human responses that bypass cognition (e.g., reflexes), we may also process this data by *thinking*, which is a more complex activity that finds patterns, assigns meaning and works with symbols and encoding (making mental organization possible).[1]

Table 8.1. Mental Activities

Mental Activities	
Sensing	Something outside of the person comes into contact with the person's capacities to receive input.
Perceiving	Some level of receptivity in the person allows the data in, and some initial sorting begins.
Thinking	Mental activity seeks patterns, assigns significance and meanings, and encodes the data for further work.

In earlier chapters we introduced cultural variations concerning the role of context, language and worldview, the importance of affect, and the relationship between the individual and the group. These and other variables create cultural distinctives in cognitive styles. It is common for certain variables to be clustered, and one schema uses labels referring to brain patterns: "left hemisphere" and "right hemisphere."

---

[1]Edward Stewart and Milton Bennett, *American Cultural Patterns: A Cross-Cultural Perspective*, rev. ed. (Yarmouth, Maine: Intercultural Press, 1991), pp. 17-19.

Table 8.2. Brain Hemispheres[a]

Left Hemisphere	Right Hemisphere
Analytic: propositions, theories	Synthetic: metaphor, narrative, poetic
Field-independent / low context	Field-dependent / high context
Rational, linear, cause-effect, sequential	Intuitive, analogic, spatial, emotive, imaging
Cognitive routines	Cognitive novelty
Predictable / permanent	Flexible / adaptive
Individualistic	Collectivistic

[a]Devorah Lieberman, "Culture, Problem Solving, and Pedagogical Style," in *Intercultural Communication,* ed. Larry Samovar and Richard Porter, 8th ed. (Belmont, Calif.: Wadsworth, 1997), p. 193; James Ashbrook, *Faith and Ministry in Light of the Double Brain* (Bristol, Ind.: Wyndham, 1989), pp. 7-17, 266-69; Elkhonor Goldberg, *The Executive Brain* (New York: Oxford University Press, 2001), p. 43.

These variables, while subject to individual differences, tend to be shaped by a culture's experiences and habits. We think, we see connections, we anticipate, we solve problems, and we are creative in ways that have been modeled for us. Our cognitive styles are formed by feedback loops—like affirmations and criticisms of those around us. When we encounter persons who work with other cognitive styles and everyone fails to adapt, we limit the possibilities for genuine collaboration. Defensiveness, insistence and disrespect can push people apart. But if we are self-aware and conscious of the interplay of variables, we can assist each other in naming these differences and benefiting from them. This kind of work is seldom easy, and it always takes longer to achieve mutual understanding; but if reconciliation and collaboration are priorities, then attentiveness to cognitive styles is essential. In chapter nine we will offer additional insights into communication; this chapter will expand on the cultural differences in perceiving and thinking. This is primarily a matter of interpretive leadership, but it has obvious implications for relational and implemental leadership.

SENSATION

We live in the midst of overwhelming sensory overload. Our sensory organs have the ability to receive and discriminate between an extraordinary amount of visual, auditory, tactile, olfactory and taste data. Most of those sensory signals are fleeting and are not part of our conscious thinking process. Nonetheless, our minds need means to organize this data into images, thoughts and feelings, which then become the basis for constructing our understanding of the world "out there." The beginning step—sensing—is trained and shaped by our experiences within our cultures.

Over a period of years a culture may develop habits that make its people attuned to sounds or sights or the feel of the air on their skin. Cultures with traditions of hunting, storytelling or ballads would have a sensitivity to auditory data. This could lead to a greater capacity to attend to the spoken word for longer periods of time or to distinguish sounds in a forest. An agrarian or fishing culture could develop sensitivities to changes in air moisture or temperature. Even over a short span of time, a group of people can develop habits concerning sensory data in an urban environment, in crowded settings, in high-violence areas or when a state of conflict is perpetuated.

There are significant implications rooted in a culture's sensory biases. For example, because we are a literate society we place a great deal of emphasis on the sense of sight. We live in a visual world, which is evident in our metaphors: to "see" is to "understand." Because writing separates the message from the messenger, we tend toward abstract systems of thought that are not always directly linked to everyday life. We tend to systematize our knowledge, to develop elaborate systems to store and retrieve this information, and to trust messages more if they are visual or in print. This emphasis on sight has been crucial in the development of modern science. But it also tends to limit the value we give to other sensations and to thinking patterns not based on sight, such as intuition or what people often call "spiritual sight" or a "sixth sense." (It also affects how Christians understand the role of the Holy Spirit.) These are also part of our sensory stimuli, but because of the way we have been taught to organize our thinking, these are often ignored in our perception process.[2]

In a multicultural church, leaders can help shape an environment in which various sensory biases are evident. A worship environment, the atmosphere for a meeting, the church's grounds or buildings, the use of visual and auditory resources, and attention to silence or to energetic music are all ingredients of cultural attentiveness.

---

[2]Paul Hiebert, *Anthropological Insights for Missionaries* (Grand Rapids: Baker, 1985), pp. 134-37.

PERCEPTION

A person's culture is involved in the perception process from the very beginning.[3] Humans are shaped by their cultures to value some types of sensory stimuli over others. Perception is not only the reception of sensory data, but it is also the valuing of data and receptivity to particular details. We all receive overwhelming sensory data, but our cultures teach us to discriminate between figure and ground. We learn to perceive and pay attention to the *figure*, like a particular smell in the wind, while the *ground* is the background, other ambient or unnoticed smells that do not become part of data we use to interpret and classify what we are experiencing. For example, clutter on a lawn or the sounds of playing children may be *figure* for some people but *ground* for others.

Different cultures teach us to value different stimuli, so that what is figure in one culture may be ground for people in another culture. This creates various types of complexities in intercultural settings. The most common is the inability to perceive (or process sensory stimuli) as people from other cultures do. Paul Hiebert's advice, that crosscultural workers recognize the difference between an *emic* (insider's view) and an *etic* (outsider's view) of a culture, is particularly important in a multicultural setting. When a person is with those who share a similar cultural formation they tend to have common perspectives on what is figure and what is ground when they experience an object or an event. They may still have many disagreements about its significance (which is more about *thinking*), but they basically saw the same thing.

An *etic* perspective changes everything. Usually cultural groups use their own perceptions to experience something or to engage another culture. With two cultures present, each is using its own perceptions as they experience the other culture. But a crosscultural worker, notes Paul Hiebert, should be trained to pay attention to these figure-ground differences. Similarly, in a multicultural setting in which persons from two or more cultures are sharing an experience, leaders need to shape the group's capacities to attend to such differences. In a way, both cultures can benefit by seeing

---

[3]Sometimes the word *perceive* refers to our reflective processes, as in "Since the lights are off, I perceive it's time to go." However, for clarity in this exposition we will use *perceive* for the initial reception of stimuli and specify the further processes as matters of conceptual work or thinking.

themselves as outsiders to the other culture; they can assume an *etic* perspective. Then, rather than each cultural group being limited to the perspectives embedded in its own knowledge and habits, they can begin testing their *etic* perspectives and thereby gain access to the other culture's perceptions.[4]

There are numerous ways that culturally embedded perceptions are a challenge to cultural diversity in a church. The smells from the kitchen, the noise level during certain hours or in particular locations, the tones of conversations, and even body language are all perceived differently by persons of different cultures. Particular figures arise that were not previously present. But one cannot assume that these figures will be perceived the same way by everyone. Two people may smell the same aroma coming from the kitchen and know that kimchi is being prepared. But for one it may elicit many fond memories and provoke hunger, while another may dislike the odor and wonder why people are messing up the church kitchen with powerful smells. This different perception might then lead to very different thoughts about what is happening and what should be done about the situation.

> *I (Juan) was part of a church-based reconciliation group after the "Rodney King riots" in Los Angeles. African American, Korean and Latino leaders came together to try to build bridges after the riots. Even though we were working with people who wanted to reconcile, we immediately found that even "simple" issues were contributing to the existing mistrust. The "serious" face of the local Korean shop owners made Latinos and African Americans feel they were not trusted; the high-touch business interaction of Latinos and the "loud" conversations among many African Americans created suspicions among Koreans about how they did business, and the dress styles of young urban African Americans and Latinos made them potential gang members in the eyes of many of the older people, no matter their background. Because the participants were all reading the circumstances very differently, it made it difficult to even begin a conversation.*

Matters of figure and ground may also affect communication. A person

---

[4]Hiebert, *Anthropological Insights for Missionaries*, pp. 94-96.

used to reading certain types of body language might quickly grasp the "real" message behind the spoken word. But because this type of body language is ground for another person, who was not raised to understand those types of messages, the message is completely misunderstood and this second person is left with an inaccurate understanding of the event.[5]

Thinking

The mental work then moves from data perception to thinking. This part of the process concerns interpretation, constructing meaning (making sense) of our perceptions, and anticipating implications and potential responses. This is a complex process that creates a network of mental connections—bundling the perception with previous experiential and mental constructs. While some of the thinking process is conscious, it is shaped by numerous subconscious habits.

> [Thinking] involves bringing to bear the stored knowledge (memory), emotional predispositions (feelings, intuition), and subjective thought processes (mindsets) on the continuous influx of new sensory/perceptual data. At the core, thinking is the mental ability to govern adaptation and to search for meaning below the sensation-driven surface and beyond the reach of facts.[6]

Because the process of perceiving is so quick, our main access for intentional work is the thinking stage of the process. Thinking is influenced by what is "out there" and by how we have been shaped by culture, society, family and experience. Interpretation, meaning and action come out of that mental process that is taking place in our mind; it is not controlled by the article or event that was experienced. Thinking is framed by the symbol systems, particularly language, that are used by our cultures to weave the fabric of meanings that make it possible to respond to the world around us.

This means that the same sensory stimuli create many different responses from people, depending on culture and experience. For one individual, a hot wind may mean that the community needs to act in certain ways for food security; to another person a hot wind brings memories of sunburn and thus prompts the purchase of lotion; and for another person

---

[5]See Stewart and Bennett, *American Cultural Patterns*, p. 127.
[6]Ibid., p. 22.

the hot wind is cause for celebrating the nearness of a summer vacation. This interpretive work is culture dependent: food, lotion and celebration are all matters of how a culture weaves the fabric of meanings.

> *The denominational leaders and I (Juan) were never able to find a positive way forward. Many of them were farm owners or were linked to farming, and many Latinos were farm workers. For the denominational leaders César Chávez represented a threat to their livelihood, while for many farm workers he represented a hope for a better future. Farm boycotts and strikes offered a way out for one group of people but represented disruptive change for the other. Though Chávez died years ago, in the San Joaquín Valley of California his name is still either a blessing or a curse, stimulating very strong reactions from both farmers and farm workers.*

The thinking process of some cultures tends toward logic (the construction and linking of ideas in various rational modes), while other cultures work more with analogs (making connections among various associations). The dominant culture in the United States tends toward the "Western mind" described by Louis Luzbetak:

> To the Western mind, to know means above all else that one observes the sensible (i.e., the empirical), forms a hypothesis, and tests it; if it survives the test, it is upheld, otherwise it is rejected and another hypothesis is proposed. ... The Western mind, more than other minds, seeks concepts representing reality, categories, principles, and theories.[7]

This can be compared with other cultures, "The Oriental mind, on the other hand, is fundamentally mythological, analogical rather than logical, relying heavily on feeling and intuition."[8] Analogic thinking processes are interested in

> type and antitype configurations, in seeing patterns in the world as traces of the creating godhead *(vestigia Dei)* left in creation, in any speculation that reveals the ordered character of the universe (numerological and astrological speculations), development of hierarchical orders, controlled allegory, relating the visible to the hidden.[9]

---

[7]Louis Luzbetak, *The Church and Cultures* (Maryknoll, N.Y.: Orbis, 1988), p. 254.
[8]Ibid.
[9]Robert Schreiter, *Constructing Local Theologies* (Maryknoll, N.Y.: Orbis, 1985), pp. 85-86.

Both of these thinking systems, logical and analog, are means for sorting and connecting perceptions. They work within particular worldviews and are framed by the symbol systems, particularly language, in which they exist. It is difficult for those raised outside of the specific cultures that use them to understand how thinking is changed by being a part of one culture or another, so this is a significant challenge for interpretive leadership.

Because the conceptual work of thinking involves symbolic systems, it means that we have to connect perceptions with images, theories, analogs or a system of abstractions. This "next stage in the mental process is the creation of complex symbol systems which can be encoded and represented in notations, signs, and symbols and shared with others."[10] Each culture produces and develops images, language, visual arts, rhythms and music, and their systems so that they can provide the means for interpretations to be processed and shared within a group. Those from outside the group not only have to learn the symbolic system (language) but also how the symbolic system is used in thinking and interpreting.

The *thinking* process also involves categories and boundaries.[11] For example, the presence of a certain person needs interpretation. Possible categories include matters of power, familiarity, social networks and related categories of memories, emotions and obligations. How someone interprets the presence of the other, and the degree to which his or her response is preconscious or carefully analyzed, are matters that are culturally formed. For example, the presence of a church's pastor will be interpreted in various ways, largely depending on ethnic background, church culture and personal experience. Does the pastor represent caring and friendship, church government bureaucracy, God's voice or a management hierarchy? When the pastor visits a member's home, is there a quick and friendly welcome or a cautious conversation about church politics? When persons need to think about a situation, the mental categories provide a way for perception to be shaped into concepts and responses. Concepts may have definite bounded categories, or there may be a continuum of gradations.

WORKING WITH DIVERSITY IN PERCEPTION AND THINKING

Stewart and Bennett point to certain patterns of perception and thinking

---

[10]Stewart and Bennett, *American Cultural Patterns*, p. 22.
[11]Ibid., pp. 26-28.

Bible Study: Acts 11:19-26; 13:1-3—The Church at Antioch

As we read through the first part of the book of Acts we find several instances of intercultural interaction and the difficulties that it created, particularly for Jewish believers who had lived all their lives in Palestine. Their perception of what God was doing in the world was framed in such a way that they had a very hard time understanding how God was also working with Gentiles. Time and again they ran up against their perceptions and thinking about how things should be. They heard the message of the gospel and experienced the work of the Holy Spirit, but their cultural and religious experiences were such that they found it difficult to accept what they saw God was doing.

The Jews who had been raised outside of Palestine had a very different perception, because of their different experience. They could see that the temple was a passing structure (Stephen; Acts 7), that one could preach to Samaritans and eunuchs (Phillip; Acts 8), and that the good news was also for Gentiles (Acts 11:19-26). So in many ways it is not surprising that the first intentionally missionary congregation is not Jerusalem but Antioch (Acts 13:1-3). Diaspora Jews who had left Jerusalem because of persecution started this congregation. Acts 13:1-3 describes a congregation with multicultural leadership.

This group of believers perceived the gospel differently. They were able to see what God was doing more broadly, and they were able to intentionally send missionaries into the Gentile world. Because they had been raised in a different cultural setting, they could hear and respond to God's word differently. The diverse community established in Antioch was then able to hear God in new ways and send out Barnabas and Saul.

1. Think of concrete ways your culture limits or expands your ability to see what God is doing. In what ways is your church more like Jerusalem or Antioch in this respect?

2. For example, are the worldwide migrations of today "figure" or "ground" in your understanding of God's mission in the world? How are they either?

3. Name a situation in your church or community in which perception affected thinking and then created tensions in your congregation? How did you resolve the problem? How were different perceptions taken or not taken into account in the solution?

that are common to the dominant U.S. culture. Priority is given to "facts," which are assumed to be measurable, reliable and equally available to anyone.[12] There is often a confidence that factual information can make life more predictable and manageable. Euro-Americans will also use counterfactual modes of thinking, in which opposites or hypotheticals are considered in a thinking process.[13]

Euro-American culture gives attention to agency and action—there are causes and we think toward our role in future causes. So we interpret facts to find causes, we speculate concerning options, then we construct procedural knowledge to fit our pragmatism. Persons of other cultures may be more attentive to relationships, to ideas or to certain observed details—and in each case, the interpretive work is different. European culture tends to be more deductive—working from concepts and ideas toward specifics. Euro-American culture usually is more inductive—taking details and constructing a theoretical framework toward action. Many Latino cultures are first aware of relationships, which convey matters of priorities and power. Again, this is not just a matter of how cultures carry out certain activities—it concerns what is initially perceived and how thinking operates.

Cognitive work in intercultural settings. Having common patterns of perception and thinking, or at least being attentive to and appreciative of various modes of thinking, are very important as people work to construct a common understanding of their experiences. United States philosophers Charles Peirce and Josiah Royce emphasize the triadic nature of knowledge. William James had explained religious insight and knowledge as the interplay of percept and concept (with a bipolar focus of the interaction between experience and the person). In this framework, one pole is the person who considers the other pole, which is the experience. But Royce claimed this was inadequate. He called for a third element, providing a schema whereby a person perceived an experience and continued to the interpretive work of explaining it to another person. In this triadic theory of knowledge (requiring one who perceives, that which is perceived and a person to whom the perception is communicated), understanding was unavailable without the conversation; learning was always communal.[14] For

---

[12]Stewart and Bennett, *American Cultural Patterns*, p. 31.
[13]Ibid., p. 32.
[14]Donald Gelpi, *Committed Worship: A Sacramental Theology for Conversing Christians* (College-

this to happen there has to be enough of a common culture and symbol system to make conversation possible. This commonality creates the space for interpreting reality, but it also limits how people in any specific culture understand and interpret their experiences. The common symbol systems that create the possibility of interpretation also limit the interpretative possibilities within the framework of a specific culture or language.

Cultures, with their languages, rituals and systems of abstract concepts, construct what is available for persons to interpret and frame perceptions in particular ways. For example, Stewart and Bennett note that "Americans tend to focus on functional, pragmatic applications of thinking; in contrast, the Japanese are more inclined to concrete description, while Europeans stress abstract theory."[15] This means that in an intercultural situation, persons from one culture may process a set of experiences by attending to description—carefully noting details (often without articulating the implications). Persons of other cultures may move quickly to problem solving or acting, while others may want to engage other persons in serious theoretical analysis. While some of these differences may also be matters of personality or training, cultures tend to shape participants toward certain emphases.

These differences often play out in almost stereotypical fashion in intercultural situations in the life of the church. The moment a problem arises, many people from the U.S. dominant culture want to find the cause and fix it. Others are immediately concerned about relationships and about power differentials in the situation. For others, the concern is maintaining the community and saving face. It is not that some people want to address the problem and others want to avoid it. This is not just a matter of how cultures carry out certain activities—it concerns what is initially perceived and how thinking operates but also what different ways of thinking define as the issue needing resolution.

Bob, an elderly African American, was chairing the deacons' meeting in a biracial Baptist church. Camille, an African American deacon, told the group that the husband and father of an African American church family

---

ville, Minn.: Michael Glazier, 1993), 1:x-xi. Gelpi is agreeing with Royce, against William James. See Josiah Royce, *The Sources of Religious Insight* (New York: Scribners, 1912).
[15]Stewart and Bennett, *American Cultural Patterns*, pp. 28-29.

had lost his job in a company downsizing, and after several months he was
still looking for work. Camille knew that the family was facing stress for a
daughter's college tuition at the city college. Ann, who was Euro-American,
started listing a number of potential resources for the family's rent, utilities
and tuition. She offered to e-mail a list to the parents. John, a Euro-Amer-
ican deacon, said he would be glad to go to the family that night and provide
a personal check for the tuition expenses. Camille became silent, and Bob
cleared his throat, displaying some discomfort. Bob then said that he ap-
preciated these offers and said he would get back to them.

Church activities, including relationships, programs and mission, arise
from a continual matrix of conversations and decisions, and these are
rooted in cognitive styles and cultural priorities. In this story, Ann and
John were culturally inclined to deal with the most obvious facts, to think
about options and to solve problems. They tended toward action. But Camille and Bob were aware of some relational and affective dimensions of
the father's situation. What were appropriate ways to help the family without undermining the father's role in the family or embarrassing the wife or
daughter? Even in a deacons' meeting that is rooted in gospel values for
generosity and interdependence, leaders need to guide the group's capacities to attend to the diverse cultural approaches to thinking.

The issue of language further complicates this. As noted in chapter
five, the grammar structures imprinted on our brains are related to these
thinking styles. The language we use frames our perception and thinking
and also affects the meanings given to words. Since the interactions with
others are often verbal, or at least include a verbal component, this process
is further complicated if people are not communicating in the same language, or in the same culturally framed version of the language, or if one
or more of those in the process are communicating through a secondary
language. It becomes much easier to draw incorrect interpretations from
experiences when there is not a shared linguistic symbol system being used
to interpret a common experience.

Finally, the earlier material on worldviews is related to perception and
thinking. A culture's worldview predisposes certain perceptions—so cultures of China, which have a worldview that includes the spirited presence
of ancestors, would attend to and categorize experiences differently than a

---

Personal Reflection/Group Exercise: Cognitive Styles

1. *Individual reflection.* Use table 8.2 on cognitive styles and brain hemispheres on page 172 and reflect on your own cognitive style. You may want to think about a crosscultural conversation that reveals ways you were perceiving and thinking differently than your conversation partners. Place yourself to the left or right (or center) of the variables. For each choice see if you can remember an example that supports your decision. (Try to imagine how the "other" would classify your style even if it is different than your self-perception.)

2. *Group discussion.* Begin your group discussion by having each person select one variable and provide a brief story that supports that choice. If you have time, continue this exercise through several more variables.

3. *Group problem solving.* Read the opening paragraph of chapter nine (p. 189). Do you align more with the African American pastors or the Euro-American pastors? Why? If you entered the argument, what would you say? What do you want the other side to understand? After everyone provides some responses, turn back to this chapter's chart on cognitive styles (p. 172) and sort out your responses. Compare your participation in this exercise with your notes from the first step of reflection.

---

strictly materialist culture. If a culture, like that of Korea, gives significant positional preference for teachers or elders, there is dissonance in U.S. classrooms when other students converse with instructors concerning disagreements. For some, this is good learning theory in practice; for Koreans or Korean Americans this can be viewed as inappropriate and disrespectful. The experience is perceived and categorized according to the cultures.

The benefits of diverse cognitive styles. Leaders need to address issues of perception and thinking in many experiences. First, Bible study itself will constantly raise these issues. With narratives, poems, letters, worship rituals, court documents, sacred legislation and prayers rooted in several cultures over two millennia, it is little wonder that we often disagree over matters of interpreting the Bible. Readers bring their own worldview to a text—and habits of perception and thinking filter what we read. As leaders guide the community in reading Scripture together, they can point to the benefits that a community of believers brings to understanding God's Word and to thinking about how to live the gospel message in their context. By listening to those who perceive the text differently, all will be challenged to read the Word anew.

But the biggest tension will often not be with the text itself but with the implications of the text for our lives today. We may all agree with the original meaning but still have to struggle with how to live out the biblical message. Because, whether relating to neighbors or to other churches or to diversity within the congregations, church participants work within the mental frameworks that they construct from their own perceptions and thought processes. Leaders need to help develop new practices and commitments for a congregation to benefit from the larger community of believers and to shape new ways of community life that are appropriate for intercultural church life.

Pastors and leaders can use the praxis cycle to help their congregation understand how differences in perception affect biblical interpretation. By naming their current understanding of Scripture (step 1) and how it was framed by their culture (step 2), interpretive leaders increase the abilities of the church. This can create the opportunity for a new reading, including the tradition and theology of the congregation and readings that come from other theological and cultural backgrounds (step 3). By having people tell how their own interpretation has been framed, the congregation can ask questions about how their own culture and experi-

At the Movies

Both of these movies invite their audiences to be attentive to differences in perception. In both, the world looks very different depending on the experiences of each protagonist.

El Norte (1983). Mayan Indian manual laborers escape a Guatemalan army massacre and decide to flee to the United States, struggling to make a new life as young, uneducated, illegal immigrants.

Smoke Signals (1998). A young Native American man sets out with another young man from the reservation to collect the pickup truck and ashes of his deceased father, and discovers his memories of his father are very different than his companion's.

ences impact biblical interpretation (step 4) and rethink how to discern Scripture's meaning in their lives and mission (step 5). The praxis cycle opens the congregation to a more perceptive interpretation of Scripture, while also helping it avoid individualistic interpretations, by drawing on its theology and tradition. This hard work opens the church to hearing anew the voice of the Spirit.

PART III

LEADERSHIP, COMMUNICATION AND CHANGE

9

INTERCULTURAL COMMUNICATION

Mark Lau Branson

New Life Church, an urban-edge megachurch, was to host a very unique meeting in October 1995. The church's roots and current membership were mainly Euro-American. For many years there had been no significant relationship with the numerous African American churches in the area. Through cautious initiatives over a period of weeks, this meeting was to be the first between a number of African American pastors and several of the church's pastoral team. Earlier on the meeting day news accounts had been featuring the acquittal of O. J. Simpson in a criminal trial concerning the murder of his ex-wife. This news, which was not on the agenda as a topic of conversation, began to dominate the meeting. It was immediately obvious that reactions split along racial lines. The Euro-American participants were troubled, even bewildered, because they believed the evidence against Simpson was overwhelming and they could not imagine how a jury would acquit him. The African American pastors were celebrating—it was profoundly heartening that this African American celebrity had been found not guilty. These positions were not lightly held—and the tension rose as the bewilderment of the Euro-Americans connected with their sense that justice had not been served, and the African American pastors sensed the insult of these Euro-Americans who could not join them in celebrating this verdict from the established criminal justice system. When the meeting broke up, relationships were apparently further apart than before.

Why would Christian leaders be unable to engage each other in conversations that create understanding and trust? In this situation everyone had access to the same basic set of facts concerning the trial. Further, they share citizenship in a society with a set of agreements about how criminal trials are to be conducted. They had the benefits of living in the same geographic area, and they all spoke English as a primary language. Finally, as Christians, they could draw on resources concerning morality and justice. But this single societal event led to a deeper wedge between two groups who had recently been motivated to build trust and partnership.

HABERMAS ON COMMUNICATIVE COMPETENCE

In chapter four, on worldviews, we introduced Jürgen Habermas's social theory, which includes three facets: lifeworlds, world concepts and communicative competence. A lifeworld, which is primarily preconscious, is the entire worldview of a group of persons, including their culture and language. World concepts are specific topics that can be lifted up for consideration. Communicative competence provides a framework for deepening the integrity and generativity of discourse concerning those topics.[1] Church leaders, in their interpretive and relational work, have a primary role in shaping environments and prompting conversations that increase the communicative competence of a congregation.

As a culture continues through generations, the lifeworld stores the interpretive work that the culture continues to shape its members with.[2] Habermas draws an analogy with the physical world to explain these concepts. Lifeworld is "the horizon within which communicative actions are 'always already' moving."[3] As we stand on the earth, we can see the horizon around us and are limited to life within those horizons. Similarly, we stand within a lifeworld and are not able to step outside of it and objectivize it. Our lifeworld is a preconscious social and personal context. Any work we do to understand, or use words, or relate to others, must be done while standing within some set of horizons. When persons are consciously problematizing a situation, or bringing it to consciousness and discourse, they are dealing with a more definable segment of their common life-

---

[1]Jürgen Habermas, *The Theory of Communicative Action*, trans. Thomas McCarthy, 2 vols. (Boston: Beacon, 1984, 1987).
[2]Ibid., 1:13, 70.
[3]Ibid., 2:119.

world. Lifeworld is in the background, assumed, and it always provides resources and inadequacies. Intercultural communication requires that we expand our lifeworlds.

Habermas seeks to make this problematizing work more thoughtful and helpful. World concepts provide conceptual access to the lifeworld, especially for "problematic situations—that is, situations that need to be agreed upon—in a lifeworld that is already substantively interpreted."[4] He describes three worlds—objective, subjective, social—and each one features its own type of speech, subject matter and validity claims. By objective world, Habermas is referring to the shared realities around us—to specific states of affairs. This *objective world* is the context of constative (descriptive) speech regarding truth claims. In other words, two persons can point to some object and begin talking about it by using descriptive speech. Their goal is to be truthful, and they are capable of assisting each other in increasing the accuracy and adequacy of how they describe the object. The *subjective world* is the realm of the inner self, the narratives, reasonings and affects of the person. This world is accessible through expressive speech, and to be valid it must be honest. The same two persons can narrate a person's history with the object, or they can express their emotions about the object. The honesty of that communication is what matters. The *social world* is interpersonal, a world of regulations and norms. Communication in the social world is an environment of regulative speech (imperatives and intentions) that shapes and embodies norms. These two persons need to decide what to do with the object, so the objective and subjective discourse set the foundations for shaping their social response.

Communicative competence requires validity in all three worlds for discourse to be valid and for understanding to be genuine. Within the context of communicative competence, the objective world is the context for creating shared propositional knowledge about a state of affairs, the subjective world is the sphere for developing mutual trust through honesty, and the social world is the setting for shared social norms concerning shared living.[5] When discourse features these measures of integrity and understanding, communicative action (cooperative) is possible.

---

[4]Ibid., 2:125.
[5]Ibid., 1:308.

Table 9.1. Habermas on Communicative Competence[a]

	Objective World	Subjective World	Social World
Type of speech	Descriptive	Expressive	Regulative
Subject matter	Propositional knowledge	Narrative and affect	Norms and intentions
Validity measurement	Truth	Honest	Just and appropriate

[a]Jürgen Habermas, *The Theory of Communicative Action*, trans. Thomas McCarthy, 2 vols. (Boston: Beacon, 1984, 1987), 2:115-97.

Crosscultural communication in churches is often subject to distortion—an experience that may include tension, a lack of trust and misunderstandings. Habermas's approach to crisis is noteworthy.[6] Each segment of his social structure (culture, society, person) is a potential site of difficulty. (In chapter three, we posited a fourth social entity—a *community*—and the disequilibrium discussed here applies to that social entity as well.) For example, persons of a culture may have migrated during a recent generation; they come into contact with other cultures; the society (governing and economic structures) contributes certain resources and challenges; individuals are caught in the midst of changing meanings, practices and the loss of coherent narratives. These "distortions" are threatening to all levels of life. The crisis itself can be identified in one of three processes: cultural reproduction (coherence of meaning, rationality), social integration (coordination in social space, solidarity) or socialization (competencies for action, responsibility). In the immigration example, parents may strive to convey to their children the meaning of kinship or work, or that relationships are more important than personal rights. Their children are exposed to the society's conflicting approaches, and they learn ways of reasoning that do not value their parent's thinking. The various adults adapt differently to the new society, so they do not agree on how to maintain friendships or what social connections are important and worthy of commitments. Disruption appears in various forms, as explained in table 9.2.

Habermas also takes the concept of "colonization" and applies it to matters of societies and cultures. While colonization has traditionally described a process of military and political conquest, enforced by an exter-

---

[6]Ibid., 2:140-43.

Table 9.2. Habermas on Manifestations of Crisis[a]

Structural components → Disturbances in the domain of ↓	Culture	Society	Person	Dimension of evaluation ↓
Cultural reproduction	Loss of meaning	Withdrawal of legitimation	Crisis in orientation and education	Rationality of knowledge
Social integration	Unsettling of collective identity	Anomie	Alienation	Solidarity of members
Socialization	Rupture of tradition	Withdrawal of motivation	Psychopathologies	Personal responsibility

[a]Habermas, *Theory of Communicative Action*, 2:143, fig. 22. Used by permission.

nal empire or government, Habermas posits the colonization of cultures (and I would add, communities) by larger societal forces. In U.S. society, for example, the normative meanings of cultures are constantly being suppressed by the society's dominant characteristics of consumer capitalism. There are numerous forces at work—a demand for mobility, cost of living that is not aligned with local wages, and a priority on the nuclear family as the center of consumption. Further, the resulting economic and relational tensions regularly lead to social unrest (in micro- and macro-groups) as individuals face psychological threats and maladaptation. For U.S. churches, cultural groups may be losing languages, traditions and practices—and those are connected to a loss of meaning. A church may live in the context of racial unrest that gets expressed in various institutional settings. Personal fears and hatred can lead to psychological difficulties. When leaders bring some carefully chosen topics into a setting that allows authentic communication, these topical explorations can guide community discourse toward important interpretive and relational gains in their conceptual worlds.

In the opening example of this chapter, a Euro-American church, founded in its own stories of migration and its cultural dominance in society, had experienced a few decades of changes in its geographical setting.

There had been tensions with nonwhite neighbors over matters of public education, city planning and political vision. They had not significantly entered into the worldviews and perspectives of others. The church's narratives—from Scripture and from some traditional meanings about reconciliation and neighbor love—provided the motivation to attempt new conversations. The African American churches, which by now had been established for several decades, brought assumptions that arose from being marginalized in the society. Their cultural narratives and their more recent church narratives indicated that they had little influence on Euro-American society. The Euro-American church, with its wealth, its organizational structures based on the norms of modern corporations, and its apparent power within societal structures, represented an entirely different set of narratives. In spite of these barriers the meeting was to represent the power of God, as known from biblical narratives, to bring about a consensus of meanings that could lead to cooperative actions. Habermas's framework is helpful for reflecting on the case study in order to discerning the crisis and how a different course might be fostered.

Habermas calls for *communicative action* rather than just strategic action. In the case-study situation, a meeting or a series of meetings was needed to explore all three *worlds* in order to shape new horizons for all participants. Their lifeworlds (worldviews), composed of narratives and values and imaginations and expectations, were different. Their only access was through world concepts—thinking, talking and learning about the worlds of the "other." Discourse would need to be crafted around objective, subjective and social realities.

To explore their subjective worlds, they needed to listen to each other's honest narratives. For example, participants could have begun with short personal narratives that feature one or two cultural traits that correlated with the gospel. Then each participant could tell one story about a time of personal tension or crisis that was centered in a crosscultural situation. This may be an experience of racism, a misunderstanding about an event or conversation, or some other story of woundedness. Additionally, each participant could narrate a positive story about boundary crossing: when had they experienced something commendable in the context of persons of another culture? More specifically, in that this initiative concerns black-white relationships, what stories were relevant to this effort? Chapter seven noted that Euro-American culture tends strongly toward individualism, and some other cultures are more aware of personal identity being embedded in larger cultural and societal groups. Therefore, this mix of positive and negative stories is most helpful when participants are encouraged to consider some experiences that would be interpreted as individual matters and others that invite consideration of structural or societal realities. How have participants experienced the presence and activities of various churches? This set of conversations is not a context for argument—rather it is the hard work of memory, storytelling and listening. Habermas sets honesty as the standard, which at times is different than truth or justice.

Participants also needed to explore their objective worlds. There is a shared context, including their city and nation, and they are participants in the outcomes of some states of affairs in those settings. These objective matters include historical narratives (national and local), societal structures (like the justice system) and the narratives of each congregation. Also relevant to these conversations is the matter of ethnicity in relationship to the history of U.S. churches. There are numerous topics here that are profoundly uncomfortable—the creation of African slavery as an economic tool, the Middle Passage, the U.S. Constitution's compromises concerning slaves, racism in church life and mission, lynchings, local exclusionary clauses in real estate, segregation in public schools followed by busing and then Euro-American withdrawal, and continued segregation among Christians on Sunday mornings. Habermas proposes that truth is pursued in these conversations. This work requires an accurate telling, cognizant of complex data, an acknowledgment and bracketing of contradictions (and decisions about what clarifications to pursue), and numerous occasions in which participants voice that they are learning (an appropriate return to subjective honesty).

Prior to the crisis meeting, numerous objective topics could have been explored over a series of conversations. Once everyone could acknowledge the crisis as it unfolded, specific topics required attention, like the history of lynchings or other failures within the society concerning the topics of murder, race, justice and inequities in the legal system. A new framework might be available for the disagreement that surfaced during the meeting. Perhaps the language of "justice" versus "fairness" is helpful. Even though *justice* in biblical narratives is a holistic term of social, moral and relational righteousness, it can be a narrower term in society, concerning technical legalities and the system that works with rules of the legal system. The object world includes the truth that Euro-American men have murdered African Americans with impunity. Sometimes the governing systems were absent, and sometimes they were culpable. This is the narrative in which the African American culture was shaped. In these histories African American men were often on trial for acts against Euro-Americans, and there was no justice, only misplaced racist revenge. Further, seldom have Euro-American men been found guilty of crimes against African Americans. For Euro-Americans the justice system has not just functioned adequately, it has displayed bias in favor of Euro-Americans. It is important to place these accounts alongside another cultural difference: Euro-Americans perceive themselves as individual entities; African Americans tend more toward identity with the group. On the day of O. J. Simpson's acquittal, the African Americans were surprised that fairness was present—that an African American on trial was not automatically executed, and that a talented (and expensive) legal team could be created and go head-to-head with a system that had seldom been fair (in their view). In light of several centuries of profound discrimination and racism, here was a single time the system finally provided a surprising conclusion. This was in contrast to Euro-American participants, who focused on the individual, as defined in the society's legal framework, and when they considered the evidence regarding the individual they could not fathom that an acquittal was just. So the African American pastors would say, "It is not of primary concern if O. J. Simpson committed the crime; finally we have a degree of fairness." The Euro-Americans believed, "The facts point to guilt, and the system failed." It is very unlikely, given years of no significant communication, that this diverse group could have reached a level of mutual understanding that evening.

The third sphere is the social world in which a group of persons is conversing about what would be just and appropriate in their own life together. Rooted in their always-moving lifeworlds, and having increased the degree of shared horizons, there can be sufficient overlap of social worlds for communicative action—that is, life together can have increasing levels of competence in communication and integrity in common life. Life together can include many common pursuits—conversation, engagement together in

Personal Reflection/Group Exercise: Communicative Competence

This is an imaginative scenario in which the instructor of this class announces several immediate changes. First, he or she has just received a new book that everyone should read, so it is being added to the required reading list and will be discussed toward the end of the course. Second, the instructor says that because some students have been uncomfortable in their discussion groups, beginning next week all groups will be homogeneous regarding gender and culture. (Or, if the groups are already homogenous, the announced change is that discussion groups are canceled.) Finally, because of some other commitments that the instructor has, weekly class time will be reduced by one third. The instructor wants student responses, and the discussion will begin in the existing small groups. (Even though this is imaginative, do what you can to feel and seriously ponder the situation.)

1. *Individual time.* Your small group will soon have time to talk about these changes. Write down your three most important comments or questions about the announced changes.

2. *Group time.* When you come together, spend about 5 minutes discussing the situation. (You do not need to deal with what you previously wrote.) After 5 minutes, sort out your conversation by trying to name whether you focused on objective, subjective or social communication. Were there subjective matters that were unexpressed but came out as efforts to shape the social directions? Can you agree on which elements fit the three spheres?

3. *Group time.* Now, go around the circle with each person, one at a time, reading their original three comments/questions. After each person, the others in the group need to classify the three items—without the author making any comments. After the three items are classified, the author provides a brief reflective commentary—agreeing or disagreeing with the classification and noting anything that he or she learned about what was originally valued as the most important considerations.

4. *Whole class.* Discuss the communication tendencies of the groups. Also discuss whether there were cultural differences concerning how the three changes were discussed.

speaking and acting on public matters, and cooperative activities among congregants. This is the realm of cooperative options and "oughts." In the case study, participants would recognize that because they live in different worlds, they ought to experiment with some set of initiatives to enlarge their lifeworlds so there is more overlap. They could develop appropriate ways of working together, and they could move toward some agreements on justice in relationship to local matters of social structures.

Communicative competence is more complex than strategic action; this framework makes it more likely that shared life includes increasing depth and cooperation. In chapter five we noted that our corporate and personal lives are largely socially constructed through language. We can create new realities as we enlarge shared language. Further, we can address distortions through communicative competence. The action orientation of Euro-American culture can undermine these pursuits; the more leisurely approaches of storytelling cultures can provide helpful means.

SOCIAL DYNAMICS

Communication always takes place in the context of numerous psychological and social factors.

Emotions. This brief exploration into crosscultural relationships and intercultural communication cannot deal adequately with the topic of emotions. A few generalities may help frame approaches to better communication.[7] The language of "I feel" has many meanings in the United States, often referring to opinions and commitments rather than to affectivity. For many Euro-Americans, emotions are to be downplayed, even denied as a significant factor. This culture tends to understand emotions as beyond our control, and, while understood as not especially valuable for reasoning and communication, emotions are often thereby more powerful while unrecognized. Some other cultures, including African Americans, Latinos and Italians, are more expressive and view Euro-Americans as cold or concealing. But other cultures, such as Japanese and some northern Europeans, view Euro-American communication as emotion-laden.

The framework of Habermas can be of assistance. Honest communication, serving the subjective world, requires that we pay attention to our

---

[7]Edward Stewart and Milton Bennett, *American Cultural Patterns: A Cross-Cultural Perspective*, rev. ed. (Yarmouth, Maine: Intercultural Press, 1991), pp. 150-51.

feelings. The stories we have received and lived bring an abundance of emotions—and those feelings shape our perceptions and actions. In its simplest form this framework will teach that the emotions of a previous experience will often surface when a similar event is experienced. So an experience of injustice, in which hurt and anger were felt, will influence the person when another event of injustice is experienced or narrated—even if this new experience is significantly different. A woundedness about being misunderstood also may lead a person to withdraw if a new situation appears to be a similar experience. The honesty that Habermas calls for is one of reporting—not blaming. All groups, in the social world, need to address matters of justice and appropriateness. But that work can be wiser if we talk about our subjective worlds so that we can then work in the context of knowing each other's stories—including each other's feelings. Groups cannot afford to ignore affective responses nor to let emotions control the conversation and the progress toward next steps. In storytelling, and in responding to each other, we benefit when we gain an adequate vocabulary, abilities to articulate how we experience our inner life and capacities to listen deeply. Then this subjective communication is placed alongside conversations that include objective communication and the pursuit of social norms.

Sympathy and empathy. *Sympathy* is a correspondence of feelings, especially sorrow, among persons who significantly share a lifeworld. Sympathy is one link in relationships that have some affinity. But when this emotional projection goes beyond our lifeworld, it easily becomes condescension, more like pity. So sympathy can be helpful when persons can assume that a given situation will create a specific emotion. But if persons are more culturally distant, those assumptions are often inaccurate, and sympathy will create more distance.

Empathy is more helpful in crosscultural relationships. Empathy requires the bracketing of our own perceptions and emotions in an effort to problematize and enter into the world of another. The assumption of empathy is that persons feel differently, that experiences and perceptions vary. In developing communicative competence, participants can listen to each other, bracket their own perceptions and emotions, attempt to see the experiences through the eyes and feelings of others, then check those perceptions in conversation. In some cultural settings this coming together may be served by some indirect styles rather than by the more Euro-American directness. It may be more appropriate to check out our empathetic responses with a third party, to see if our understanding is growing, then to decide what is appropriate for direct communication.

Reverend Frank Jackson, an African American pastor in Oakland, who had been shaped in a cultural narrative in which random violence, unjust legal systems and oppressive economics had been realities, saw television coverage of the beginning violence in Los Angeles (1992).[8] Policemen had been acquitted of wrongdoing in the videotaped beating of Rodney King. As Pastor Jackson watched reports of the spreading Los Angeles uprising, he began calling Korean American pastors in Oakland. He had already developed these relationships over a period of years—so he knew that the television reports would create fear that street violence might be aimed at Korean American citizens and stores in Oakland. He was viscerally connected to the frustrations of African Americans, and he was relationally and theologically connected to Korean churches. (He had come to faith while stationed as an Army soldier in Korea.) Responding to his phone calls, within a couple of hours a group of Korean American and African American pastors planned a rally for downtown Oakland. They brought together their congregations for a time of worship and prayer with the news media present. Oakland never exploded, largely because anyone checking local television saw a large multicultural group of Oakland Christians being led in worship and prayer by Korean American and African American pastors.

Pastor Jackson moved from sympathy to empathy, and such empathetic communication can make a difference. This story shows the benefits of the full communicative competence posited by Habermas—there was a history of subjective storytelling, an adequate basis of seeing the state of affairs similarly, and a quick sense of what they ought to do.

Power. Communication takes place in the context of power—the structural powers of societies, the power of meaningful cultural narratives, the power of personal loyalties. Habermas's exposition on colonization provides one framework for how churches can understand power.

---

[8]The late Rev. Frank Jackson was pastor of Faith Presbyterian Church, Oakland, California.

The pressures of any society bear on cultures and communities. United States churches have been shaped in the context of societal narratives— Euro-American dominance, manifest destiny, nationalism, entrenched racism, the rise of modern capitalistic corporations, success and meaning largely defined in terms of consumerism, along with other elements of late modernity such as expressive individualism and functional rationalism.[9] Some of these traits have been structured into church organizations. Further, the interaction among peoples is shaped by the power dynamics of the lifeworld.

Habermas notes that structural and historic colonization becomes internalized by participants. In other words, the societal dominance of Euro-Americans, even when mitigated by later narratives or laws or personal convictions, is still present *internally*—within the assumptions and language and practices of the people. This means that intercultural communication must be constantly attentive to the embedded barriers—the assumptions about superiority or inferiority, the habits of procedures, and the imaginations about what is good. One example of this is the negative spiral that easily develops between Euro-Americans and persons of other cultures. Euro-American communication is often oriented toward problem solving, an approach that comes from functional rationalism and an orientation to action (like fixing things). Non-Euro-Americans often carry a sense of suspicion that is based on previous narratives and experiences of oppression. So a critique by a Euro-American triggers suspicion by others—and the communication is inadequate for the needed shift of lifeworlds that might make communicative action possible. In addition, Euro-American communication often gives a priority to persuasion, based in precise data, which can exhibit a disinterest in relational, emotional or contextual matters. When persons of different cultures are working together to form a faith community, the power styles of one culture (based in Euro-American dominance) and the power styles of another (based in relationships) can easily collide.

In a Midwest Asian American church that had previously been Japanese American, a Japanese American board member proposed the creation of a

---

[9]Manifest destiny is a theologically and socially grounded belief that the United States was "destined" to include territory from the Atlantic Ocean to the Pacific Ocean.

*new fund to promote ministry among children and youth. She wanted to
provide the funds herself, and she specified that the youth committee would
set up a separate account and have discretion over expenditures. Many
Japanese American churches form various committees and groups to establish and control checking accounts. This decentralizing of control seems to
be rooted in the experiences of the internment in which thousands of Japanese Americans lost control over their homes, businesses and churches. In
this church a decade of restructuring the finances prompted by regulatory
requirements had been led by a Chinese American businessperson. This
new proposal created tension because board members agreed with the goals,
and they appreciated the proposed contribution, but the proposed structure
was exactly what they had spent years correcting. When this difficulty was
voiced, the woman who had brought the proposal complained that the
board was dictatorial and did not trust other church members. Attempts to
form alternative solutions were rejected; anything but the original proposal was suspected of an abuse of power. Stories about previous grievances
were also recalled—such as an incident in which a memorial fund for a
relative had not been satisfactorily administered.*

This story displays numerous levels of narratives, and each story carried
certain understandings about power. Japanese Americans, like other minority groups, had few institutions within their own control, so an ethnic-
specific church can be a unique location for cultural norms that is pro-
tected from the society. Sometimes the norms of society (or from
denominational structures) are avoided—until the church experiences
some level of ethnic diversity. In this case the dispersion of control over
funds, the connections between individuals and organizational management, and shared understandings about agendas and priorities are all important. When churches are increasingly multicultural, structures need to
change, but, as we will explain more in chapter ten, there are often no
obvious technical answers. However, an emphasis on communicative competence, using all three of Habermas's worlds, is essential no matter what
the organizational rules are to be. If the larger goal is that of shaping a
church to discern and participate in God's initiatives, then we need to pay
attention to the role of power as we converse about our objective, subjective
and social worlds.

Relational context. For much of Euro-American communication, context is seldom a major consideration. Communication is focused on a topic, preliminaries are avoided or brief, the conversation is linear and there is little patience for digressions. In Latino and Middle Eastern cultures, conversation begins with inquiries about family or other personal matters. Time is given to greeting rituals and general inquiries. This communication concerning social context provides cues concerning mental states, social networks, motivations and potential creative options. Such contextual matters then shape the rest of the conversation. For Euro-Americans conversations are determined to be either action oriented or generically relational, but these forms do not tend to mix.

> *I (Juan) am part of a new network of African American and Latino pastors in greater Los Angeles that has come together to address common concerns in our communities (gang violence, economic injustice and immigration reform). There have been several attempts at building these types of relationships in the past. Short-term relationships have been established to respond to specific crisis, but once the urgency passes, the efforts have disappeared. So we decided that we needed to approach this effort differently. We get together to eat in churches and restaurants, in small groups and large groups. As we take time to eat, read the Bible and pray together, we have been able to begin to address our common concerns. As we tell our stories and share how we understand Scripture, we are getting to know each other and have begun establishing the long-term relationships we will need to go forward.*

Churches that seek to create intercultural life will need to surface these stylistic issues. Most situations will benefit if time is given to social and personal communication—which can often be embedded in times for food and prayer. Churches, as communities of primary relationships, should be contexts for the complexities of many-layered communication. This comprehensive approach would also value clarity and even precision when communication is dealing with social cooperation. All cultures have tendencies to make assumptions about agreements—like the results of some conversation. If intercultural communication is to thrive, participants will learn how to determine adequate clarity while also honoring the values of

Bible Study: Luke 10:25-37—
A Lawyer Questions Jesus

[25]Just then a lawyer stood up to test Jesus. "Teacher," he said, "what must I do to inherit eternal life?" [26]He said to him, "What is written in the law? What do you read there?" [27]He answered, "You shall love the Lord your God with all your heart, and with all your soul, and with all your strength, and with all your mind; and your neighbor as yourself." [28]And he said to him, "You have given the right answer; do this, and you will live."

[29]But wanting to justify himself, he asked Jesus, "And who is my neighbor?" [30]Jesus replied, "A man was going down from Jerusalem to Jericho, and fell into the hands of robbers, who stripped him, beat him, and went away, leaving him half dead. [31]Now by chance a priest was going down that road; and when he saw him, he passed by on the other side. [32]So likewise a Levite, when he came to the place and saw him, passed by on the other side. [33]But a Samaritan while traveling came near him; and when he saw him, he was moved with pity. [34]He went to him and bandaged his wounds, having poured oil and wine on them. Then he put him on his own animal, brought him to an inn, and took care of him. [35]The next day he took out two denarii, gave them to the innkeeper, and said, 'Take care of him; and when I come back, I will repay you whatever more you spend.' [36]Which of these three, do you think, was a neighbor to the man who fell into the hands of the robbers?" [37]He said, "The one who showed him mercy." Jesus said to him, "Go and do likewise."

Jesus' life and teachings created different responses among those who heard about him. In this situation a lawyer begins a conversation in which the subject matter (connecting personal justification with social responsibility) presents material for all three spheres of Habermas's communicative action model.

1. Begin by naming details that are related to the effectiveness of communication in the passage. What was the original purpose of the conversation? What do we know about social positions and careers? How does the

---

lawyer's goal shift early in the conversation? What is the geographic context, and what historical events make that important?

2. There is movement in the conversation among the three worlds of Habermas's model (subjective, objective, social). Discuss how you would assign verses to the three kinds of communication.

3. Jesus introduces a matter of objective reality (the barriers of culture biases) that will shift the communication concerning both subjective and social worlds. Discuss how this opens the opportunity for "communicative competence."

4. Jesus told a parable to change the conversation. What role does this play in the overall pursuit of good communication?

---

and learning from social, contextual conversation.

One framework, noted especially in chapters six and seven, concerns individualism versus collectivism. Some cultures focus primarily on an individual's benefits, rights, choices, status and options. Other cultures place more attention on the group's identity, well-being, synergism and opportunities. These differences are critical in communication because they shape priorities concerning what information matters, how roles are addressed and what expectations are appropriate. A whole group may be attentive to the shame or honor of one member and, as a group, they will tend to communicate in ways that protect each person because the group "identifies" with each individual. Or, conversely, a group might give priority to identifying actions that indicate individual blame or accomplishment, and they may do this with little attention to how that affects individuals. There are strengths and challenges to both styles; anyone who shapes a group's conversations needs to be attentive to how these variables affect communication. How can objective, subjective and social frameworks serve intercultural communication? Can you perceive what is happening during conversation in these three spheres? What questions or procedures or exercises can deepen the adequacy and integrity of these facets of communication? Try drawing three circles on a board, explaining these types of communication, and ask participants to categorize the elements of their conversation. Be aware that different cultures will feel more "at home" in one of the spheres, and most will have some immediate sense of cultural "oughts" (fitting Habermas's social sphere) that will need to be translated through the other two frameworks before the whole group can shape a new direction for everyone. Leaders need to develop their own communicative practices as well as the habits of the church.

PRACTICES OF ATTENTIVENESS

Each cultural variable that we have noted in earlier chapters will affect intercultural communication. Throughout the book, especially in chapters four through eight, we have worked to promote an attentiveness to the factors that contribute to boundary crossing and intercultural life. Many of these elements can be listed as potential barriers to appropriate and effective communication. Table 9.3 provides a partial list.[10]

The work of leaders to shape intercultural communication in faith communities is a complex and multifaceted task. The goal is attentiveness—to God, to congregation, to oneself, to cultures, to power, to consequences. The following topics provide a suggestive list that, though not exhaustive, calls attention to some critical areas.

Oneself. What are the cultural patterns you bring to the conversations? If you were able to watch yourself from a balcony, listening into communication, what might you observe about yourself and your interactions? Do you understand how you communicate respect or disrespect? Can you identify your assumptions as explained in chapters four to eight, especially those that differ from others? How do you work with embedded assumptions about superiority and inferiority? What do you need to problematize in order to nurture better communication? The work of critical self-reflection requires commitment, constant learning and the courage to experiment.

Empathy. How can you foster your own empathy for others? What can you do to nurture empathy among other participants? While personal and group narratives are needed to build trust, they can also (unfortunately) become a collection of dueling stories ("I was also wounded") that actually lead to an inwardness that limits empathy. Biblical narratives, read along-

---

[10]LaRay Barna provides a similar, helpful list in "Stumbling Blocks in Intercultural Communication," in *Intercultural Communication*, ed. Larry Samovar and Richard Porter, 8th ed. (Belmont, Calif.: Wadsworth, 1997), pp. 370-79. Also see Richard Brislin and Tomoko Yoshida, eds., *Improving Intercultural Interactions: Modules for Cross-Cultural Training Programs* (Thousand Oaks, Calif.: Sage, 1994).

Table 9.3. Barriers to Intercultural Communication

Assumed differences and similarities

Languages that are similar but different

Inadequate attention to translation in multilingual conversations

Misunderstood gestures

Lack of reflection on one's own culture

Unreflective individualism or collectivism

Differences concerning power distance

Assumptions about superiority and inferiority

Defensive or offensive affective environment

Different worldviews

Different cognitive styles

Assumptions about roles and authority

Unexamined or unarticulated values and goals

Unexamined effects and misuse of power

Lack of empathy

---

side our own stories, can break unhealthy patterns if we can see how God works to shape responsible love even when there is disagreement among groups concerning how to calculate debts.

Cognition. What does the conversation reveal about various cognitive styles? How can you name the benefits of the differences ("John, I can hear that you care about . . .")? When is it helpful to indicate differences ("You both bring important priorities, so we need to learn from what you see and figure out a way forward")? The cognitive styles chart in chapter eight can help you identify variables and increase the communication capacities of the group.

Power. How is power operating in your setting? What narratives— societal, cultural, personal—have shaped the interplay? Who is making what kind of assumptions? How are decisions made? What role do organizational structures play? How does language reveal power dynamics? Power can be overt or covert; it can come in the forms of one of the cultures or in the habits of the larger society (as noted in Habermas's explanation about "internalized colonization"). You also work in the midst of the power of God's Spirit and the power of biblical narratives, so a primary work of the group is to discern and participate in what God is initiating.

Community. Based on our earlier discussions about church as a primary community, how might you discern the assets and challenges that each culture brings into your communication? How can you problematize specific experiences and concepts so the community can learn to relativize cultural norms in favor of a more generative life together? What practices do the various cultures bring into the interaction that could serve everyone? There may be people around you who can offer cultural explanations or who can be bridge builders for trust and cooperation.

Gratitude. How can questions and conversations surface the most valuable and generative characteristics of groups and individuals? What narratives, traits and commitments are available for Christian faithfulness and intercultural life? Interpretive leaders can help shape questions about specific cultures or intercultural experiences so that a church learns about God's initiatives and human faithfulness. For example, participants could work with these questions: What have been your most encouraging experiences in crosscultural relationships? How have persons of other cultures helped you learn about faith and Christian living? What do you believe are some important characteristics of your culture that can help shape intercultural life? Gratitude is not just a demeanor, rather it is a practice that

At the Movies

What disparities are notable in the objective, subjective and social worlds of these narratives? When do preconscious notions come to the surface, and when do they remain buried?

Dances with Wolves (1990). Lieutenant John Dunbar, sent to a remote Civil War outpost, befriends wolves and Sioux Indians, and gradually sheds his "white man's" ways, then is tested as the Army advances into the plains and upon what has now become his family.

Born in East LA (1987). A Mexican American caught up in an immigration raid is wrongly deported as an illegal immigrant, with no way of proving he is an American citizen, and is forced to sneak his way back home.

guides a church's actions as we identify and receive God's grace; it is required if we are to gain the knowledge we need. This kind of questioning and a process for working with the resulting discoveries and perspectives is called "appreciative inquiry."[11]

---

[11]See Mark Lau Branson, *Memories, Hopes, and Conversations: Appreciative Inquiry and Congregational Change* (Herndon, Va.: Alban, 2004); and Mark Lau Branson, "Gratitude as Access to Meaning," in *The Three Tasks of Leadership*, ed. Eric Jacobsen (Grand Rapids: Eerdmans, 2009) pp. 148-59.

10

LEADING CHANGE

Mark Lau Branson

Second Street Church was historically Euro-American and had watched their neighborhood and much of the city become increasingly Latino. Their Sunday morning attendance dropped below eighty, and their pastor prepared them for his retirement. He preached often on how God leads God's people through changes, and he encouraged them to hire a new pastor who had experience in Latino communities. He emphasized the theological basis for ethnic diversity and engaging their context in new ways. Several months later they called Ramón, a third-generation Mexican American, who had been an assistant pastor in a Latino church across the state. That church had welcomed a few biracial families, and Ramón voiced a strong commitment to diversity.

When asked, pastors can create very long lists of the activities they are expected to do: preach, teach, counsel, evangelize, officiate, lead worship, manage meetings, provide administrative oversight, inspire faith, visit homes and hospitals, and be involved in the community. The expectations of a church's members and board might be clear and explicit, but there are usually unnamed expectations that are rooted in the church's history and preferences. Leadership, like other topics, needs to be studied as an element of our context—the societal context as well as cultural and local contexts. Modernity shaped expectations concerning leadership in the United States. Modern management theory often focuses on the leader's responsibilites to predict, command and control, which leads to the adoption of strategic planning. Consumerism, as embraced by churches, led to the framework of marketing with terms like *seeker-sensitive*, and the church is simply one more organization that is marketing goods and services.[1] The church's self-understanding as a volunteer organization emphasizes that obligations are minimized and members are "free agents." Given these cultural influences, what kind of leadership is needed to help shape churches in the midst of significant cultural changes and ethnic diversity?

During the first months of his work at Second Street Church, Ramón focused on conversations with individuals and families, in cafes or at home with Lisa (his wife). When Ramón and Lisa (gently) let it be known that they welcomed invitations into members' homes, they experienced a slow increase in such invitations. In all of these conversations they asked for stories—about ancestors and migrations, marriages and families, neighbors and neighborhoods, work and school. They also asked about the ups and downs of the church's narrative—the comings and goings of members and pastors. These conversations were taking place in the midst of regular church activities, and Ramón would comment on the gifts he observed and the commitment he saw among members and leaders.

The work of leaders

- Prioritize conversations.
- Use a diversity of locations.
- Encourage opportunities to be in homes.
- Ask about personal and family stories.
- Ask about church stories.
- Notice and articulate the strengths and gifts of the church.

This chapter will use numerous episodes from the story of Second Street Church and Ramón, their new pastor.[2] Following many episodes of the story a few key leadership practices will be noted in lists ("The work of

---

[1] George Hunsburger, *The Church Between Gospel and Culture*, ed. George Hunsburger and Craig Van Gelder (Grand Rapids: Eerdmans, 1996), p. 337.

[2] This sequence of stories is compiled from numerous experiences we have had and research we have done. Our intent is not to provide a model to be copied—the leadership approach we advocate specifically opposes importing answers from elsewhere. Each church has the work of discerning its own vocation. This chapter, when linked with the other chapters, provides a process for that discernment and engagement. For frameworks and skills regarding church transformation in the midst of a changing environment, see Alan Roxburgh, *Missional Map-Making* (San Francisco: Jossey-Bass, 2010).

leaders"). Important theoretical materials will be explained throughout the chapter.

From these conversations, Ramón was learning how the neighborhood changes had affected the church and its members. This church had had an important role in the community during the one hundred years of its life—its members had been leaders in government, schools and businesses. Their children had attended the local schools; their church had been the center of community events. Then, more recently, many children of church families had relocated elsewhere with their own families. Demographic shifts meant that schools and civic life were no longer familiar, and members felt they had a diminishing witness in the community. Then, with lots of prayer, they began to think more seriously about taking steps toward being a racially inclusive church. That led to calling Ramón as their pastor.

The work of leaders

- Pay attention to the changing relationships between church and context
- Note trends with generations, demographics and civic life
- Learn how the church learns and what influences its imagination

This chapter builds on the leadership triad that was introduced in chapter one. We will offer a sequence of phases or steps that are important for those who want to lead a church through significant transformation. Throughout this chapter, we assume the specific frameworks and perspectives of preceding chapters. This process is not about experts who tell us the truth and solve our problems—it is about leaders who shape an environment and provide resources so a plural leadership becomes normative.

LEADERSHIP TRIAD

The leadership triad, as explained in chapter one, includes interpretive, relational and implemental spheres of work. Interpretive leadership shapes a leadership team and a whole congregation to pay attention to and interpret texts and contexts, all in service of attending to and being responsive to God's initiatives. Relational leadership focuses on human connections and synergism toward an embodiment of gospel reconciliation and love. Implemental leadership guides, reforms and initiates activities and structures so that the church embodies the gospel.

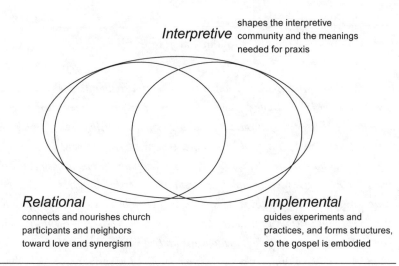

Figure 10.1. Leadership triad

Interpretive leadership. *Interpretive leadership* is about understanding and shaping meanings. What does it mean to be a church? How do the particulars of our theological heritage help us listen to God and participate in God's mission to our context? What do we need to know about this context? What narratives and information help us know our neighbors, ourselves and the movements of the Spirit? An interpretive leader shapes a "community of interpreters" who discovers what it needs to know in the midst of study and ministry. The praxis cycle of chapter one listed various important resources for interpretive work.

Ramón already knew that the racial demographics of the city had significantly changed during the last thirty years, but he did not have details. He talked with some members about early families, called on the local librarian concerning the region's history, and met with a couple of local Latino pastors. Whenever possible he asked at least one other church leader to join with him. Helen, a retired teacher who was on the church board, suggested that a couple of teenagers might be interested in getting statistics from the school system, so Ramón asked them to buy some pizza and meet with the teens to discuss some research.

The work of leaders

• Find numerous sources for information on the context

- Learn from other churches and their leaders
- Ask leaders and members to join you in research

In sermons and Bible studies Ramón would ask participants to discern what God was doing in the Bible passage and to reflect on how it gave them clues to their own church life and community. A Sunday morning Bible study, which had usually drawn a handful of old-timers, was now attracting most of the board members. Ramón decided to focus on Acts 6:1-7, a passage about how the early church faced questions concerning priorities and leadership in a crosscultural environment. After reading the text, Ramón ask everyone to read the same passage silently, paying special attention to how the passage dealt with cultural issues. This approach gave everyone time to think and reflect more before the discussion began. After a few minutes of silence, Ramón said, "The early church was shaped in the midst of the Holy Spirit's work to cross old cultural boundaries. The story of Pentecost in Acts 2 emphasizes the Spirit's grace for Hellenists, those Jews whose roots were in nations throughout the Roman Empire. What does this Acts 6 story tell us about what they were learning?" Member of the class spent an hour asking questions and making observations about the story. They made connections between Jesus' teachings and money, the responsibilities of leaders, how marginalized persons decide to voice their concerns and the way decisions were made. They continued working with the same passage for the next few weeks. They made observations about the text: boundary-crossing activities affected the whole community, the new leaders did not stay with their original job descriptions, and some behaviors seemed to bring more conversions. (We will return to this passage later in this chapter.)

The work of leaders

- Weave together the Bible stories with the stories of the church and community
- Give participants time to make observations and connections

In the practical theology cycle of chapter one, interpretive leadership moves from descriptive work in step 1 to research and meaning-making in steps 2, 3 and 4. This includes the work of analyzing sociocultural resources, studying Scripture, and recalling personal and congregational stories.

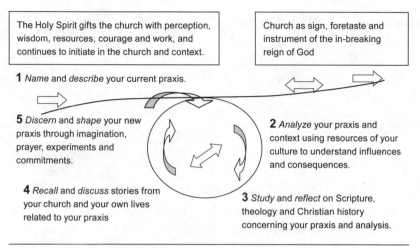

The Holy Spirit gifts the church with perception, wisdom, resources, courage and work, and continues to initiate in the church and context.

Church as sign, foretaste and instrument of the in-breaking reign of God

1 *Name* and *describe* your current praxis.

5 *Discern* and *shape* your new praxis through imagination, prayer, experiments and commitments.

2 *Analyze* your praxis and context using resources of your culture to understand influences and consequences.

4 *Recall* and *discuss* stories from your church and your own lives related to your praxis

3 *Study* and *reflect* on Scripture, theology and Christian history concerning your praxis and analysis.

Figure 10.2. Practical theology steps

Interpretive leadership requires that leaders gain abilities to observe and interpret the current life of the church—its activities, its relationships, even its imagination. This work, like all other interpretive activities and the entire practical theology cycle, has the goal of shaping a church that discerns God's initiatives with them and their context and then enters more faithfully into that mission. This attention to observing and analyzing the current life of the church is what Ronald Heifetz calls the "balcony perspective." Heifetz and his colleague Marty Linsky, both of the Kennedy School of Government at Harvard University, write,

> Achieving a balcony perspective means taking yourself out of the dance, in your mind, even if only for a moment. The only way you can gain both a clearer view of reality and some perspective on the bigger picture is by distancing yourself from the fray. Otherwise, you are likely to misperceive the situation and make the wrong diagnosis, leading you to misguided decision about where and how to intervene.[3]

By developing "balcony" habits, church leaders can become more attentive and perceptive. Interpretive leadership is about "meaning making," and it is always rooted in the ground realities. As a church's awareness and competencies are shaped, the participants actually construct a social world. We are

---

[3]Ronald Heifetz and Marty Linsky, *Leadership on the Line* (Boston: Harvard Business School, 2002), p. 53. We recommend this book for church leaders.

borrowing this framework from what is called "social construction," which asserts that "human behavior must be understood by taking the point of view of those experiencing it, because they are the ones that give meaning to that experience, as it takes place in a precise context."[4] Our ideas about church, gospel, leadership and mission are all constructed by a group of people (like a church) who live and work together as a community of praxis.

In every conversation, during meetings and worship, in both casual and formal settings, pastors need to observe and interpret what is happening. They also seek to shape the interpretive capacities of a group of leaders and of the whole church. This balcony work also requires them to be very aware of responses and reactions—not to be overly sensitive but to discern how persons, conversation topics and organizational elements are interacting.

In order to increase the number of persons involved in formative conversations, Ramón assembled an "appreciative inquiry" group of six current and former board members. They wrote several questions in order to learn about the church's most life-giving characteristics and experiences: (1) In all of your experiences at Second Street Church, when were you most engaged and most encouraged? What people or events shaped that experience? (2) Concerning our fellowship, when we are at our best, how to we relate to each other? How have members cared for each other or worked well together? (3) Concerning our relationships with others, what have been our best experiences of connecting with those around us, in our neighborhood and town? When we are at our best, how have we lived and expressed the gospel to those around us? (4) Consider any relationships you have had with persons of other cultures. What experiences have been the most engaging, enlightening and encouraging? (5) As you reflect on the cultural diversity in our church and neighborhood, what three wishes do you have for us and how we live and work together and for how we reach out to our neighborhoods?

The appreciative inquiry (AI) group spent an evening interviewing each other in dyads and then reporting to their whole group what they heard from each other. Then they created a list of persons they would try to interview during the next month. As the interviews proceeded, they kept hearing ripples of their

---

[4]Sonia Ospina and Ellen Schall, "Perspectives on Leadership," *Leadership for a Changing World*, September 2001 <www.leadershipforchange.org/insights/conversation/files/perspectives.php3>. The authors refer to the work of Wilfred Drath and Charles Paulis, *Making Common Sense: Leadership as Meaning-Making in a Community of Practice* (Greensboro, N.C.: Center for Creative Leadership, 1994).

conversations as these stories spread beyond the conversations they initiated. Ramón asked this team to continue to work together. He gave them more tools for writing about what they were learning, and he helped them gather some other groups that were composed of persons who had expressed similar interests in their answers. Then he led them in a process of helping a couple of these groups to shape experiments that were built on the stories and wishes they had shared.

The work of leaders

- Ask questions that elicit the most life-giving narratives and traits of the church
- Provide training and opportunities that increase the value of conversations
- Move from conversations to small-scale experiments shaped by participants

When churches are in the midst of significant transitions, often accompanied by anxieties, it is important to discover how God has already provided narratives and traits that can fund the transformation. Because anxieties often draw attention to problems and organizational deficits, leaders need to give unique and sustained attention to the resources that are already present by the grace of God. Appreciative inquiry is a powerful and encouraging process for engaging an increasing number of participants in conversations, interpretive exercises and experiments.[5]

All of this interpretive work needs the sensitivities and competencies discussed in earlier chapters concerning cultural variables. The stories we tell and the interpretations we hold have been shaped by our cultures. But because we have been created with capacities to listen and learn, we can have our own interpretive horizons changed in the midst of the praxis cycle.

Relational leadership. Ramón learned from Helen that the principal was Latino. Frank, another member of the church board and a retired businessman, owned a parking lot that was used for a weekly farmer's market. Throughout his first year Ramón kept building relationships, learning about connections, asking

---

[5]See Mark Lau Branson, *Memories, Hopes, and Conversations: Appreciative Inquiry and Congregational Change* (Herndon, Va.: Alban, 2004). This book involves an extended case study at a Japanese American church that was in a transition toward greater ethnic diversity. Also see Mark Lau Branson, "Gratitude as Access to Meaning," in *The Three Tasks of Leadership*, ed. Eric Jacobsen (Grand Rapids: Eerdmans, 2009), pp. 148-59. Additional resources on appreciative inquiry are available at <http://appreciativeinquiry.case.edu/>.

for stories during and after church meetings, prompting conversations that con-
nected the Bible and people's lives, and creating various clusters of members and
neighbors for conversation. Because the church had not previously included per-
sons who could not speak English, Ramon personally provided translation be-
tween English- and Spanish-speakers or he arranged for others to translate.

The work of leaders

- Pay attention to relational connections
- Notice community connections
- Make new relationships and nurture existing networks

Relational leadership concerns all the human connections—families
and friends, groups and networks. In chapter six we noted that relationships in U.S. culture have been shaped in ways that are different than in
many other cultures. There are two primary influences on how the majority culture understands relationships, both embedded in modernity:
instrumental rationality and expressive individualism. Instrumental rationality, arising from scientific rationalism, focuses on causality and
influences a society's pursuits of resources and security. Expressive individualism is rooted in Romanticism, which sought to restore elements of
human emotions, sensuality and relationality to Enlightenment rationalism but has sometimes resulted in rather thin understandings concerning the bonds of human beings. Attention to biblical narratives and instructions concerning relationships can bring rich and generative
resources into a faith community concerning our own relationships.
What was Jesus thinking when he created the group of twelve that included a tax collector, who was colluding with Rome, and zealots, who
sympathized with those promoting a militant uprising? How does the
Spirit intervene in Antioch to create a new community among persons
who would not previously have accommodated each other (Acts 11; 13)?
What happens when the gospel redefines the relationship between a
landowning Christian and his runaway slave (Philemon)? Trust is built
when we listen to each other. Innovation happens when relationships are
woven with new patterns.

Ramón asked Helen to get an appointment for them with the school principal.

When they met, Ramón asked the principal how churches were supporting the school and what opportunities the principal could imagine. Ramón learned about some simmering issues about racism that affected the schools, including the challenges he faced concerning immigration (documented and undocumented). Over the next year this led Ramón and Helen to meet other volunteers, pastors and youth who shared their concerns for the kids in the school. When Ramón spoke about these people and activities in a sermon (about Jeremiah's letter concerning seeking the shalom of the city [Jer 29]) several other members approached Helen about how they could help. They discovered new relational connections with teachers and a member of the school board. During these months, several students and adults became Christians. This also motivated Ramón and others to begin talking about experiments they might try concerning some bilingual activities during worship.

The work of leaders

- See the community through the eyes of others
- Continue shaping new conversations and explore opportunities
- Build trust through listening and caring
- Connect on-the-ground stories with biblical stories
- Address complex issues by broadening awareness and trying experiments

A church's social imaginary—about what it means to be church and what it means to be a church in this particular context—is nourished and changed by various perspectives that are available from diverse peoples. This allows a church to deal with the complexities of their increasingly intercultural life. These complexities also mean that disagreements and conflicts are surfaced—some rooted in ethnocentrism, some simply displaying human habits that had not benefited from adequate reflection.

Ramona (Ramón and Lisa's daughter) and several youth had become involved in the research concerning local schools. With Helen they invited some parents to meet for a couple of Saturday mornings to talk about the demographic research. Ramona prepared snacks, and they spent their time getting to know each other and discussing their research. After the second meeting Ramón had a Saturday visitor to his office. Richard and his wife Sharon knocked on his door, and Sharon was very tense. After some nervous small talk she asked Ramón, "Do those kids have to use the kitchen and cook their food here?" Ramón was confident his daughter was being respectful of the church property, but he was not surprised that something about the kitchen was creating anxiety. "Is something missing? Did they leave a mess?" Sharon was having a hard time expressing her specific concerns. Finally she said, "When we have our members here, especially for an important gathering, they shouldn't have to deal with strange smells. Some of our women are coming to cook, and I know they will be uncomfortable." Ramón knew from Sharon's language ("our members" and "strange smells") that the cultural diversity was a frustrating experience for her.

The work of leaders

- Attend to discomfort—in yourself and others
- Clarify surface issues
- Identify perspectives and habits that contribute to the tension

Many churches that engage multicultural life will experience conflicts that can be mistaken as small or incidental but in fact are important. Some of the most common conflicted experiences (apart from worship) include kitchens, adults supervising children, attire, clocks, and assumptions and experiences concerning power. Throughout this book we have provided ways to deepen understanding and shape new options

Since those of us in the United States are shaped in a national culture that places too much weight on individual rights and on matters of personal comfort, church leaders will need to continually emphasize that discomfort is to be embraced and that a changing social imaginary will call on us to set aside our individual or ethnocentric claims to preferences. Because there are numerous ways that cultural norms vary, relational leadership needs to be shaping leaders and the whole congregation to give time to new relationships that are more adequate for God's call on us. Even though some members will resist, and some churches experience complete sabotage, if leaders can shape a growing percentage of participants that are committed and increasingly skilled, then the barriers will be lessened.

Implemental leadership. Implemental leadership attends to creating, modifying, and working with activities and structures so that the Spirit's provisions of meanings and relationships are embodied in the life of the church. In the midst of activities, conversations and studies, leaders can learn about the convictions and experiences behind the church's structures and activities, including how organizational behaviors have led to positive or negative outcomes. This work sets the stage for modifying some practices and shaping new experiments.

During the worship service, after the opening music, the Sunday school teachers and the kids left the sanctuary for their own classes. Several parents discussed ways that worship could be more generationally inclusive, and Ramón asked this group to continue discussing their ideas. He also asked them to talk about what was most important in their memories of worship and to pay attention to anything that they thought was influenced by their cultures.

The work of leaders

- Note practices that are rooted in societal and cultural norms
- Encourage and protect voices that explore change
- Shape conversations by suggesting autobiographical resources
- Expand the perspectives of those in discussions about change

With the permission of the board, the exploratory group decided to try some experiments—some concerning cultural matters and others concerning the participation of children and youth. In order to provide time for ongoing creativity and evaluation, they spaced these experiments over a few months. This also gave them time to include others in the planning and leadership. Ramón suggested they check with Helen to see if she knew of someone at the school who was especially knowledgeable about relevant developmental issues that could help them. He also said that some of them may want to get a couple of high schoolers and make a Sunday morning trip to his previous church, which was primarily Latino with a growing number of Euro-Americans. They began some experiments with artwork, group interaction with Scripture after a short sermon, drama and music that engaged the diversity of worshipers.

The work of leaders

- Encourage experiments
- Connect intercultural initiatives with other topics needing attention
- Increase the number of leaders and connect them with each other

- Shape a community that learns from others
- Increase intergenerational partnerships

Sometimes implemental leadership works on the most complex and traditional church practices, like worship services or the governing structures. At other times implemental leadership focuses on simple or temporary activities—like scheduling some appointments or asking a group to read an article or visit another church.

In the work of Heifetz and Linsky, changes are classified as either technical or adaptive. A technical change (which requires technical leadership) is appropriate when goals, methods and skills are understood and available. Technical challenges may be difficult but are within the understanding and capacities of the group, or the group can easily obtain the knowledge and skills needed.[6] Church leaders need to be adept at technical challenges, and those skills need to be constantly increased and spread throughout the church. There are cultural differences concerning how we approach technical work—everything from decision making to timing to types of participation involve cultural patterns. Churches that are learning intercultural life will always be increasing their awareness of differences and their capacities to shape cooperative work. When adaptive challenges are engaged, those technical skills and the fruit of good technical work will shape an environment with more trust and confidence. But the adaptive challenge itself is one for which there are no roadmaps.[7]

An adaptive challenge is one that will require that the church move toward a future that it cannot see, become something different, learn things it does not know and innovate beyond the current imagination. As Ronald Heifetz asks, "Does making progress on this problem require changes in people's values, attitudes, or habits of behavior?" If so, the challenge is adaptive. A primary job of leadership is to identify adaptive challenges, to distinguish them from technical work and to shape the organization and its environment so that the approach, pace, feedback loops and constant learning are appropriate to the challenge. An adaptive situation cannot be met by incremental adjustments or improvements on current

---

[6]Heifetz and Linsky, *Leadership on the Line*, pp. 11-20.
[7]This explanation and table 10.1 are based on Ronald Heifetz, *Leadership Without Easy Answers* (Cambridge, Mass.: Belknap Press of Harvard University, 1994), pp. 73-88; and Heifetz and Linsky, *Leadership on the Line*, pp. 13-30.

Table 10.1 Technical Versus Adaptive Challenges

Technical Challenge	Adaptive Challenge
• Clear goals	• Murky future
• Known methods	• Unknown road
• Current knowledge	• New learning
• Available resources	• Resources not identifiable
• Familiar roles	• Unfamiliar roles
• Adequate competencies	• Competencies not developed
• Predictable and manageable change	• Unpredictable and uncontrollable change
• "We are who we need to be."	• "We need to become different."

practices. Adaptive leadership will help name such a challenge and shape the environment and resources so a new imaginary emerges and new practices are employed.

Although in this discussion we are explaining adaptive leadership in relationship to implemental leadership, it also has implications for interpretive and relational leadership. Two key activities for adaptive leadership have been noted—*get on the balcony* (something leaders need to do frequently) and *discern the adaptive challenge* (which comes from continual individual and corporate reflection).[8] Heifetz and Linsky note other essential leadership activities. Adaptive leadership must *manage the holding environment* by keeping other organizational activities going in a way that serves organizational viability while freeing attention and resources for the adaptive challenge.[9] This "holding environment" includes all of the usual structures, activities and relationships. Leaders may provide management either in the usual ways or by providing new approaches as adjustments are made. All organizations periodically face stress, but an adaptive challenge always signals the presence of increased external and internal pressures. Adaptive leaders *regulate stress levels.*[10] In informal conversations and at meetings, in supervising staff and volunteers, and in managing familiar activities and innovating experiments, leaders can increase organizational stress or lower it—and there are times for both. People and organizations need pressure to change—so leaders need to

---

[8]Heifetz and Linsky, *Leadership on the Line*, pp. 55-62.
[9]Ibid., pp. 102-7.
[10]Ibid., pp. 107-16.

decide when and where to increase the stress. In a multicultural environment a diverse leadership is needed to monitor and guide when adaptive stresses are experienced. Threats or challenges need to be named, new activities need to be tested, and people need to risk new responsibilities. But there are also times to reduce the stress by offering assurance, providing the voice of trusted persons, offering important information, or shaping activities or pacing that reduce the temperature. The capacities of the church are increased when leaders demonstrate their own abilities for taking the heat. In the midst of adaptive change there are always technical challenges—and good management of those technical tasks will reduce stress. Overall the organization's capacity for stress is increased when relationships are deepened and trust is increased.

Leaders shape the process when they *focus attention and deepen conversations*.[11] The attention of a church is shaped by stories, information and experiences. Ramón focused attention on worship by creating new conversations, giving some participants the permission to innovate, and creating opportunities for new experiences and learning. The complexities of both intergenerational and intercultural issues were named. The whole church's attention was engaged simply because experiments were obvious during Sunday morning gatherings. No doubt stressed increased when percussion instruments were available to kids and the normal 11 a.m. ending time became permeable. But stress was reduced when innovations were limited to a monthly worship service and even the experimental services had numerous familiar elements.

Adaptive challenges require that the organization become reconfigured as more participants actively innovate and assume leadership responsibilities. Those leading the process need to *give the work back to the people*, including the work of observing and interpreting the context and the challenges and the work of reinventing the organization's structures and practices.[12] Ramón did this with parents, youth and the board. In these actions he modeled another essential practice—*protect leadership voices from below*.[13] We believe God places gifts, perspectives, connections and imagination through-

---

[11]Heifetz and Linsky provide basic means for "interventions" that shape a group's work; ibid., pp. 134-39; see also pp. 154-60.

[12]Ibid., pp. 123-39.

[13]Ronald Heifetz and Donald Laurie, "The Work of Leadership," *Harvard Business Review* 75, no. 1 (1997): 129-30. This article is an excellent summary of Heifetz's *Leadership Without Easy Answers*.

out a church. Organizational history and habits often limit the creativity and energy that is available. Adaptive leaders invite and support the voices and experiments of those not previously empowered and then weave new avenues and structures suitable to the ongoing changes.

Leadership is increasingly dispersed in a healthy, adapting organization. This is not anarchy—there is an overall coherence as leaders work together in interpretive, relational and implemental activities. Another term for this is *plural leadership*, and in multicultural situations it is especially important. We have emphasized that practical theology requires the whole church to be shaped by praxis—the continual cycle of study/reflection and engagement/action. Leadership is about shaping the organizational environment so that the church as a whole, and various configurations of groups within the church, are learning how to discern the initiatives of the Holy Spirit in their midst and in their neighborhoods and are developing experiments and

Table 10.2 Leading Adaptive Change

Leading Adaptive Change
• Get on the balcony.
• Discern the adaptive challenge.
• Manage the holding environment.
• Regulate stress levels.
• Focus attention/deepen conversations.
• Give the work back to the people.
• Protect leadership voices coming from below.

Personal Reflection/Group Exercise: Experiences with Leadership

Reflect on your own experiences with leaders, then discuss your observations with others.

1. Recall a situation when you were especially appreciative of a leader—what factors mattered to you? What value did you attach to goals and successes? How much did you focus on how you were treated?

2. Reflect on situations in which the elements of the leadership triad were well done. Can you provide specific examples?

3. Reflect on your own leadership—any situation in which your contributions shaped the activities of others. What do you remember about your activities in relationship to the leadership triad?

practices that increase everyone's participation in God's grace. The three spheres of leadership activities—interpretive, relational, implemental—are always necessary and must cohere. The fabric of the church is torn when the integral connections among these leadership spheres are lost; the meanings (about what it means to be a church in mission in a location) must enliven the relationships (with mutual accountability, learning, trust, partnerships, love) so that the gospel is apparent in activities and structures. Many persons will formally and informally provide leadership as a church's faithfulness increases.

TRANSFORMING AN ORGANIZATION

Challenges can arise because a church's context has changed or because a church's commitments shift so that they are motivated to pay more attention to the diverse world of their context. In chapters two and three we emphasized a missional ecclesiology and noted some contextual elements that churches in the United States are facing. Alan Roxburgh, Fred Romanuk and M. Scott Boren explain the adaptive and technical processes for transforming a church. While traditional strategic planning is inadequate for this work, they demonstrate how leaders can shape the learning environment in a way that leads to new praxes in a church.[14] They assume that congregations are dealing with contexts that have been changed and that leaders need to develop new capacities to guide and motivate participants as they engage that environment. The same steps are relevant to a church that has existed in a diverse environment but is coming to a new commitment to engage that diversity missionally and in their own congregational makeup.

The phases of organizational transformation include awareness, understanding, evaluation, experiments and commitment.[15] The method of practical theology that we provided in chapter one can easily be paralleled with these phases. This process is not linear; rather, it features zigzags and loops. A church's *awareness* may begin as a neighborhood changes, as biblical passages are studied or when the Holy Spirit prompts some members. Church participants and leaders can choose denial or avoidance, but if

---

[14]Alan Roxburgh and M. Scott Boren, *Introducing the Missional Church* (Grand Rapids: Baker, 2009) pp. 123-96; and Alan Roxburgh and Fred Romanuk, *The Missional Leader* (San Francisco: Jossey-Bass), pp. 79-104. Theoretical background is adapted from the work of Everett Rogers, *The Diffusion of Innovation* (New York: Free Press, 2003); see esp. chaps. 1, 5, 7.

[15]Roxburgh and Boren, *Introducing the Missional Church*, p. 136

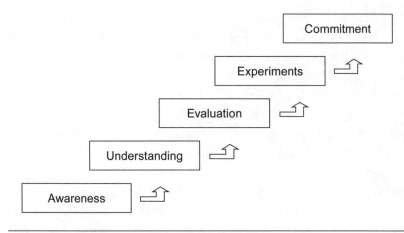

Figure 10.3 Stages of organizational transformation

missional transformation is to be realized, this awareness increases attentiveness—a more intentional focus of thinking, conversing and reflecting, whether the new situation is welcomed or not. Attentiveness and conversations lead toward *understanding*. This understanding needs to include a deeper thoughtfulness concerning the church and its environment. Many of our chapters provide perspectives and frameworks to help churches gain a deeper understanding about themselves and their neighbors.

When the youth reported to the board of Second Street Church concerning the demographics of the schools, they also talked about their own crosscultural friendships. The board was learning that the younger generation actually enjoyed numerous crosscultural friendships. Frank, the retired businessman, had recently told Ramón that many community businesses were changing. He was aware that the farmer's market on his lot now included more diversity of foods. Ramón asked him to see what he could learn, so he visited many of them and spoke with managers and owners about their work and their customers.

The work of leaders

- Make known crosscultural experiences among church members
- Encourage curiosity
- Engage neighbors in conversations about their work and lives

Tim, a high school junior who was gaining skills as an artist, had an idea about connecting these questions about ethnicity with worship and the sanctuary. He heard how Frank's observations got everyone talking about stores and cross-cultural acquaintances. So he met with Frank, and they hosted a Sunday luncheon in which they invite everyone to draw maps of any group of streets and blocks that they called their "neighborhood." They provided large sheets of paper, color markers, glue and magazines to cut up. Each map could include whatever the participant knew about schools, parks, community activities, businesses, friendships and families. The maps were displayed around the room, and everyone talked about what they created. Ramón then asked if the maps could be placed in the sanctuary for the next Sunday. Then Ramón preached from some stories about how Jesus and his followers had different kinds of encounters and conversations in various towns. The youth led a time a prayer for all these neighbors and neighborhoods. The creativity of the artwork and the specificity of the names of streets, parks and schools made concrete connections between their sanctuary and their community.[16]

The work of leaders

- Increase the number of persons thinking about the neighborhoods
- Use different media to encourage participation
- Connect conversations about the context with worship and liturgy

As awareness and understanding grow, leadership needs to provide opportunities for *evaluation* concerning the church's history and theology, their environment and situation, their challenges and opportunities. This evaluation focuses on reconsidering the church's identity and calling. Steps 2 through 4 of the practical theology method are important for this process. Because transformation is often about adaptive changes, the church will not benefit from grandiose strategic plans or quick fixes. That is why *experiments* are so important. The church's board and other groups of participants can turn their imaginations to basics—what does the gospel look like in neighborliness, in hospitality, in connecting with and serving the poor, in stepping outside their comfort zone into new situations? Experiments can be one-time actions or a series of events. These engagements

---

[16]This artistic approach to expression and conversations was actually designed and implemented by Leiko Yamamoto Pech, a liturgical and community artist.

Bible Study: Acts 6—An Experiment in Change

Change often begins when previously stifled voices gain a new hearing. We noted in the Bible study of Acts 2 (see p. 18) that there were numerous neighborhoods around Jerusalem composed of Hellenistic immigrants. For various cultural reasons many of these residents were elderly, and that is the background for Acts 6. This study will use the five steps of transformation to examine the passage. You will need to be analytical and imaginative as you engage this study.

Read Acts 6:1.

1. Obviously the Hellenist widows were aware of their own hunger. What would have kept others from knowing or responding? How might the awareness have spread?

2. What sociocultural factors and elements of Jesus' teachings were relevant to this situation as awareness led to understanding and evaluation?

Read Acts 6:2-4.

3. This awareness, understanding and evaluation eventually spread from some group of Hellenists to the ears of the Twelve. Their own understanding and awareness led to an experiment. Describe major elements of their approach and discuss what you believe was important as well as the basis for your views. (Note what the Twelve valued and discuss the power dynamics of the story.)

Read Acts 6:5-7.

4. Discuss the responses of community. Since this was mainly an experiment concerning implemental leadership, why was it important that the new procedures be announced so publicly?

Read Acts 6:8-10.

5. Compare the job description that the apostles gave to the group of Hellenist men with the work that Stephen actually did. How is this experiment transforming the church?

    Through the rest of chapters 6 and 7, Stephen preaches, faces accusations and is stoned to death. Depending on time allotted, read from these chapters and then focus on Acts 8:1-4

6. Discuss why the increasing persecution allowed the Twelve to stay in Jerusalem but the Hellenist believers scattered. What are some of the missional results of the experiment begun in chapter 6? What cultural factors play into this continuing story?

and actions will contribute to the ongoing discernment process as the church gains new capacities to attend to what God is doing and wants to do in and through the church. (Chapter eleven features practical ideas for leading change.)

Second Street Church followed their school connections and developed a partner-ship with a neighboring church for after-school mentoring and recreation for a primary school. The youth provided mentoring, and some retirees brought re-freshments. They realized that they also wanted to connect with the parents of the kids—so several adults got involved in order to initiate conversations and offer refreshments. They quickly learned which families lived near church families— providing opportunities for building relationships. Over a period of several months these conversations deepened crosscultural friendships, inspired ways for new partnerships to invest in the schools, and several new families were drawn into church life.

The work of leaders

- Shape opportunities for both side-by-side work and face-to-face con-versations
- Encourage more connections between families and households
- Partner with other churches
- Evaluate initiatives and discern new opportunities

As we noted in chapter two, an assumption of missional ecclesiology is that the needed insights, experiences and imagination are among the ordi-nary people of the church. Some of these experiments will lead to *commit-ments* that will reshape the church. Some commitments are to people and organizations; some are to activities and ways of life. If transformation is genuine, it goes to the being, habits and character of the church and its members.

STAYING THE COURSE

Church transformation is never smooth—experiments fail, people are of-fended, some of the most promising leaders get weary. In a society where monthly reports and quick fixes are expected, the complex and slower work of transformation will be discouraging for many. Developing intercultural life, in which cultural diversity is apparent internally and externally—in relationships, language, structures, activities, decision making and leadership—is never done. Challenges will always appear. Humans will hurt each other. Sin messes every initiative. Good ideas will lack resources. However, we believe that when churches are committed to gospel reconciliation, when we take risks that are rooted in God's call on us, then grace is adequate. When we hurt each other the gospel calls for truth and forgiveness and new faith. Discouragement can lead us to dependence on the graces God provides through worship, prayer, friends and the Holy Spirit's ministry. Mistakes and failures lead us to new learning, wisdom and innovation.

We have written several times that leadership is about shaping environments in which the everyday people of the church find that their own imaginations can be engaged by God's initiatives for them and their neighbors. That environment necessarily includes words and actions of encouragement, confession, vision, forgiveness, risk, lament and celebration. Leaders do not need to know the way—we just need the capacities to encourage and guide connections, to link Scripture and context, to engage neighbors and members, and to sanction questions and insights and innovations. The process cycles of practical theology and the five steps of transformation, when fully employed, will indicate resources and activities as the whole church adopts a deepening praxis of intercultural life.

At the Movies

In the activities of these protagonists, note elements of the leadership triad and the phases of transformation.

Bread and Roses (2000). Two Latina sisters working as janitors, one of whom is an illegal immigrant, are set on a collision course that mirrors the conflict between workers and management when they are caught up in a fight for the right to unionize.

Gandhi (1982). Biography of Mohandas Gandhi, the famed leader of the fight for Indian independence from the British through nonviolent protest.

Stand and Deliver (1988). A dedicated inner-city math teacher inspires his dropout-prone students to learn algebra and calculus using unconventional methods, and they do so well that they are accused of cheating.

11

PRACTICES FOR THE CALLING

Juan Francisco Martínez

A N ANALOGY THAT HAS BEEN VERY HELPFUL to me in understanding how to be effective in multicultural praxis is the "cultural tool kit."[1] Michael Emerson and Christian Smith use it in *Divided by Faith* as a way to describe why majority-culture and African American evangelicals find it so difficult to effectively relate to each other.[2] According to them a part of the problem is that majority-culture evangelicals do not have the proper tools to understand the dynamic of race relations in the United States. Because of this, they are unable to respond in ways that address the problem of structural racism.

The tool-kit analogy is useful in demonstrating that we need specific and varied knowledge and skills, and the ability and willingness to use them. If we only have hammers in our tool kit we tend to treat every intercultural issue as a nail. We need multiple strategies to effectively analyze and interpret intercultural relations. Of course, the tool-kit analogy can give the impression that intercultural issues are merely technical problems that can be solved if we use the proper tool in the correct way. The reality is much more complex. Effective leaders need competencies in technical understanding, analysis, and managing life and ministry in a changing environment. They need adaptive approaches, as described in chapter ten. But they also need to have a heart for others, knowing that even when

---

[1]Sociologist Ann Swidler advanced this phrase in "Culture in Action: Symbols and Strategies," *American Sociological Review* 51 (1986): 273-86.

[2]Michael Emerson and Christian Smith, *Divided by Faith: Evangelical Religion and the Problem of Race in America* (New York: Oxford University Press, 2000).

something requires a technical approach, attention to relationships cannot be omitted. Nonetheless, the complexities of the issues we face are such that the most important thing a leader can learn in response to our changing world is discernment linked with multiple practices.

Some of the practices we need to learn to use are obvious. For example, on most Sundays I attend an early morning Korean-language church service before going to my Latino congregation. Because I only understand a little Korean (I am studying the language), I often miss cultural clues. An important tool in intercultural church relations is the willingness to learn the language of the other and to value it in ministry. Though a person may never become an expert, a willingness to learn provides a bridge and an initial level of understanding.

But I also need to learn to how to "read" cultural patterns so that I can relate more effectively to my Korean sisters and brothers. As we have written, this includes attention to worldview, relational approaches and other specifics of Korean life and culture. I have to be proactive in taking the time to understand Korean culture and how it is being lived out in Los Angeles today.

I also need to use the same practices in my own Latino congregation. Even though outsiders might assume Latinos are culturally very similar, I need to be sensitive to the very real differences between a Mexican American and a Mexican immigrant, or between that Mexican immigrant and a young person whose parents were born in Chile. I preach regularly in a congregation that has this type of cultural variety, so I need strategies to communicate the gospel in a multicultural setting.

Throughout the book we have referred to issues, practices and attitudes that facilitate boundary crossing, the understanding of cultural differences and their implications, how to acknowledge the other, and an understanding of the polycentric identity of most U.S. ethnic minority people. We provided a practical theology model for pastors and other leaders to address the intercultural challenges of ministry in the United States today. We also described many of the basic cultural differences that make effective intercultural relations so complex. Every chapter also included activities, Bible studies and reflections that you can use in your church or other ministry setting to build intercultural understanding.

In this last chapter we want to provide practices that will help you effectively address the types of issues we have been describing throughout the book. We have learned all of them from others and have already referenced some of them. So this final chapter will summarize, expand and add to practical approaches we have already provided. This focus on implemental leadership is intended to deepen a church's interpretive and relational capacities for intercultural life.

Bible Study: Revelation 7:9-10— Walking in the Light of God's Future

[9]After this I looked, and there was a great multitude that no one could count, from every nation, from all tribes and peoples and languages, standing before the throne and before the Lamb, robed in white, with palm branches in their hands. [10]They cried out in a loud voice, saying, "Salvation belongs to our God who is seated on the throne, and to the Lamb!"

The book of Revelation constantly juxtaposes scenes from earth with scenes from God's heaven—with the assumption that these visions do not present a dualistic worldview but invite us to see their dynamic relationship. Even as the situation becomes more difficult and persecution is more severe on earth, Christians are invited to continue believing in God's future through scenes from God's perspective. The throne vision of Revelation 7:9-10 is particularly important for what we have been addressing in this book. The seer describes a worship scene with all of the diversity of his known world united around worship of the Lamb. He is very clear in using all of the terms at his disposal to emphasize that all human diversity is present. This is not a melting pot but humans who are very different. What unites them is not uniformity but a common vision and purpose.

1. How do we envision what God is doing in the world in relation to human diversity? How does this perspective affect what I want the church to look like?

2. How does my church reflect or not reflect Revelation 7:9-10? Why?

3. How does this vision affect my understanding of what intercultural church life should look like?

While individuals can work with these practices, we believe they will be most effective when used within an interpretive community, a community of meaning. Pastors and church leaders need to shape communities of meaning (i.e., churches) but also need to be shaped by them in the process of interacting together. It is within congregational life and intercongregational life that these practices will be most effective, as communities of faith use them for praxis and culture creation.

Sharing Cultural Narratives

Testimonies have always been an important part of my Latino Protestant church tradition. People share conversion stories, how God has responded to their prayer requests and other ways they have seen God present in their lives. These testimonies affirm the faith and commitments of those who are following Christ together.

But narratives, stories and testimonies are also very important in developing a common story in the life of any local church. Churches have their own stories and histories. Many older churches were started by a specific ethnic community and tell their history in light of that community's experiences. But as people from other ethnicities and experiences come into the life of the church their stories also need to be incorporated so that the story becomes broader.

We need to listen to other's narratives because these "are the cultural framework in which individuals interpret their social situations, imagine themselves in other situations, and make choices about who they want to be and how to behave."[3] By inviting church members to tell their cultural narratives and to listen to those of others we expand our understanding of each other and of how we see ourselves in the world. Learning how to tell my own cultural story and how to listen to others' narratives gives a very important message within the life a church. On the one hand it makes me think about how I "imagine myself." But it also says that all members are important in a congregation's broader story.

To share my cultural story is to take time to see how I have been formed and informed by my background. We are all children of specific families, cultures and experiences. By taking the time to develop and tell my own

---

[3]Robert Wuthnow, *American Mythos: Why Our Best Efforts to Be a Better Nation Fall Short* (Princeton, N.J.: Princeton University Press, 2006), p. 59.

story I have the opportunity to see how my past shapes who I am today, in good and bad ways. It is an invitation to affirm my identity, but also to understand how my identity has been formed, and how I use my past to explain who I am in the world.

In our congregation we have multinational mission festivals every year. This is a great place for people from different countries to talk about their country of origin and about how they came to the United States. We always "celebrate" all of the national holidays of the countries represented in our congregation, another excellent place for personal storytelling. New members' classes are also an important time for people to narrate their autobiographies, including their walk with God and their ethnic and cultural roots. This should include a recognition that God was walking with them even before they had an encounter with the gospel.

Rereading U.S. History

Many people feel excluded from the life of a church because their story never becomes a part of the larger story of the church. But this is part of a larger problem, because churches are part of a society and a country that also tells its own story in ways that can exclude people. The official national narrative tells us who is considered important to the national identity and who the heroes and villains are. This official narrative indicates how the presence and activities of each ethnic group is described and who makes those determinations. The reason for this is that history is never just about what happened in the past—it always includes interpretation. The person or persons telling the history have to decide which events to include, which to exclude and how to define the importance of events within the larger narrative.

For example, U.S. history usually begins with the English colonies in Jamestown and Plymouth and follows the story of English immigrants who founded the country and defined its institutions. Immigrants from Europe are seen as people who wanted to break from a European past and build a new future as Americans. Western migration opened new opportunities in the vast frontier to expand this great nation blessed by God. We are from all over the world, but together we choose to be Americans and work together toward the common good of our country. We bring our own previous national identities to this country and join together, leaving behind previous identities to become "American."

This "official" story presents U.S. history largely as the story of European migration through the eastern seaboard. The heroes and heroines of this story are those whose story "fits" within this narrative. They are presented as crucial players in forming and shaping this country. Those who do not come from this background are either ignored, maligned or have their stories told only in light of the "official" story. The history of Native peoples, African slaves, pre-Jamestown European immigrants from Spain (sometimes via Mexico) and France, plus other southern European, Latin American or Asian immigrants might be included, but principally as a sideline to the principal narrative.

But the U.S. narrative looks very different if told from the perspectives of the minority peoples of this country. A crucial practice in intercultural relations in the life of the church is to understand and help others understand the history of the United States from a broader perspective. If people are invisible in the "official" national narrative, it is easier for them to be invisible in the life of a local church. It is important to tell the European narrative, but also the narratives of those who have been traditionally excluded from the U.S. story. By rereading the American story and including the perspective of ethnic minorities we are bringing these peoples into the larger U.S. narrative. Doing this both expands and changes the story. It also obligates us to reinterpret its meaning and to think differently about what the future might look like. It creates "a larger memory" upon which to build toward a future in which all can be included.[4]

Today there are many good movies (including documentaries) that tell the U.S. story from the perspective of minority peoples. By watching such movies and having people from those cultural and ethnic backgrounds "interpret" the stories, a church can provide a voice for those traditionally excluded. Churches can also take field trips to cultural landmarks that can serve as places for extended reflection. For example, the Catholic missions of colonial California invite us to understand the native peoples who are tied to them to this day, to ask questions about Spanish colonial evangelization methods, and to consider how native peoples and Mexicans lost their lands after 1848.[5]

---

[4]This idea from comes Ronald Takaki, *A Larger Memory: A History of Our Diversity, With Voices* (Boston: Little, Brown, 1998).
[5]There are a number of good books that can help develop discussions on alternative readings of

REREADING SCRIPTURE FROM
A MULTICULTURAL PERSPECTIVE

Not only do we need to retell our national story, but we also need to reread the Bible together. Christians confess that the Bible has a transcultural message. But it was written in concrete cultural settings, and we read it from within our own cultural reality. An important task in the process of multicultural church ministry is to read and study the Bible, taking into account both the biblical social context and our own context today. The hermeneutical task applies both to the Bible and to the community reading and interpreting it.

Because we often read the Bible as an ahistorical document, we ignore the historical and social location of the actors or the writers and miss much of the message. Sometimes we also assume that we can find a single "objective" understanding that stands on its own, independent of the social location of the interpreter. In the United States this has usually meant that Eurocentric or U.S.-centric, male interpretations of Scripture were considered normative, without recognizing how readers and their specific contexts affected their interpretation of Scripture.

Throughout the book, we have invited you to reread specific biblical passages in light of the intercultural questions we have been asking. This process has invited you to see the specific biblical narrative differently. But it is also an invitation to recognize that our "social location" (chap. 6) and perceptions (chap. 8) influence what we see in the Bible and what we consider important from the biblical text. Biblical scholars can help us take the biblical context more seriously. But in Bible studies in intercultural contexts we need to make sure that minority voices are given a space. It is not that their interpretation will be the most accurate but that the community of believers needs all the voices of the church if it is to effectively hear the Word of the Lord for today.

Learning to reread the Bible will feel jarring for some, particularly those

---

the history of the United States. Ronald Takaki's books *A Different Mirror* and *A Larger Memory*, which have been mentioned previously, are two good places to begin. Scholastic Books has also published the "Dear America" and the "I Am America" series, which are very good books for children and intergenerational groups. Another important, though more complex, discussion can be based on books, often hard to find, on the specific religious histories of different ethnic groups in the United States. How have the groups reflected the gospel? How have they been far from the ideal of the gospel?

who are used to a specific reading of Scripture that fits their social and cultural location. But as communities of faith reread the Bible with an intercultural sensitivity, they encounter a new richness in Scripture as its formative role is expanded in a multicultural community of believers. The Spirit speaks anew to a new generation that seeks to be faithful to the biblical message.

As we have noted throughout the book, this way of reading Scripture is crucial because, on the one hand, God is at work in all cultures, so it is possible to find understandings and practices in any culture that draw us toward God. But all cultures are also distorted by sin, so the gospel constantly needs to challenge those practices that reflect fallenness instead of God's grace. Paul Hiebert uses the term *critical contextualization* to describe this process by which one seeks to incarnate the gospel in another cultural setting without falling into syncretism or assuming that our own cultural framework accurately reflects the gospel. This tool both invites me to see how the gospel is distorted by my own culture and how to understand the culture of the other so that the gospel is good news for both.[6]

The pulpit is a crucial place for this culturally intelligent reading of Scripture to be modeled. In *Preaching to Every Pew: Cross-Cultural Strategies*, authors James Nieman and Thomas Rogers mention ethnicity as one of the four types of differences common in many churches that need to be taken into account when we are publicly proclaiming God's Word. The other three are class differences, diversity in belief systems (even among people of similar theological formations) and a general sense of displacement (not only among immigrants). They provide a series of concrete suggestions under each of these categories. Preaching that uses communication styles and illustrations from the various cultural experiences of the audience will both connect the message with the people and also connect the people with each other as they learn to value the experiences of the other. That is how a church can be a sign of God's future and a witness to God's mission in the world.[7]

HOSPITALITY TO SHALOM

Elizabeth Conde-Frazier presents a concrete process within which to

---

[6]Paul Hiebert, *Anthropological Insights for Missionaries* (Grand Rapids: Baker, 1985).
[7]James R. Nieman and Thomas G. Rogers, *Preaching to Every Pew: Cross-Cultural Strategies* (Minneapolis: Fortress, 2001), esp. pp. 147-53.

frame all of the practices mentioned in this chapter and throughout the book. In "From Hospitality to Shalom," she presents a spirituality for multicultural living.[8] The goal is to start at biblical hospitality and move through encounter, compassion, passion and finally to arrive at biblical shalom. As people who take seriously the implications of biblical hospitality we are called to new levels of commitment to the other, and these steps lead to other commitments and practices. This journey of conversion leads us to a situation in which we begin to approximate God's shalom in our intercultural relations.

Creating specific opportunities for hospitality in multiple directions creates the opportunity for encounter. In many cultural settings, common meals or shared meals in homes will be a great way to start. This shared hospitality can be linked to telling cultural autobiographies or watching movies together. By making sure that these activities happen across cultural lines, such activities can create spaces for encounter to begin. This can be a place for sharing stories, family pictures, cultural symbols and making the time for people to interpret them to others.

Recognizing the importance of this process helps us get beyond symbolic ethnicity and symbolic cultural interaction. When we only focus on the external products of a culture, such as food or music, "we give lip service to diversity, but when it come down to it, cultural differences amount to cigar-store Indians and made-in-China menorahs." We enjoy the experience, but we can never get to the "sustained inter-ethnic dialogue that pluralism requires." Going from hospitality to shalom requires deep personal interaction that can challenge the contradictions of our underlying cultural assumptions about the other.[9] In this process we can learn from our brothers and sisters and grow in relationship to each other.

Life Together: Worship, Prayer and Planning

Our corporate life needs to get beyond symbolic ethnicity through how we worship, pray and study the Bible together. At the beginning of the book we wrote about how our assumptions of what the United States "should"

---

[8]Elizabeth Conde-Frazier, "From Hospitality to Shalom," in *A Many Colored Kingdom: Multicultural Dynamics for Spiritual Formation*, ed. Elizabeth Conde-Frazier, S. Steve Kang and Gary Parrett (Grand Rapids: Baker, 2004).

[9]Wuthnow, *American Mythos*, pp. 183-84, 220.

look like will tend to influence what we think churches should look like. Some churches seek to attract people from different cultural backgrounds but then expect them all to assimilate into the church's culture. Others practice forms of symbolic ethnicity by including some songs or musical instruments that reflect the diversity of the community. The challenge is to get beyond these models toward a common life that reflects a cultural partnership where all the cultural communities represented become a part of the planning and the decision-making process of the congregation.

C. Michael Hawn draws on the "Nairobi Statement on Worship and Culture" of the Lutheran World Federation to invite us to develop worship styles that are transcultural, contextual, countercultural and crosscultural. In his book *One Bread, One Body: Exploring Cultural Diversity in Worship*, Hawn studies four United Methodist churches that are trying to be culturally conscious in worship, then he develops a series of steps that churches can take to develop cultural partnerships in worship. The process starts with a culturally diverse informed leadership willing to develop liturgy and worship spaces that reflect the diversity of the congregation. Their experiments may begin with symbolic ethnicity, but they work to include the deeper interpretative framing so that corporate worship moves from hospitality to shalom.[10]

This is particularly important in decision making. Most churches use processes that reflect the cultural bias of their leaders. Churches can begin breaking out of that tendency by consciously changing the process. For example, the practical theology spiral presented in the first chapter can serve as a model for decision making by repeating the cycle until all voices are incorporated before going forward. The congregation can also allow for experiments (chap. 10) that provide spaces for various cultural expressions.

Decision-making meetings can also be broken up into small groups, sometimes intentionally monocultural and sometimes intentionally multicultural, to provide various venues for the different cultural communication models. Such practices can help ensure that those from the dominant culture, who best understand the process, do not end up framing and dominating decision making.

---

[10]See C. Michael Hawn, *One Bread, One Body: Exploring Cultural Diversity in Worship* (Herndon, Va.: Alban Institute, 2003). Several of Eric Law's books on multicultural communities also include worship and Bible study activities that facilitate intercultural church life.

MODELS OF BEING CHURCH IN A MULTICULTURAL SETTING

It is not sufficient to say that churches need to be different in a multicultural environment. There are many different ways to form Christian communities in the midst of ethnic and cultural diversity. The various models present opportunities and also challenges in the process of seeking to be faithful to the gospel. We invite you to look at what others are already doing around the United States. Our prayer is that this will stimulate your thinking so that you can begin to imagine new ways of being church together.

Earlier in the book we referenced Manuel Ortiz's *One New People*, in which he outlines two basic types of multicultural congregations: multicongregational churches and multiethnic single congregational models.[11] Under these basic types he describes three multicongregational models: renting, celebration and integrative. He also recognizes the difficulty of clearly defining what constitutes a "real" multiethnic congregation. Some churches have diversity in the audience but have a dominant cultural model for worship and decision making, while others consciously attempt to reflect diversity in leadership, public worship and decision-making processes. Each model addresses some aspects of interethnic relations and raises other questions, which may be theological or sociological. It is also true that multicongregational integrative models or consciously diverse multiethnic congregations are the most difficult to develop and maintain. By taking various models into account we have the opportunity to address the myriad opportunities and challenges of being church in a multicultural setting. Mark and I participate in different types of intercultural churches and recognize that each model offers opportunities and limitations in living out effective intercultural life. In the midst of globalized and transnational populations it is likely that each of these models will continue to be used in the United States in the foreseeable future.

But we also need a new generation of leaders who will be able to push out beyond the "accepted" models and think about church communities in new ways. Given the reality of globalization we can anticipate more intercultural interaction, not less, in the future. We need new models of church that can address the increasingly multilingual, transnational, network-

---

[11]Manuel Ortiz, *One New People: Models for Developing a Multiethnic Church* (Downers Grove, Ill.: InterVarsity Press, 1996).

based reality of many people. These churches will need to be "glocal" (global and local), recognizing both the need to minister to their geophysical parish and to the network relationships of people that cross national boundaries. The distinction between mission as something done beyond national borders and ministry done in one's own neighborhood and country needs to disappear as churches learn to minister outside of the categories that congregations have taken for granted for so long.[12]

That new generation will lead by interpreting these new realities, connecting the diverse peoples that are now living near each other, and organizing them to work together toward what God is doing in the world

---

Personal Reflection/Group Exercise:
Experiments in Intercultural Life

In this last exercise we are including a series of reflection questions that can help us think about how to use some of the tools presented in this chapter.

1. In the introduction you read both Mark and Juan's cultural autobiographies. What do you learn about how each imagines himself in U.S. society? What does your own autobiography tell you about how you see yourself in U.S. society?

2. Which people in your church tend to be excluded from the "official" narrative of the United States? How does that affect their place in the life of your church?

3. What would be the best space for people to share their cultural narratives in your church? What could be an initial experiment in your church?

4. What are the most promising ways that your church can create experiments that bring people together across generational lines—for books or movies or personal stories?

5. What other steps are a priority for you regarding intercultural life in your church and in other social contexts?

---

[12]See Juan Francisco Martínez, *Walk with the People: Latino Ministry in the United States* (Nashville: Abingdon, 2008), for potential models that arise from within the transnational Latino/a community. Oscar García-Johnson's book *The Mestizo/a Community of the Spirit: A Postmodern Latino/a Ecclesiology* (Eugene, Ore.: Pickwick, 2008), provides a solid theological framing for these new ways of thinking about the church and its mission.

(leadership triad). By using the practical theology cycle in this process these leaders and congregations will be able to hear God's Spirit speaking in new ways and inviting them to serve in new ways for the glory of God and for the service of others in the name of Christ.

The throne vision in Revelation 7:9-10 provides us with a glimpse of where God is guiding our world. Since this is the direction we have been pointing to throughout the book, we end here. May God's Spirit guide us to making this vision a reality.

> After this I looked, and there was a great multitude that no one could count, from every nation, from all tribes and peoples and languages, standing before the throne and before the Lamb, robed in white, with palm branches in their hands. They cried out in a loud voice, saying, "Salvation belongs to our God who is seated on the throne, and to the Lamb!"

For Further Reading

Conde-Frazier, Elizabeth, S. Steve Kang and Gary Parrett. *A Many Colored Kingdom: Multicultural Dynamics for Spiritual Formation*. Grand Rapids: Baker, 2004.

Hawn, C. Michael. *One Bread, One Body Exploring Cultural Diversity in Worship*. Herndon, Va.: Alban Institute, 2003.

Hiebert, Paul. *Anthropological Insights for Missionaries*. Grand Rapids: Baker, 1985.

Law, Eric. *The Bush Was Blazing But Not Consumed*. Atlanta: Chalice Press, 1996.

Nieman, James, and Thomas Rogers. *Preaching to Every Pew: Cross-Cultural Strategies*. Minneapolis: Fortress, 2001.

Ortíz, Manuel. *One New People: Models for Developing a Multiethnic Church*. Downers Grove, Ill.: InterVarsity Press, 1996.

APPENDIX

THEOLOGICAL RESOURCES

IN THE PRACTICAL THEOLOGY CYCLE, churches work with the theological resources in their own ecclesial heritage and with other theological writings relevant to their topic. There is no systematic way to create a comprehensive repertoire of theology—but we can prompt and fund this work by providing a collection of statements from contemporary writers. We are not claiming that any statement is a full exposition, but we do believe each writer is addressing an important aspect of these topics. In chapter one, we stated that theology is always contextual, and that is true of these writers. We have noted their ethnic heritages to draw attention to this factor, and we have selected writers who were addressing the U.S. context during the last three decades.

THEOLOGY

"There are no neutral starting points from which to engage in the work of theology. . . . Christian theology is an ongoing, second-order, contextual discipline that engages in the task of critical and constructive reflection on the beliefs and practices of the Christian church for the purpose of assisting the community of Christ's followers in their missional vocation to live as the people of God in the particular social-historical context in which they are situated."

John Franke (Euro-American—German), *The Character of Theology* (Grand Rapids: Baker, 2005), p. 44.

"The single most critical challenge of Hispanic American theology is to find the courage and discernment to make God, Jesus Christ, the reign of God, salvation, and so forth, not just interesting topics of philosophical reflection, but most urgently issues of life and death. Hispanic theology must present a word of hope and life in the face of the death-dealing powers and principalities that daily assault humankind."

Loida Martell-Otero (Latina—Puerto Rican), in *Teología en Conjunto*, ed. José David Rodríquez and Loida Martell-Otero (Louisville: Westminster John Knox, 1997), p. 157.

"Real engagement among theologies and theologians would mean that a multiplicity of methods would be examined, that different social locations would be analyzed, and that the theological praxis of different communities of struggle would become intrinsic to theological education. Engagement among different theologies would prevent us from falling into total relativity and individualism since all engagement is, in a sense, a calling to accountability."

Ada María Isasi-Díaz (Latina—Cuban), in Ada Isasi-Díaz and Fernando Segovia, *Hispanic/Latino Theology* (Minneapolis: Augsburg Fortress, 1996), p. 373.

"How is this new perspective formed? What are the theological sources? Latinas take into account people's cultural and historical experiences. This involves practices of faith, reflections, symbols, rites, music, art, *pathos* and oral story, in other words, a testimony. The theological epistemology includes the interpretation of these practices in order to bring the knowledge of the faith. Revelation is fundamental for our conversation about the knowledge of God by faith. This does not only communicate a *corpus* of knowledge, but the self-revelation of God within history, which has its climax in Jesus of Nazareth. This understanding about the revelation implies the combination of a cognitive knowledge of God jointly to a personal relation of God with humanity."

Elizabeth Conde-Frazier (Latina—Puerto Rican), in Jorge Maldonado and Juan Martínez, *Vivir y Servir* (Clarence, N.Y.: Kairos, 2007), pp. 147-48.

God

"God's character is not simply to be admired. It is also to be copied. Therefore, immediately after God is described as partial to strangers, the believers are exhorted: 'You shall also love the stranger, for you were strangers in the land of Egypt' (Deut 10:19). Justice and benevolence were always to be extended to the newcomers, because all Hebrews were once, and still were, newcomers: 'You shall not deprive a resident alien or an orphan of justice. . . . Remember that you were a slave in Egypt' (Deut 24:17-18)."

Aída Besançon Spencer (Latina—Dominican), in Aída Besançon Spencer and William David Spencer, *The Global God* (Grand Rapids: Baker, 1998), pp. 98-99.

"The traditional term used to express the loving presence of God is 'immanence.' For African-American theologians God's immanence refers to the fact that God is present in the experience of black people. Unless God is truly present in the lives and struggles of people, then the whole notion of an efficacious God is threatened with irrelevance. . . . Immanence, moreover, means that God suffers with suffering humanity, at the side of those seeking freedom and liberation when possible, and those seeking succor and survival when necessary."

James Evans (African American), *We Have Been Believers* (Minneapolis: Augsburg Fortress, 1992), p. 71.

CREATION AND THE IMAGE OF GOD

"Humanity was made in the image of God. While our Western individualism will focus our attention of the personal reflection of the *imago Dei* in the individual, we need to see the image of God expressed as a corporate reflection. . . . The cultural mandate culminates in the image of a multicultural gathering of believers in Revelation 7:9, . . . [which] speaks of a multicultural future for the church, a gathering together of various cultures for the worship of God. . . . As individuals and people created in the image of God and as people who have been given a cultural mandate, we have the capacity, and even an obligation, to bring our cultural expression of faith to the mosaic that culminates in Revelation 7."

Soong-Chan Rah (Korean American), *The Next Evangelicalism* (Downers Grove, Ill.: InterVarsity Press, 2009), pp. 133-34.

SIN

"Sin—disobedience to God—creates divisions, separations, alienations, polarizations, and fragmentations. Sin splits us up into conflicting camps and plants hostility in our hearts. Sin breeds fear, discrimination, bitterness, and illogical, irrational prejudices. All of these spin-offs of sin hinder reconciliation and solidarity. Sin tears up, disrupts, disconnects, and puts us at odds with one another."

Samuel George Hines (African American—Jamaican), in Samuel George Hines and Curtiss Paul DeYoung, *Beyond Rhetoric* (Valley Forge, Penn.: Judson Press, 2000), p. 26.

COVENANT

"The breaking of treaties, or covenants, has caused a huge chasm of distrust and great animosity in the hearts of Native people toward Whites. The U.S. government broke more than 98 percent of all the hundreds of treaties—signed and ratified by Congress—made with the sovereign First Nations of North America. . . . The sin of covenant breaking is one of the conditions to which God relinquishes His people because of their rejection of who He is: . . . "They are gossips, slanderers, God-haters, insolent, arrogant and boastful; . . . they are senseless, faithless, heartless, ruthless . . .' (Rom 1:29-31, *NIV*). 'Faithless' in this passage is translated from the Greek *asunthetos*, meaning 'not agreed' or 'treacherous to compacts.' In the *King James Version* this word is translated 'covenant breakers.' All true believes are in covenant with God through Jesus Christ and the New Covenant. They are also in covenant relationships with each other. Our Christian covenant contains some good tools for us to use for walking in unity and breaking down barriers and walls between brethren. . . . From His first covenant with Adam, all God's covenants have revealed and expressed His desire and intention to have loving relationships with people. I believe a primary influence, emphasis and focus of our covenant in Christ should be its power to produce unity and oneness among His people. . . . Making and keeping covenants reveal many aspects of the nature of our Creator. Our heavenly Father makes, keeps, initiates and enables covenant; therefore, as His people, so should we."

Richard Twiss (Native American—Rosebud Lakota/Sioux), *One Church, Many Tribes* (Ventura, Calif.: Regal, 2000), pp. 177-79.

TRINITY

"The relationships within the Trinity require a differentiation of persons.

. . . They share in the divine nature, and yet the Persons have their own uniqueness also. . . . The unity of the Trinity coexists with and requires diversity. The church is to reflect the diversity found in the Trinity. . . . By looking at the nature of the Trinity, we are able to more clearly understand the nature of the church. We must see relationality, presence, equality, non-domination, unity, and differentiation in the nature of the church if the church is to correspond to the Trinity."

Robert Muthiah (Asian American—Malaysian, German, Scottish), *The Priesthood of All Believers in the Twenty-First Century* (Eugene, Ore.: Pickwick, 2009), p. 68.

SPIRIT

"The Spirit as the giver of faith, hope, and love makes it possible for us not only to overcome the oppressive forces that seek to dehumanize us, the Spirit makes it possible for us to liberate our oppressor because we can overcome the sinful tendency to oppress others."

Loida Martell-Otero (Latina—Puerto Rican), in *Teología en Conjunto*, ed. José David Rodríquez and Loida Martell-Otero (Louisville: Westminster John Knox, 1997), p. 63.

"The actual appearances of the Spirit in Scriptures show up primarily in relation to *specific contexts* and *particular communities* of faith. It is important to attend to the actual working of the Spirit within these contexts and among these communities in order to understand the Spirit's ministry. The practices of the Spirit that are evident provide the raw material for coming to a deeper understanding of the ministry of the Spirit. This approach . . . takes seriously what is going on within the life of a faith community within a particular context."

Craig Van Gelder (Euro-American—Dutch, German), *The Ministry of the Missional Church* (Grand Rapids: Baker, 2007), p. 25.

INCARNATION

"Diametrically opposed to the characteristics of mobility, and a spiritual numbness and apathy arising from mobility, are the characteristics of the body of Christ. Instead of upward mobility, there is the doctrine of the incarnation. Instead of a seeking of comfort through geographic and technological mobility, there is Jesus' willingness to suffer and die on the cross.

Mobility may be a high value in our contemporary culture, but the value of the kingdom of God and the example of Jesus Christ is the incarnation. As Christ chose to dwell among people and live in the flesh with all its limitations, the doctrine of incarnation would demand that the body of Christ (his church) would dwell among those enduring suffering."

Soong-Chan Rah (Korean American), *The Next Evangelicalism* (Downers Grove, Ill.: InterVarsity Press, 2009), pp. 151-52.

CROSS

"Jesus' death on a cross is the paradigm for faithfulness to God in this world. The community expresses and experiences the presence of the kingdom of God by participating in 'the *koinonia* of his sufferings' (Phil 3:10). Jesus' death is consistently interpreted in he New Testament as an act of self-giving love, and the community is consistently called to take up the cross and follow in the way that his death defines."

Richard Hays (Euro-American—Scottish, English, Dutch), *The Moral Vision of the New Testament* (San Francisco: HarperSanFrancisco, 1996), p. 197.

"Within the pages of the New Testament, the saving significance of the death of Jesus is represented chiefly (though not exclusively) via five constellations of images. These are each borrowed from significant spheres of public life in ancient Palestine and the larger Greco-Roman world: the court of law (e.g., justification), commercial dealings (e.g., redemption), personal relationships (whether among individuals or groups—e.g., reconciliation), worship (e.g., sacrifice), and the battleground (e.g., triumph over evil). . . . [These] views of the atonement as set forth by the various New Testament writings are the product of mission mindedness, of working to articulate the nature of the faith in terms that made sense to persons seeking to live in missionary outposts in the ancient world. The significance of Jesus' death 'for us' can never be exhausted or captured, so early theologians searched the conceptual encyclopedia of their day in order to communicate in ever-widening circles the nature of God's good news in Christ. Such a range of metaphors was useful not only in proclaiming the meaning of the cross to potential Christians but was also serviceable in the resulting archipelago of local Christian communities. . . . If we would follow the path of the New Testament writers, the metaphors we deploy would be at home, but never too comfortable, in our settings. Those writers sought, and we seek not only to be understood by but also to shape people and social systems around us."

Joel Green (Euro-American—English, French) and **Mark Baker** (Euro-American— German, Irish, English, Dutch), *Recovering the Scandal of the Cross* (Downers Grove, Ill.: InterVarsity Press, 2000), pp. 97, 114-15.

"The death of Jesus must be understood first and foremost as the result of a conflict between the historical Jesus and the powerful elite of his day. Jesus and the Jewish leaders met in conflict primarily over their views of God. In other words, the *historical* conflict that led to Jesus' death was precipitated by a *theological* conflict. . . . However, first-century Palestine did not permit the bifurcation of theology and politics. Therefore, although theology lay at the base of the conflict, politics was its medium. Jesus was brought to trial initially for blasphemy, a theological crime, but he was convicted as king of the Jews, a political charge. From the standpoint of the leaders, Jesus' death was necessary because he simultaneously undermined their religiopolitical leadership and conscientized the poor to resist oppression."

Priscilla Pope-Levison (Euro-American—German, Swedish) and **John Levison** (Euro-American—Italian, English), *Jesus in Global Contexts* (Louisville: Westminster John Knox, 1992), pp. 169-70.

RESURRECTION

"Despite the discontinuity between the spheres of the historical and risen Jesus, it is the same person, with the same opposition to oppressive ideologies and institutions, who lives beyond the grave. In three respects, the resurrection continues rather than concludes the relationship between Jesus and justice. First, the resurrection *validates* the life and death of Jesus. . . . Second, the resurrection gives the words and deeds of Jesus *universal* validity. . . . Third, the resurrection sets in motion an inexorable movement toward final liberation and reconciliation because it anticipates *within history* the future reign of God."

Priscilla Pope-Levison (Euro-American—German, Swedish) and **John Levison** (Euro-American—Italian, English), *Jesus in Global Contexts* (Louisville: Westminster John Knox, 1992), p. 174.

ESCHATOLOGY AND THE REIGN OF GOD

"To participate in the Reign of God means to participate in God's rule. It is to take seriously God's call as a church to be a community of the Spirit *in* the world and a community of the Spirit *for* the world. This participation implies there is no area of life where the rule of God cannot be exercised."

Eldin Villafañe (Latino—Puerto Rican), *The Liberating Spirit* (Grand Rapids: Eerdmans, 1993), p. 196.

"The church is to be a sign of God's eschatological reconciliation of the world, and therefore a community in which 'there is no longer Jew or Greek, there is no longer slave or free, there is no longer male and female; for all of you are one in Christ Jesus' (Gal 3:28). Thus the church's unity at table across ethnic boundaries is an outward and visible sign of the breaking down of these barriers, a prefiguration of the eschatological banquet of the people of God."

Richard Hays (Euro-American—Scottish, English, Dutch), *The Moral Vision of the New Testament* (San Francisco: Harper SanFrancisco, 1996), p. 440.

"What, then, can the life of the baptized community be but a sharing in the eschatological freedom of the risen Lord? Hence the New Testament language that describes the situation of the baptized displays a daring intensity and exaltation. . . . In three Pauline Epistles, passages appear linking baptism with the breakdown in Christ of the classic social and natural barriers that separate Greeks from Jews, slaves from free men, and males from females—all the baptized are one (or one body) in Christ. . . . This was a new era in time, inaugurated by Jesus' resurrection, in which the ordinary distinctions of creation (male-female) and of society (Greek-Jew; slave-free) were superseded because unity in the body of Christ took their place."

James McClendon (Euro-American—Scottish), *Ethics: Systematic Theology* (Nashville: Abingdon, 2002), p. 257.

"The astonishing claims made about the church in the Gospel of Mathew: 'You are the salt of the earth. . . . You are the light of the world' (5:13-14) are not due to the church's wisdom, piety, or goodness but to its redemptive relationship with Jesus Christ. A community that has died and risen with Christ is freed from the desire to secure and protect its own life and well-being. The confidence to challenge the established way of the world is due to the belief that Jesus has made a difference: in him God's saving future has invaded the present. Through his words and actions, the promised kingdom has been inaugurated. God's liberating and invigorating new social order has begun. The calling of the church is to be a real, visible, tangible, capable of being experienced—though not yet perfected—actualization of the reign of God in the world."

Inagrace T. Dietterich (Euro-American—English, German), in James V. Brownson et al., *StormFront: The Good News of God* (Grand Rapids: Eerdmans, 2003), pp. 110-11.

PENTECOST

"The church, though Jewish by origin and context, transforms at Pentecost into a polyphonic-multiracial cultural community. The Pentecost is the *formative biblical narrative* revealing how the Spirit intersected a cultural milieu, respecting, embracing, and affirming its various and multiple stories and identities. Such a diverse socio-cultural setting is portrayed with the following words: '. . . there were dwelling in Jerusalem Jews, devout men from every nation under heaven . . .' (Acts 2:5). The Pentecost Story offers, then, a rich cultural vision in which a diverse cultural geography was constructed by the power of the Spirit into the Christian community."

Oscar Garcia-Johnson (Latino—Honduran), *The Mestizo/a Community of the Spirit* (Eugene, Ore.: Pickwick, 2009), p. 82.

"Cruciformity—life as conformity to the crucified Jesus—is the visible side of the Pentecost experience. . . . Cruciform life is life as embodiment of Jesus' cross in community. Hence, this existential-cultural way of life belongs to the *created visible* realm."

Oscar Garcia-Johnson (Latino—Honduran), *The Mestizo/a Community of the Spirit: A Postmodern Latino/a Ecclesiology of the Spirit* (Eugene, Ore.: Pickwick, 2009), p. 86.

CHURCH

"[The] Christian community, since its beginning, represents a cultural space where multiple matrices of identities find commonality and affirmation in the Spirit of Christ, as the transcendent socializing-formative agent. The Spirit acts in both directions simultaneously: it creates a common space for being-in-community and affirms the distinctiveness of each cultural reality within the whole through a polyphonic proclamation of Jesus. Commonality, in the Latino/a sense, implies *convivencia* (life together). Affirmation of diversity means both affirmation of the *person in the diverse body* and also affirmation of *diversity in* the person. These affirmative movements by the Spirit imply a great deal of empathy, relationality, and spirituality. In short, all this is only possible within community."

Oscar Garcia-Johnson (Latino—Honduran), *The Mestizo/a Community of the Spirit: A Postmodern Latino/a Ecclesiology of the Spirit* (Eugene, Ore.: Pickwick, 2009), p. 109.

"The church is the *Koinonia* of the Spirit. It is the unique *locus* of the Spirit's activity in the world. . . . It is that community which acknowledges Jesus Christ as savior and Lord, and through whom the pneumatic (risen) Christ is mediated by the Spirit. As God's colony in a human world, it is *both* a model and a sign of redeemed and transformed relationships—it is a *Koinonia* of the Spirit and *Koinonia* with fellow Christians. It witnesses to the Reign of God's reality, by its very existence a 'sacrament' in and to the world."

Eldin Villafañe (Latino—Puerto Rican), *The Liberating Spirit* (Grand Rapids: Eerdmans, 1993), pp. 216-17.

"When a congregation is a contrast community in comparison to the dominant culture, the dominant culture often resists. . . . So, when congregations, by their life and ministry, give collective witness to Jesus Christ, they are taking risks—physical, financial, social. When their distinctive conduct goes against the grain of society's norms, they many be looked down on or treated unjustly. When they challenge the powers of the world, the powers may fight back."

Lois Barrett (Euro-American—English, Irish, German, Dutch), *Treasure in Clay Jars: Patterns in Missional Faithfulness* (Grand Rapids: Eerdmans, 2004), p. 76.

BAPTISM

"Baptism is not the formation of new, isolated selves; it is, rather, the formation of a new people, the Body of Christ, by the power of the Spirit. As such, baptized believers are becoming holy by learning to live together as forgiven and forgiving people in mission to the world. That is, baptism signifies the transformation of individual selves through their initiation into the friendships and practices of eschatological Christian community, the horizons of which are ever-expanding."

L. Gregory Jones (Euro-American—Welsh, German), *Embodying Forgiveness: A Theological Analysis* (Grand Rapids: Eerdmans, 1995), p. 167.

FELLOWSHIP/TABLE

"The word *koine* means common. . . . The multiracial church encourages participation from every believer regardless of their diverse backgrounds. In the fellowship of a multiracial congregation, not only does each person have access to the same Christ but the multiracial vision calls for substantial and persistent sacrifice and sharing with one another. . . . One tributary of this image of *koinonia* is table fellowship. The table of God's community is open to everyone. In fact, this openness was a charge that Jesus' enemies made against Him (Matt 11:19; Luke 7:34). . . . Although the primary target of Jesus' earthly ministry was the Jews, Jesus intermittently reached out to the Gentiles at pivotal points in His ministry (see Mark 7:24-30; Luke 7:1-10; John 4:12, 20-26). Jesus' parable of the great banquet (Luke 14:15-24) reiterated Isaiah's prophecy that the Messiah 'will prepare a feast for all peoples' (Isa 25:6) which stood in sharp contrast to the popular rabbinic understanding of the promised Messianic banquet."

Rodney M. Woo (Asian American—Chinese), *The Color of Church: A Biblical and Practical Paradigm for Multiracial Churches* (Nashville: B & H, 2009), p. 52.

RECONCILIATION

"Reconciliation is the way of the cross—love pressing its way even in the face of death. . . . The reconciler recognizes and believes that reconciliation is God's one-item agenda. God is the author of reconciliation. People only carry out the reconciling process that God initiated. Reconciliation begins between God and human beings, through the atonement of Jesus Christ, and then is channeled through us to each other by the empowerment of the Holy Spirit."

Samuel George Hines (African American—Jamaican), in Samuel George Hines and Curtiss Paul DeYoung, *Beyond Rhetoric* (Valley Forge, Penn.: Judson Press, 2000), p. 3.

"Godly reconciliation, then, brings about a radical change in us so that all persons can rightly relate to God the Father, through Jesus Christ the Son, by the power of the Holy Spirit. . . . The church as a family, with unity in diversity, bears the responsibility to make reconciliation a manifested reality. God's plan has no room for any church fellowship to be intentionally and exclusively limited to race or other ethnic interests, however historically justified and culturally expedient those divisions may seem to be."

Samuel George Hines (African American—Jamaican), in Samuel George Hines and Curtiss Paul DeYoung, *Beyond Rhetoric* (Valley Forge, Penn.: Judson, 2000), pp. 21-22.

"This 'reconciliation' (*diallassomai* as in Matthew 5:24) was an 'in house' action. Paul expanded this concept to apply to Jew and Gentile by relating it to the individual's reconciliation with God. If Jews and Gentiles were reconciled to God, they were therefore automatically reconciled to each other. In fact, Paul went so far as to say that out of these two groups of people God created 'one new humanity' superseding the categories of Jew and Gentile. To follow Jesus Christ was to embrace the restoration of true humanity."

Curtiss Paul DeYoung (Euro-American—Dutch, English), *Reconciliation: Our Greatest Challenge—Our Only Hope* (Valley Forge, Penn.: Judson Press, 1997), p. 50.

"Paul's understanding of unity and the need for reconciliation expanded beyond the relationship between Jews and Gentiles. He also recognized that this ministry of reconciliation included breaking down the dividing walls between men and women, slave and free, and all other groups of people who were estranged or separated (Galatians 3:28). Reconciliation was to be applied to concrete human situations. The purpose of reconciliation was (and is) to repair the damage of division and to restore the reality of oneness. Paul's message was oneness, unity—reconciliation."

Curtiss Paul DeYoung (Euro-American—Dutch, English), *Reconciliation: Our Greatest Challenge—Our Only Hope* (Valley Forge, Penn.: Judson, 1997), p. 52.

JEW-GENTILE RELATIONS

"While the issue of Jewish-Christian relations is of great ethical importance in its own right, there is still more at stake in this discussion, because the New Testament's treatment of the relation between Jew and Greek unavoidably becomes a paradigm for the Christian response to ethnic and racial divisions of all sorts."

Richard Hays (Euro-American—Scottish, English, Dutch), *The Moral Vision of the New Testament* (San Francisco: HarperSanFrancisco, 1996), p. 409.

"The New Testament can be shown in quite a powerful way to present an argument for the transcending of ethnic divisions *within the church*. Paul at Antioch opposed Peter to his face because he and his party had withdrawn from table fellowship with Gentile Christians. Paul saw this not merely as a social affront to the Gentile converts but as a betrayal of the truth of the Gospel (Gal. 2:11-14)."

Richard Hays (Euro-American—Scottish, English, Dutch), *The Moral Vision of the New Testament* (San Francisco: HarperSanFrancisco, 1996), p. 439.

FORGIVENESS

"This brings us to [another] feature of the practice of reconciling forgiveness. We typically need one another to help us narrate the truth of our lives, both in praise and penitence; further, we must recognize the authority that others, and most determinatively the Church, must have if we are *all* mutually to engage in this practice. The practice of reconciling forgiveness presumes our acknowledgment that any of us may *not* have the best or most truthful perspective on our own life or on the issue we face. We often find it difficult to know even where to begin in gaining such truthful perspective. Yet those involved in the practices of Christian community often find this in surprising ways and places."

L. Gregory Jones (Euro-American—Welsh, German), *Embodying Forgiveness: A Theological Analysis* (Grand Rapids: Eerdmans, 1995), p. 187.

FAMILY

"The familial terms *brother, sister, mother, father, friend,* and *neighbor* are now reinterpreted and redefined by Jesus. As a result of the blood of Christ all believers are transformed into a new household of reconciliation and solidarity. The community of Christ is the conduit of convergence for the great rivers of humanity. This new relationship to the body of Christ now takes priority over all other human relationships, such as family, race, culture, gender, and nation."

Rodney M. Woo (Asian American—Chinese), *The Color of Church: A Biblical and Practical Paradigm for Multiracial Churches* (Nashville: B & H, 2009), p. 51.

CONVERSION

"The Petrine or Markan paradigm of conversion focuses on Peter's conversion as a process of transformation until there is a conversion of his inner self. As Christian educators, we are to prepare people not only for an initial encounter with Jesus as Savior but also for an ongoing process of turning from sin to God. Conversion . . . is an ongoing journey into the mystery of the reign of God. . . . The life we appropriate in conversion involves turning to God and God's world and work, changing our minds, and adopting a new worldview so that we ally ourselves with the values and life of commitment associated with the realm of God."

Elizabeth Conde-Frazier (Latina—Puerto Rican), *A Many Colored Kingdom: Multicultural Dynamics for Spiritual Formation* (Grand Rapids: Baker, 2004), p. 112.

ANNOTATED BIBLIOGRAPHY

Tʜʀᴏᴜɢʜᴏᴜᴛ ᴛʜᴇ ʙᴏᴏᴋ, ᴡᴇ ʜᴀᴠᴇ ɴᴏᴛᴇᴅ important books in lists and footnotes. This extended list does not include all of those resources but focuses on our recommendations under four specific areas of study.

AMERICAN STUDIES AND ETHNICITY

Cornell, Stephen, and Douglas Hartmann. *Ethnicity and Race.* Newbury Park, Calif.: Pine Forge, 2007. Explores the various forces that construct ethnic and racial identities over time at the group level, such as politics, social institutions, culture and labor markets.

Gallagher, Charles A., ed. *Rethinking the Color Line.* 3rd ed. New York: McGraw-Hill, 2007. A compilation of writings from selected race scholars providing an overview of the racial dynamics characteristic of American society.

Omi, Michael, and Howard Winant. *Racial Formation in the United States.* New York: Routledge, 1994. Posits ways in which racial categories are created, maintained and transformed at the individual and group level through racial projects.

Stewart, Edward C., and Milton J. Bennett. *American Cultural Patterns.* Rev. ed. Yarmouth, Maine: Intercultural Press, 1991. A helpful analysis of white American middle-class patterns of thinking and behavior compared with other cultures.

Takaki, Ronald. *A Different Mirror.* Rev. ed. New York: Back Bay, 2008. A very readable narration of America's history with attention to perspectives of oppressed minority groups.

———. *A Larger Memory.* New York: Back Bay, 1998. Helps the reader develop awareness and empathy by experiencing America through the personal stories of individuals from minority cultures.

Wuthnow, Robert. *American Mythos*. Princeton, N.J.: Princeton University Press, 2006. Examines the narratives and embedded cultural assumptions, from the viewpoint of immigrants, that both legitimize American society and prevent it from fully realizing its ideals.

ANTHROPOLOGY AND WORLDVIEW

Eriksen, Thomas Hylland. *Small Places, Big Issues*. London: Pluto, 2001. An introduction to cultural anthropology, providing insights into different cultural subsystems such as economics, marriage and family, religion, power and organization, modes of thought, and ethnicity.

Hiebert, Paul G. *Transforming Worldviews*. Grand Rapids: Baker Academic, 2008. Hiebert's magnum opus discussing how missionaries can work toward the spiritual transformation of worldviews to induce lasting spiritual change.

Lingenfelter, Sherwood G. *Transforming Culture*. Grand Rapids: Baker Academic, 1998. Assists Christian missionaries in interpreting and understanding the social structures, characteristics and practices of different culture groups.

Strauss, Claudia, and Naomi Quinn. *A Cognitive Theory of Cultural Meaning*. New York: Cambridge University Press, 1998. The first four chapters present an excellent description of how individuals and groups make meaning in their contexts.

SOCIETY, RACE AND CHRISTIANITY

Christerson, Brad, Korie L. Edwards and Michael O. Emerson. *Against All Odds*. New York: New York University Press, 2005. Highlights common hindrances and enablements to racial integration in evangelical institutions.

Emerson, Michael O., and Christian Smith. *Divided by Faith*. New York: Oxford University Press, 2000. This seminal work is a must read, highlighting the reciprocal relationship between American evangelicalism and the forces of racialization in American society and the evangelical church.

Kidd, Colin. *The Forging of Races*. New York: Cambridge University Press, 2006. Kidd demonstrates the frequent negative influences that Western

Protestant theologizing has had on modern constructions of race and racial categorization.

Metzger, Paul L. *Consuming Jesus*. Grand Rapids: Eerdmans, 2007. Traces how consumerism, market forces and the homogeneous unit principle have contributed toward race and class divisions in the American church.

Priest, Robert J., and Alvaro L. Nieves, eds. *This Side of Heaven*. New York: Oxford University Press, 2006. This compilation covers several essential topics including racial dynamics in congregations, developing multicultural competencies and theological reflection.

Rah, Soong-Chan. *The Next Evangelicalism*. Downers Grove, Ill.: Inter-Varsity Press, 2009. This provocative book prophetically calls the church to shed its Western cultural captivity and embody diversity, reconciliation, and justice.

Sechrest, Love L. *A Former Jew*. New York: T & T Clark, 2009. Discusses the Pauline understanding of Christianity as a third race and its ethical implications for the contemporary American church.

Sharp, Douglas R. *No Partiality*. Downers Grove, Ill.: InterVarsity Press, 2002. Integrates biblical theology and the social sciences to provide a comprehensive theology of race and racial reconciliation for the church.

FORMING MULTIETHNIC CONGREGATIONS

Anderson, David. *Multicultural Ministry*. Grand Rapids: Zondervan, 2004. Anderson is pastor of a multicultural congregation in Maryland and part of the Willow Creek Association. Using a dance analogy the author invites churches to find their rhythm using his experience as a base.

Blount, Brian K., and Lenora Tubbs Tisdale, eds. *Making Room at the Table*. Louisville: Westminster John Knox, 2001. A compilation exploring practical issues that can make worship more inclusive for groups that have been marginalized or excluded.

Cha, Peter, S. Steve Kang and Helen Lee. *Growing Healthy Asian American Churches*. Downers Grove, Ill.: InterVarsity Press, 2006. Discusses eight key values relating to the identity and mission of Pan-Asian multicultural congregations, such as overcoming toxic shame through a life of grace, the values and practices of healthy leaders, and nurturing intergenerational relationships.

Conde-Frazier, Elizabeth, S. Steve Kang and Gary A. Parrett. *A Many Colored Kingdom*. Grand Rapids: Baker Academic, 2004. Provides valuable insights for those involved in teaching or spiritual formation ministry in multicultural settings.

Deymaz, Mark. *Building a Healthy Multi-Ethnic Church*. New York: John Wiley, 2007. The author draws on his experience as pastor of Mosaic Church in Little Rock, Arkansas. Uses a similar framework to that developed by George Yancey.

DeYoung, Curtiss Paul, Michael O. Emerson, George Yancey and Karen Chai Kim. *United by Faith*. New York: Oxford University Press, 2003. Provides an introduction to the history and current state of multiethnic congregations in the United States

Edwards, Korie L. *The Elusive Dream*. New York: Oxford University Press, 2008. A somewhat pessimistic view highlighting interracial churches' struggles to negotiate structural barriers like white hegemony.

Emerson, Michael O. *People of the Dream*. Princeton, N.J.: Princeton University Press, 2006. Significant research into congregations that are multiracial, including the beliefs and practices that both hinder and facilitate the formation of these congregations.

Garces-Foley, Kathleen. *Crossing the Ethnic Divide*. New York: Oxford University Press, 2007. A case study detailing how a Pan-Asian church has worked through issues of ethnic diversity and reconciliation as it has transitioned into a more ethnically inclusive model of multiethnic ministry.

Kujawa-Holbrook, Sheryl. *A House of Prayer for All Nations*. Herndon, Va.: Alban Institute, 2002. Based on six case studies, this book discusses how multiracial congregations have overcome unhealthy institutional habits by intentional practices such as sharing a rich symbolic life together, cultivating spiritual stamina and knowing their history.

Martínez, Juan. *Walk with the People*. Nashville: Abingdon, 2008. A description of ministry across the multiethnic and multicultural complexity of ministry among Latinos. Addresses the profound differences among Latinos and their implications for ministry.

Ortiz, Manuel. *One New People*. Downers Grove, Ill.: InterVarsity Press,

1996. Discusses several practical insights and models for developing multiethnic congregations, including multicongregational approaches.

Woo, Rodney. *The Color of Church.* Nashville: B & H Academic, 2009. Provides an in-depth biblical rationale for multiracial congregations and an insightful look at how one church transitioned into multiracial ministry; includes discussion questions after each chapter to promote dialogue among a church's leadership and congregants.

Yancey, George. *One Body, One Spirit.* Downers Grove, Ill.: InterVarsity Press, 2003. Provides seven essential principles for those developing a multiracial church, such as intentionality, inclusive worship, an overarching goal and diverse leadership. The author on race as the defining factor in understanding differences and the challenges of working together.

INTERCULTURAL LEADERSHIP AND COMMUNICATION

Bordas, Juana. *Salsa, Soul, and Spirit: Leadership for a Multicultural Age.* San Francisco: Berrett-Koehler, 2007. Draws on African American, Hispanic and Native American leadership values and practices to construct a theory of leadership for multicultural organizations.

Connerley, Mary L., and Paul B. Pedersen. *Leading in a Diverse and Multicultural Environment.* Thousand Oaks, Calif.: Sage, 2005. Provides an effective three-stage model for developing multicultural leadership competencies centering on awareness, knowledge and skills.

Foster, Charles R. *Embracing Diversity.* Herndon, Va.: Alban Institute, 1997. Stresses the importance of leaders in multicultural congregations employing the linking practices of embracing, welcoming and hospitality to accept racial and cultural others.

Gudykunst, William, Stella Ting-Toomey and Tsukasa Nishida. *Communication in Personal Relationships Across Cultures.* Thousand Oaks, Calif.: Sage, 1996. Provides valuable insights into the communication practices of non-Western cultures.

Hofstede, Geert, and Gert Jan Hofstede. *Cultures and Organizations.* 2nd ed. New York: McGraw-Hill, 2004. An extremely valuable text describing how national and cultural dimensions like power distance, social roles, individualism or collectivism, and uncertainty avoidance affect organizations.

Law, Eric. *The Wolf Shall Dwell with the Lamb*. Atlanta: Chalice, 1993. Analyzes the use and misuse of power while providing practical tools for transforming power relationships in multiethnic congregations. (Other books by Law are also recommended.)

Livermore, David. *Cultural Intelligence*. Grand Rapids: Baker Academic, 2009. Important theoretical and practical materials for engaging in cross- or multicultural ministry; presents a praxis model for developing cultural competency.

Samovar, Larry A., Richard E. Porter and Edwin R. McDaniel. *Intercultural Communication*. Boston: Wadsworth, 2008. A large and valuable reader providing practical strategies for communicating effectively in various cultural and organizational contexts.

ETHNIC RECONCILIATION AND CONFLICT MEDIATION

Augsburger, David W. *Conflict Mediation Across Cultures*. Louisville: Westminster John Knox, 1992. A practical and readable resource providing valuable insights into conflict resolution patterns across different cultures.

Barnes, Sandra L. *Subverting the Power of Prejudice*. Downers Grove, Ill.: InterVarsity Press, 2006. Fusing theological and sociological insights, this book discusses the reasons for prejudice and practical ways to transform it.

DeYoung, Curtiss Paul. *Reconciliation: Our Greatest Challenge—Our Only Hope*. Valley Forge, Penn.: Judson, 1997. Rooted in Scripture, De-Young's message about the barriers and hard work of reconciliation comes from a life-long commitment to racial boundary crossing.

Hines, Samuel, and Curtiss Paul DeYoung. *Beyond Rhetoric: Reconciliation as a Way of Life*. Valley Forge, Penn.: Judson, 2000. This unique, coauthored book, rooted in a crossgenerational, biracial partnership, explores theological, congregational and practical matters of reconciliation.

Lederach, John Paul. *Preparing for Peace*. Syracuse, N.Y.: Syracuse University Press, 1995. An extremely valuable resource that provides both theoretical and practical resources for training people to resolve cross-cultural conflict utilizing local cultural resources.

Salter McNeil, Brenda, and Rick Richardson. *The Heart of Racial Justice*. 2nd ed. Downers Grove, Ill.: InterVarsity Press, 2009. Goes beyond social models of racial reconciliation rooted in interpersonal or institutional change by developing a model of racial healing rooted in God's story.

Yancey, George. *Beyond Racial Gridlock*. Downers Grove, Ill.: InterVarsity Press, 2006. Yancey describes four common ideologies concerning racial dynamics in American society and constructs his own view, building on biblical and sociological principles.

Name and Subject Index

European immigrants, 13, 14, 15, 19, 86, 89, 138, 236, 237

experiment (church ministry), 8, 9, 27, 34, 44, 45, 47, 49, 54-55, 92, 93, 100, 101, 110, 112, 113, 144, 149, 198, 206, 213-31, 241, 243

expressive language. *See* language

fair play, 149-51

feelings. *See* emotions

figure and ground, 174, 179

Fisher, Glen, 118

food, 12, 38, 74, 88, 107, 144, 159, 176, 177, 203, 220, 227, 240

forgiveness, 46, 51, 81, 102, 231, 255, 257

Franklin, Benjamin, 19, 85, 158

Freire, Paulo, 40, 41, 51, 97

French, 15, 85, 86

friend (friendship), 20, 21, 22, 28, 40, 53, 56, 63, 64, 73, 74, 76, 101, 110, 132, 141, 142, 144-46, 148, 149, 169, 178, 192, 218, 228, 230, 231, 255, 257, 277

Fuller Theological Seminary, 21, 25, 28

functional(ist), 68, 75, 106-7, 152, 181, 201

generosity, 38, 51, 135, 182

geography, 18, 42, 74-76, 79, 81, 82, 87, 193, 205, 249, 253

Gordon, Milton, 15, 16n5, 17, 89

gospel, 17, 19, 36, 42, 49, 59, 63

grace, 12, 17, 54, 61-63, 102, 168, 209, 214, 226, 231, 239, 262

Greek (language), 18, 68, 124, 128-29, 248

Greeks. *See* Jew-Gentile relations

ground. *See* figure and ground

Guder, Darrell, 65, 66n8, 69n14, 76

Habermas, Jürgen, 10, 98-101, 106, 190-206, 208

habits 17, 34, 37, 42, 44, 51, 56, 63, 88, 99, 112, 155, 169n7, 172, 173, 175, 176, 183, 201, 206, 208, 215, 219,

220, 222, 225, 230, 262

Hawn, C. Michael, 241, 244

Heifetz, Ronald, 215, 222, 223, 224n11, 224n14

Hiebert, Paul, 79, 118, 119n6, 136n1, 141, 143n11, 146, 150n17, 152n19, 157n5, 173n2, 174, 175n4, 239, 244, 260

Hispanic. *See* Latino

holding environment. *See* leadership

Holy Spirit, 12, 17, 18, 34, 36, 38, 41n5, 42, 44, 45, 46, 54, 55, 56, 57, 61-63, 65, 66, 71, 72, 73, 74, 93, 101, 111, 135, 156-57, 168, 173, 179, 185, 208, 213, 214, 215, 218, 220, 225, 226, 231, 239, 244, 249, 252, 253, 254, 255, 256

homogeneity, homogeneous, 13, 14, 15, 36, 37, 38, 45, 132, 164, 197

Homogenous Unit Principle (HUP), 11, 17, 52, 261

hospitality, 42, 51, 73, 143, 149, 228, 239-40, 241

Huntington, Samuel, 16n5, 126, 138n3

identity, 12, 19, 22, 23, 24-25, 38, 48, 53, 57n12, 60, 61, 63, 67, 69, 71n16, 81, 85-89, 90, 91, 93, 126, 131, 136, 183n3, 163, 168, 193, 195, 196, 205, 228, 233, 236, 261

imagination, 34, 39, 45, 49, 56, 70-74, 76, 83, 86, 105, 115, 201, 212, 215, 222, 224, 228, 230, 231

immigrants, immigration, 13, 14, 15, 23, 29, 36, 38, 67, 78, 80, 81, 86, 87, 89, 94, 106, 110, 129, 130, 134, 138, 142, 162, 163, 169, 184, 192, 195, 203, 207, 208, 218, 219, 231, 233, 236, 237, 239, 246, 260, 263

incarnation, 49, 60, 249-50

individualism, 27, 140, 151, 155, 154-60, 162, 166, 168, 169, 172, 185, 201, 205

mythic, 27, 160-63

individuality, 7, 154-69

intercultural, 9, 10, 12, 13, 15, 16, 26,
27, 28, 30, 38, 48-54, 60n2, 62, 70,
71n16, 78, 81, 85, 87n14, 89-94, 105,
112, 114, 128, 141, 146, 147, 148, 149,
152, 155, 166-8, 174, 179, 180-84,
189-209, 219, 221, 222, 231, 232-34,
237, 238, 240, 241n10, 242-43,
263-64
    barriers, 10, 103, 139, 194, 201,
    204-5, 206, 207
    See also multicultural

InterVarsity Christian Fellowship, 20, 21

intuitive (intuition), 172, 173, 176, 177

Jamestown, 236, 237

Japanese, 109, 181, 198

Japanese American(s), 19, 22, 29, 73-74,
147, 201-2, 217n5

Jeremiah, 34, 50, 73, 75, 219

Jesus Christ, 8, 12, 19, 37, 38, 40, 45,
59, 60, 61, 63, 65, 66, 68, 73, 75, 90,
91, 102, 110, 122, 124, 125, 156, 157,
167, 168, 204-5, 214, 218, 228, 229,
246, 248, 249, 250, 251, 252, 253,
254, 255, 256, 257, 258

Jew-Gentile relationships, 36-38, 90,
103, 135-36, 156-57, 179, 252,
256-57, 261

Jones, Absalom, 16

justice, injustice, 17, 34n2, 51, 63, 64,
68, 141, 142, 149n16, 165, 169, 189,
190, 195, 196, 198, 199, 203, 247,
251, 261

King, Martin Luther, Jr., 20

kingdom of God. *See* reign of God

Korean (language), 120, 233

Korean Americans, 92, 175, 183, 200,
233

language (types), 100, 132, 190-91

language(s), 8, 14, 17, 18, 26, 37, 38, 87,
88, 89, 98, 101, 107, 114-31, 132, 133,
134, 148, 158, 171, 175, 176, 178, 181,
182, 193, 190, 198, 207, 220, 231,

233, 234, 244, 252

Latin America, 15, 67n11, 130, 137,
142

Latino(s)/Hispanic(s), 16, 21, 22, 23,
25, 29, 33, 48, 67n11, 69, 70n15, 78,
82, 86-88, 92, 100, 114, 115, 122,
123, 126, 129, 130, 132, 133, 138,
163, 165, 166, 169, 170, 175, 177, 198,
203, 210, 213, 217, 233, 254, 262

leaders, leadership 12-13, 19, 26-27, 39,
41-42, 46, 51, 54-57, 62-63, 67,
70-74, 76, 98, 100, 103, 110, 112-13,
115, 121, 123, 130, 133, 137, 148,
149, 152, 155, 159, 166, 168, 172, 173,
174, 182, 183-84, 190, 193, 206,
206-8, 210
    adaptive, 222-26
    balcony perspective, 206, 215-16,
    223, 225
    holding environment, 223, 225
    implemental, 55, 56-57, 172, 212,
    220-26, 229
    interpretive, 55-56, 99, 133, 152,
    172, 177-78, 180, 184, 190, 193,
    208, 212-17, 226
    leading change, 27, 54, 208-31
    relational, 55, 56, 141, 143, 212,
    217-20, 226
    technical, 222-23, 224, 226, 232-33
    triad, 54-57, 212-26

lectio, 72-73

lifeworld, 98-101

Linsky, Marty, 215, 222-24

Locke, John, 157

Lone Ranger, 162

Luzbetak, Louis, 98, 104-5, 177

majority culture, 144, 145, 146, 165

meals. *See* food

melting pot, 15, 89, 234

memory, 81, 176, 195

Mennonite(s), 13, 16, 51, 159

metaphor(s), 39, 40, 44, 63, 68, 167,
172, 173, 250

Scripture Index

THE
MISSIONAL
NETWORK

A network of leaders across North America and the UK committed to a practical and biblical/theological engagement with the missional conversation in the church.

MISSIONAL PERSPECTIVE

TMN frames its processes, tools, and resources within a robust biblical and theological missional perspective—God's mission in the world and the church's participation in this mission. An organizational understanding of systems is used in relation to these frames to support transformation across local, regional and national church bodies.

RESOURCES FOR TRANSFORMATION

TMN offers a variety of well tested tools and resources that can assist church organizations and their leaders engage in intentional processes of missional innovation and transformation. These resources support the consulting/coaching processes TMN makes available for systems change.

CONSULTING AND COACHING

TMN provides both consulting and coaching to support the transformation of church systems at all levels. The consulting is designed to build the capacity of church systems to engage in systemic missional transformation. The coaching is designed to walk along side leaders in strengthening their skills and capacities for leading in the midst of change.

PUBLISHING

TMN has a Writing/Publishing Team made up of a broad, cooperative table of church leaders—pastors, teachers, and practitioners that produces a book series and other printed resources to deepen the missional conversation while informing system transformation from a biblical and theological perspective.

TMN ASSOCIATES AND PARTNERS

TMN consists of a team of associates and partners who are part of and have a deep understanding of the historical development of denominations as faith traditions and polities. In all its work this team takes seriously the traditions and histories of each church system viewing it as helpful gift to the larger church.

INTERNATIONAL

TMN is an international organization that works with church leaders in North America, the UK and Europe to understand the particular ways in which the Gospel interacts with the churches and cultures in these locations, with a view towards the transforming of Western cultures.

The Missional Network

404 Macbeth Crescent
West Vancouver, BC
V7T 1V7 Canada
office@themissionalnetwork.com
www.themissionalnetwork.com
Phone: 604-762-6354

**Join the conversation
and find additional resources**

You've read *Churches, Cultures and Leadership,*
now continue the conversation at
www.churchesculturesleadership.com

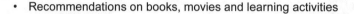

We have provided new materials, including:

- Video interviews with pastors

- Recommended documentaries

- Links to informative websites

- Recommendations on books, movies and learning activities

And we want your contributions, such as:

- Engaging in conversations about the book's theories and resources

- Linking readers to your videos, curriculum and websites

- Recommending books, movies, exercises and activities

- Telling us your stories about classrooms and churches